本书出版得到《大中华文库》出版经费资助

大 中 华 文 库
LIBRARY
OF CHINESE CLASSICS

大中华文库

汉英对照

LIBRARY OF CHINESE CLASSICS

Chinese-English

老 子
Laozi

亚瑟·韦利　　英译

陈鼓应　　今译

傅惠生　　校注

Translated into English by Arthur Waley

Translated into Modern Chinese by Chen Guying

Revised and Annotated by Fu Huisheng

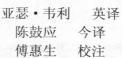

湖南人民出版社

Hunan People's Publishing House

外文出版社

Foreign Languages Press

First Edition 1999

ISBN 7-5438-2089-7/B.50
© 1999 Hunan People's Publishing House

Published by
Hunan People's Publishing House
  66 Zhanlanguan Road, Changsha 410005, Hunan, China
Foreign Languages Press
  24 Baiwanzhuang Road, Beijing 100037, China
  http: // www. flp. com. cn
Printed by
Shenzhen Jiaxinda Printing Co., Ltd.,Shenzhen, China
Printed in the People's Republic of China

总　序

杨牧之

《大中华文库》终于出版了。我们为之高兴，为之鼓舞，但也倍感压力。

当此之际，我们愿将郁积在我们心底的话，向读者倾诉。

一

中华民族有着悠久的历史和灿烂的文化，系统、准确地将中华民族的文化经典翻译成外文，编辑出版，介绍给全世界，是几代中国人的愿望。早在几十年前，西方一位学者翻译《红楼梦》，书名译成《一个红楼上的梦》，将林黛玉译为"黑色的玉"。我们一方面对外国学者将中国的名著介绍到世界上去表示由衷的感谢，一方面为祖国的名著还不被完全认识，甚而受到曲解，而感到深深的遗憾。还有西方学者翻译《金瓶梅》，专门摘选其中自然主义描述最为突出的篇章加以译介。一时间，西方学者好像发现了奇迹，掀起了《金瓶梅》热，说中国是"性开放的源头"，公开地在报刊上鼓吹中国要"发扬开放之传统"。还有许多资深、友善的汉学家译介中国古代的哲学著作，在把中华民族文化介绍给全世界的工作方面作出了重大贡献，但或囿于理解有误，或缘于对中国文字认识的局限，质量上乘的并不多，常常是隔靴搔痒，说不到点子上。大哲学家黑格尔曾经说过：中国有最完备的国史。但他认为中国古代没有真正意义上的哲学，还处在哲学史前状态。这么了不起的哲学家竟然作出这样大失水准的评论，何其不幸。正如任何哲学家都要受时间、地点、条件的制约一样，黑格尔也离不开这一规律。当时他也只能从上述水平的汉学家译过去的文字去分析、理解，所以，黑格尔先生对中国古代社会的认识水平是什么状态，也就不难想象了。

中国离不开世界，世界也缺少不了中国。中国文化摄取外域的新成分，丰富了自己，又以自己的新成就输送给别人，贡献于世界。从公元 5 世纪开始到公元 15 世纪，大约有一千年，中国走在世界的前列。在这一千多年的时间里，她的光辉照耀全世界。人类要前进，怎么能不全面认识中国，怎么能不认真研究中国的历史呢？

二

中华民族是伟大的，曾经辉煌过，蓝天、白云、阳光灿烂，和平而兴旺；也有过黑暗的、想起来就让人战栗的日子，但中华民族从来是充满理想，不断追求，不断学习，渴望和平与友谊的。

中国古代伟大的思想家孔子曾经说过："三人行，必有我师焉。择其善者而从之，其不善者而改之。"孔子的话就是要人们向别人学习。这段话正是概括了整个中华民族与人交往的原则。人与人之间交往如此，在与周边的国家交往中也是如此。

秦始皇第一个统一了中国，可惜在位只有十几年，来不及作更多的事情。汉朝继秦而继续强大，便开始走出去，了解自己周边的世界。公元前 138 年，汉武帝派张骞出使西域。他带着一万头牛羊，总值一万万钱的金帛货物，作为礼物，开始西行，最远到过"安息"（即波斯）。公元前 36 年，班超又率 36 人出使西域。36 个人按今天的话说，也只有一个排，显然是为了拜访未曾见过面的邻居，是去交朋友。到了西域，班超派遣甘英作为使者继续西行，往更远处的大秦国（即罗马）去访问，"乃抵条支而历安息，临西海以望大秦"（《后汉书·西域传》）。"条支"在"安息"以西，即今天的伊拉克、叙利亚一带，"西海"应是今天的地中海。也就是说甘英已经到达地中海边上，与罗马帝国隔海相望，"临大海欲渡"，却被人劝阻而未成行，这在历史上留下了遗恨。可以想见班超、甘英沟通友谊的无比勇气和强烈愿望。接下来是唐代的玄奘，历经千难万险，到"西天"印度取经，带回了南亚国家的古老文化。归国后，他把带回的佛教经典组织人翻译，到后来很多经典印度失传了，但中国却保存完好，以至于今天，没有玄奘的《大唐西域记》，印度人很难编写印度古代史。明代郑和"七下西洋"，把中华文化传到东南亚一带。鸦片战争以后，一代又一代先进的中国人，为了振兴中华，又前赴后继，向西方国家学习先进的科学思想和文明成果。这中间有我们的领导人朱德、周恩来、邓小平；有许许多多大科学家、文学家、艺术家，如郭沫若、李四光、钱学森、冼星海、徐悲鸿等。他们的追求、奋斗，他们的博大胸怀，兼收并蓄的精神，为人类社会增添了光彩。

中国文化的形成和发展过程，就是一个以众为师，以各国人民为师，不断学习和创造的过程。中华民族曾经向周边国家和民族学习过许多东西，假如没有这些学习，中华民族决不可能创造出昔日的辉煌。回顾历史，我们怎么能够不对伟大的古埃及文明、古希腊文明、古印度文明满怀深深的感激?怎么能够不对伟大的欧洲文明、非洲文明、美洲文明、澳洲文明,以及中国周围的亚洲文明充满温情与敬意?

中华民族为人类社会曾作出过独特的贡献。在15世纪以前,中国的科学技术一直处于世界遥遥领先的地位。英国科学家李约瑟说:"中国在公元3世纪到13世纪之间,保持着一个西方所望尘莫及的科学知识水平。"美国耶鲁大学教授、《大国的兴衰》的作者保罗·肯尼迪坦言:"在近代以前时期的所有文明中,没有一个国家的文明比中国更发达,更先进。"

世界各国的有识之士千里迢迢来中国观光、学习。在这个过程中,中国唐朝的长安城渐渐发展成为国际大都市。西方的波斯、东罗马,东亚的高丽、新罗、百济、南天竺、北天竺,频繁前来。外国的王侯、留学生,在长安供职的外国官员,商贾、乐工和舞士,总有几十个国家,几万人之多。日本派出"遣唐使"更是一批接一批。传为美谈的日本人阿部仲麻吕(晁衡)在长安留学的故事,很能说明外国人与中国的交往。晁衡学成仕于唐朝,前后历时五十余年。晁衡与中国的知识分子结下了深厚的友情。他归国时,传说在海中遇难身亡。大诗人李白作诗哭悼:"日本晁卿辞帝都,征帆一片远蓬壶。明月不归沉碧海,白云愁色满苍梧。"晁衡遇险是误传,但由此可见中外学者之间在中国长安交往的情谊。

后来,不断有外国人到中国来探寻秘密,所见所闻,常常让他们目瞪口呆。《希腊纪事》(希腊人波桑尼阿著)记载公元2世纪时,希腊人在中国的见闻。书中写道:"赛里斯人用小米和青芦喂一种类似蜘蛛的昆虫,喂到第五年,虫肚子胀裂开,便从里面取出丝来。"从这段对中国古代养蚕技术的描述，可见当时欧洲人与中国人的差距。公元 9 世纪中叶，阿拉伯人来到中国。一位阿拉伯作家在他所著的《中国印度闻见录》中记载了曾旅居中国的阿拉伯商人的见闻：

——一天，一个外商去拜见驻守广州的中国官吏。会见时，外商总盯着官吏的胸部，官吏很奇怪，便问："你好像总盯着我的胸，这是怎么回事？"那位外商回答说："透过你穿的丝绸衣服，我隐约看到你胸口上长着一个黑痣，这是什么丝绸，我感到十分惊奇。"官吏听后，失声大笑，伸出胳膊，说："请你数数吧，看我穿了几件衣服？"那商人数过，竟然穿了五件之多，黑痣正是透过这五层丝绸衣服显现出来的。外商惊得目瞪口呆，官吏说："我穿的丝绸还不算是最好的，总督穿的要更精美。"

——书中关于茶(他们叫干草叶子)的记载，可见阿拉伯国家当时还没有喝茶的习惯。书中记述："中国国王本人的收入主要靠盐税和泡开水喝的一种干草税。在各个城市里，这种干草叶售价都很高，中国人称这种草叶叫'茶'，这种干草叶比苜蓿的叶子还多，也略比它香，稍有苦味，用开水冲喝，治百病。"

——他们对中国的医疗条件十分羡慕，书中记载道："中国人医疗条件很好，穷人可以从国库中得到药费。"还说："城市里，很多地方立一石碑，高 10 肘，上面刻有各种疾病和药物，写明某种病用某种药医治。"

——关于当时中国的京城，书中作了生动的描述：中国的京城很大，人口众多，一条宽阔的长街把全城分为两半，大街右边的东区，住着皇帝、宰相、禁军及皇家的总管、奴婢。在这个区域，沿街开凿了小河，流水潺潺；路旁，葱茏的树木整然有序，一幢幢宅邸鳞次栉比。大街左边的西区，住着庶民和商人。这里有货栈和商店，每当清晨，人们可以看到，皇室的总管、宫廷的仆役，或骑马或步行，到这里来采购。

此后的史籍对西人来华的记载，渐渐多了起来。13世纪意大利旅行家马可·波罗，尽管有人对他是否真的到过中国持怀疑态度，但他留下一部记述元代事件的《马可·波罗游记》却是确凿无疑的。这部游记中的一些关于当时中国的描述使得西方人认为是"天方夜谭"。总之，从中西文化交流史来说，这以前的时期还是一个想象和臆测的时代，相互之间充满了好奇与幻想。

从16世纪末开始，由于航海技术的发展，东西方航路的开通，随着一批批传教士来华，中国与西方开始了直接的交流。沟通中西的使命在意大利传教士利玛窦那里有了充分的体现。利玛窦于1582年来华，1610年病逝于北京，在华20余年。除了传教以外，做了两件具有历史象征意义的事，一是1594年前后在韶州用拉丁文翻译《四书》，并作了注释；二是与明代学者徐光启合作，用中文翻译了《几何原本》。

西方传教士对《四书》等中国经典的粗略翻译，以及杜赫德的《中华帝国志》等书对中国的介绍，在西方读者的眼前展现了一个异域文明，在当时及稍后一段时期引起了一场"中国热"，许多西方大思想家的眼光都曾注目中国文化。有的推崇中华文明，如莱布尼兹、伏尔泰、魁奈等，有的对中华文明持批评态度，如孟德斯鸠、黑格尔等。莱布尼兹认识到中国文化的某些思想与他的观念相近，如周易的卦象与他发明的二进制相契合，对中国文化给予了热情的礼赞；黑格尔则从他整个哲学体系的推演出发，认为中国没有真正意义上的哲学，还处在哲学史前的状态。但是，不论是推崇还是批评，是吸纳还是排斥，中西文化的交流产生了巨大的影响。随着先进的中国科学技术的西传，特别是中国的造纸、火药、印刷术和指南针四大发明的问世，大大改变了世界的面貌。马克思说："中国的火药把骑士阶层炸得粉碎，指南针打开了世界市场并建立了殖民地，而印刷术则变成了新教的工具，变成对精神发展创造必要前提的最强大的杠杆。"英国的哲学家培根说：中国的四大发明"改变了全世界的面貌和一切事物的状态"。

三

大千世界，潮起潮落。云散云聚，万象更新。中国古代产生了无数伟大科学家：祖冲之、李时珍、孙思邈、张衡、沈括、毕升……，产生了无数科技成果：《齐民要术》、《九章算术》、《伤寒杂病论》、《本草纲目》……，以及保存至今的世界奇迹：浑天仪、地动仪、都江堰、敦煌石窟、大运河、万里长城……。但从 15 世纪下半叶起，风水似乎从东方转到了西方，落后的欧洲只经过 400 年便成为世界瞩目的文明中心。英国的牛顿、波兰的哥白尼、德国的伦琴、法国的居里、德国的爱因斯坦、意大利的伽利略、俄国的门捷列夫、美国的费米和爱迪生……，光芒四射，令人敬仰。

中华民族开始思考了。潮起潮落究竟是什么原因？中国人发明的火药，传到欧洲，转眼之间反成为欧洲列强轰击中国大门的炮弹，又是因为什么？

鸦片战争终于催醒了中国人沉睡的迷梦，最先"睁眼看世界"的一代精英林则徐、魏源迈出了威武雄壮的一步。曾国藩、李鸿章搞起了洋务运动。中国的知识分子喊出"民主与科学"的口号。中国是落后了，中国的志士仁人在苦苦探索。但落后中饱含着变革的动力，探索中孕育着崛起的希望。"向科学进军"，中华民族终于又迎来了科学的春天。

今天，世界毕竟来到了 21 世纪的门槛。分散隔绝的世界，逐渐变成联系为一体的世界。现在，全球一体化趋势日益明显，人类历史也就在愈来愈大的程度上成为全世界的历史。当今，任何一种文化的发展都离不开对其它优秀文化的汲取，都以其它优秀文化的发展为前提。在近现代，西方文化汲取中国文化，不仅是中国文化的传播，更是西方文化自身的创新和发展；正如中国文化对西方文化的汲取一样，既是西方文化在中国的传播，同时也是中国文化在近代的转型和发展。地球上所有的人类文化，都是我们共同的宝贵遗产。既然我们生活的各个大陆，在地球史上曾经是连成一气的"泛大陆"，或者说是一个完整的"地球村"，那么，我们同样可以在这个以知识和学习为特征的网络时代，走上相互学习、共同发展的大路，建设和开拓我们人类崭新的"地球村"。

西学仍在东渐，中学也将西传。各国人民的优秀文化正日益迅速地为中国文化所汲取，而无论西方和东方，也都需要从中国文化中汲取养分。正是基于这一认识，我们组织出版汉英对照版《大中华文库》，全面系统地翻译介绍中国传统文化典籍。我们试图通过《大中华文库》，向全世界展示，中华民族五千年的追求，五千年的梦想，正在新的历史时期重放光芒。中国人民就像火后的凤凰，万众一心，迎接新世纪文明的太阳。

1999 年 8 月

PREFACE TO THE
LIBRARY OF CHINESE CLASSICS

Yang Muzhi

The publication of the *Library of Chinese Classics* is a matter of great satisfaction to all of us who have been involved in the production of this monumental work. At the same time, we feel a weighty sense of responsibility, and take this opportunity to explain to our readers the motivation for undertaking this cross-century task.

1

The Chinese nation has a long history and a glorious culture, and it has been the aspiration of several generations of Chinese scholars to translate, edit and publish the whole corpus of the Chinese literary classics so that the nation's greatest cultural achievements can be introduced to people all over the world. There have been many translations of the Chinese classics done by foreign scholars. A few dozen years ago, a Western scholar translated the title of *A Dream of Red Mansions* into "A Dream of Red Chambers" and Lin Daiyu, the heroine in the novel, into "Black Jade." But while their endeavours have been laudable, the results of their labours have been less than satisfactory. Lack of knowledge of Chinese culture and an inadequate grasp of the Chinese written language have led the translators into many errors. As a consequence, not only are Chinese classical writings widely misunderstood in the rest of the world, in some cases their content has actually been distorted. At one time, there was a "*Jin Ping Mei* craze" among Western scholars, who thought that they had uncovered a miraculous phenomenon, and published theories claiming that China was the "fountainhead of eroticism," and that a Chinese "tradition of permissiveness" was about to be laid bare. This distorted view came about due to the translators of the *Jin Ping Mei (Plum in the Golden Vase)* putting one-sided stress on the raw elements in that novel, to the neglect of its overall literary value. Meanwhile, there have been many distinguished and well-intentioned Sinologists who have attempted to make the culture of the Chinese nation more widely known by translating works of ancient Chinese philosophy. However, the quality of such work, in many cases, is unsatisfactory, often missing the point entirely. The great philosopher Hegel considered that ancient China had no philosophy in the real sense of the word, being stuck in philosophical "prehistory." For such an eminent authority to make such a colossal error of judgment is truly regrettable. But, of course, Hegel was just as subject to the constraints of time, space and other objective conditions as anyone else, and since he had to rely for his knowledge of Chinese philosophy on inadequate translations it is not difficult to imagine why he went so far off the mark.

China cannot be separated from the rest of the world; and the rest of the world cannot ignore China. Throughout its history, Chinese civilization has enriched itself by absorbing new elements from the outside world, and in turn has contributed to the progress of world civilization as a whole by transmitting to other peoples its own cultural achievements. From the 5th to the 15th centuries, China marched in the front ranks of world civilization. If mankind wishes to advance, how can it afford to ignore China? How can it afford not to make a thoroughgoing study of its history?

2

Despite the ups and downs in their fortunes, the Chinese people have always been idealistic, and have never ceased to forge ahead and learn from others, eager to strengthen ties of peace and friendship.

The great ancient Chinese philosopher Confucius once said, "Wherever three persons come together, one of them will surely be able to teach me something. I will pick out his good points and emulate them; his bad points I will reform." Confucius meant by this that we should always be ready to learn from others. This maxim encapsulates the principle the Chinese people have always followed in their dealings with other peoples, not only on an individual basis but also at the level of state-to-state relations.

After generations of internecine strife, China was unified by Emperor

Qin Shi Huang (the First Emperor of the Qin Dynasty) in 221 B.C. The Han Dynasty, which succeeded that of the short-lived Qin, waxed powerful, and for the first time brought China into contact with the outside world. In 138 B.C., Emperor Wu dispatched Zhang Qian to the western regions, i.e. Central Asia. Zhang, who traveled as far as what is now Iran, took with him as presents for the rulers he visited on the way 10,000 head of sheep and cattle, as well as gold and silks worth a fabulous amount. In 36 B.C., Ban Chao headed a 36-man legation to the western regions. These were missions of friendship to visit neighbours the Chinese people had never met before and to learn from them. Ban Chao sent Gan Ying to explore further toward the west. According to the "Western Regions Section" in the *Book of Later Han*, Gan Ying traveled across the territories of present-day Iraq and Syria, and reached the Mediterranean Sea, an expedition which brought him within the confines of the Roman Empire. Later, during the Tang Dynasty, the monk Xuan Zang made a journey fraught with danger to reach India and seek the knowledge of that land. Upon his return, he organized a team of scholars to translate the Buddhist scriptures, which he had brought back with him. As a result, many of these scriptural classics which were later lost in India have been preserved in China. In fact, it would have been difficult for the people of India to reconstruct their own ancient history if it had not been for Xuan Zang's *A Record of a Journey to the West in the Time of the Great Tang Dynasty*. In the Ming Dynasty, Zheng He transmitted Chinese culture to Southeast Asia during his seven voyages. Following the Opium Wars in the mid-19th century, progressive Chinese, generation after generation, went to study the advanced scientific thought and cultural achievements of the Western countries. Their aim was to revive the fortunes of their own country. Among them were people who were later to become leaders of China, including Zhu De, Zhou Enlai and Deng Xiaoping. In addition, there were people who were to become leading scientists, literary figures and artists, such as Guo Moruo, Li Siguang, Qian Xuesen, Xian Xinghai and Xu Beihong. Their spirit of ambition, their struggles and their breadth of vision were an inspiration not only to the Chinese people but to people all over the world.

Indeed, it is true that if the Chinese people had not learned many things from the surrounding countries they would never have been able to produce the splendid achievements of former days. When we look back upon history, how can we not feel profoundly grateful for the legacies of the civilizations of ancient Egypt, Greece and India? How can we not feel fondness and respect for the cultures of Europe, Africa, America and Oceania?

The Chinese nation, in turn, has made unique contributions to the community of mankind. Prior to the 15th century, China led the world in science and technology. The British scientist Joseph Needham once said, "From the third century A.D. to the 13th century A.D. China was far ahead of the West in the level of its scientific knowledge." Paul Kennedy, of Yale University in the U.S., author of *The Rise and Fall of the Great Powers*, said, "Of all the civilizations of the pre-modern period, none was as well-developed or as progressive as that of China."

Foreigners who came to China were often astonished at what they saw and heard. The Greek geographer Pausanias in the second century A.D. gave the first account in the West of the technique of silk production in China: "The Chinese feed a spider-like insect with millet and reeds. After five years the insect's stomach splits open, and silk is extracted therefrom." From this extract, we can see that the Europeans at that time did not know the art of silk manufacture. In the middle of the 9th century A.D., an Arabian writer includes the following anecdote in his *Account of China and India*:

"One day, an Arabian merchant called upon the military governor of Guangzhou. Throughout the meeting, the visitor could not keep his eyes off the governor's chest. Noticing this, the latter asked the Arab merchant what he was staring at. The merchant replied, 'Through the silk robe you are wearing, I can faintly see a black mole on your chest. Your robe must be made out of very fine silk indeed!' The governor burst out laughing, and holding out his sleeve invited the merchant to count how many garments he was wearing. The merchant did so, and discovered that the governor was actually wearing five silk robes, one on top of the other, and they were made of such fine material that a tiny mole could be seen through them all! Moreover, the governor explained that the robes he was wearing were not made of the finest silk at all; silk of the highest grade was reserved for the garments worn by the provincial governor."

The references to tea in this book (the author calls it "dried grass") reveal that the custom of drinking tea was unknown in the Arab countries at that time: "The king of China's revenue comes mainly from taxes on salt and the dry leaves of a kind of grass which is drunk after boiled water is poured on it. This dried grass is sold at a high price in every city in the country. The Chinese call it 'cha.' The bush is like alfalfa, except that it bears more leaves, which are also more fragrant than alfalfa. It has a slightly bitter taste, and when it is infused in boiling water it is said to have medicinal properties."

Foreign visitors showed especial admiration for Chinese medicine. One wrote, "China has very good medical conditions. Poor people are given money to buy medicines by the government."

In this period, when Chinese culture was in full bloom, scholars flocked from all over the world to China for sightseeing and for study. Chang'an, the capital of the Tang Dynasty was host to visitors from as far away as the Byzantine Empire, not to mention the neighboring countries of Asia. Chang'an, at that time the world's greatest metropolis, was packed with thousands of foreign dignitaries, students, diplomats, merchants, artisans and entertainers. Japan especially sent contingent after contingent of envoys to the Tang court. Worthy of note are the accounts of life in Chang'an written by Abeno Nakamaro, a Japanese scholar who studied in China and had close friendships with ministers of the Tang court and many Chinese scholars in a period of over 50 years. The description throws light on the exchanges between Chinese and foreigners in this period. When Abeno was supposedly lost at sea on his way back home, the leading poet of the time, Li Bai, wrote a eulogy for him.

The following centuries saw a steady increase in the accounts of China written by Western visitors. The Italian Marco Polo described conditions in China during the Yuan Dynasty in his *Travels*. However, until advances in the science of navigation led to the opening of east-west shipping routes at the beginning of the 16th century Sino-Western cultural exchanges were coloured by fantasy and conjecture. Concrete progress was made when a contingent of religious missionaries, men well versed in Western science and technology, made their way to China, ushering in an era of direct contacts between China and the West. The experience of this era was embodied in the career of the Italian Jesuit Matteo Ricci. Arriving in China in 1582, Ricci died in Beijing in 1610. Apart from his missionary work, Ricci accomplished two historically symbolic tasks — one was the translation into Latin of the "Four Books," together with annotations, in 1594; the other was the translation into Chinese of Euclid's *Elements*.

The rough translations of the "Four Books" and other Chinese classical works by Western missionaries, and the publication of Père du Halde's *Description Geographique, Historique, Chronologique, Politique, et Physique de l'Empire de la Chine* revealed an exotic culture to Western readers, and sparked a "China fever," during which the eyes of many Western intellectuals were fixed on China. Some of these intellectuals, including Leibniz, held China in high esteem; others, such as Hegel, nursed a critical attitude toward Chinese culture. Leibniz considered that some aspects of Chinese thought were close to his own views, such as the philosophy of the *Book of Changes* and his own binary system. Hegel, on the other hand, as mentioned above, considered that China had developed no proper philosophy of its own. Nevertheless, no matter whether the reaction was one of admiration, criticism, acceptance or rejection, Sino-Western exchanges were of great significance. The transmission of advanced Chinese science and technology to the West, especially the Chinese inventions of paper-making, gunpowder, printing and the compass, greatly changed the face of the whole world. Karl Marx said, "Chinese gunpowder blew the feudal class of knights to smithereens; the compass opened up world markets and built colonies; and printing became an implement of Protestantism and the most powerful lever and necessary precondition for intellectual development and creation." The English philosopher Roger Bacon said that China's four great inventions had "changed the face of the whole world and the state of affairs of everything."

3

Ancient China gave birth to a large number of eminent scientists, such as Zu Chongzhi, Li Shizhen, Sun Simiao, Zhang Heng, Shen Kuo and Bi

Sheng. They produced numerous treatises on scientific subjects, including *The Manual of Important Arts for the People's Welfare, Nine Chapters on the Mathematical Art, A Treatise on Febrile Diseases* and *Compendium of Materia Medica*. Their accomplishments included ones whose influence has been felt right down to modern times, such as the armillary sphere, seismograph, Dujiangyan water conservancy project, Dunhuang Grottoes, Grand Canal and Great Wall. But from the latter part of the 15th century, and for the next 400 years, Europe gradually became the cultural centre upon which the world's eyes were fixed. The world's most outstanding scientists then were England's Isaac Newton, Poland's Copernicus, France's Marie Curie, Germany's Rontgen and Einstein, Italy's Galileo, Russia's Mendelev and America's Edison.

The Chinese people then began to think: What is the cause of the rise and fall of nations? Moreover, how did it happen that gunpowder, invented in China and transmitted to the West, in no time at all made Europe powerful enough to batter down the gates of China herself?

It took the Opium War to wake China from its reverie. The first generation to make the bold step of "turning our eyes once again to the rest of the world" was represented by Lin Zexu and Wei Yuan. Zeng Guofan and Li Hongzhang started the Westernization Movement, and later intellectuals raised the slogan of "Democracy and Science." Noble-minded patriots, realizing that China had fallen behind in the race for modernization, set out on a painful quest. But in backwardness lay the motivation for change, and the quest produced the embryo of a towering hope, and the Chinese people finally gathered under a banner proclaiming a "March Toward Science."

On the threshold of the 21st century, the world is moving in the direction of becoming an integrated entity. This trend is becoming clearer by the day. In fact, the history of the various peoples of the world is also becoming the history of mankind as a whole. Today, it is impossible for any nation's culture to develop without absorbing the excellent aspects of the cultures of other peoples. When Western culture absorbs aspects of Chinese culture, this is not just because it has come into contact with Chinese culture, but also because of the active creativity and development of Western culture itself; and vice versa. The various cultures of the world's peoples are a precious heritage which we all share. Mankind no longer lives on different continents, but on one big continent, or in a "global village." And so, in this era characterized by an all-encompassing network of knowledge and information we should learn from each other and march in step along the highway of development to construct a brand-new "global village."

Western learning is still being transmitted to the East, and vice versa. China is accelerating its pace of absorption of the best parts of the cultures of other countries, and there is no doubt that both the West and the East need the nourishment of Chinese culture. Based on this recognition, we have edited and published the *Library of Chinese Classics* in a Chinese-English format as an introduction to the corpus of traditional Chinese culture in a comprehensive and systematic translation. Through this collection, our aim is to reveal to the world the aspirations and dreams of the Chinese people over the past 5,000 years and the splendour of the new historical era in China. Like a phoenix rising from the ashes, the Chinese people in unison are welcoming the cultural sunrise of the new century.

August 1999

前　言

　　《老子》又叫《道德经》，作者老聃。

　　历史上学者们曾长期争论是否确有老聃其人，《道德经》是否老聃所写。这主要是因为历史上第一个为老子作传的司马迁在《史记·老庄申韩列传》中提到三个"老子"，即老聃、老莱子和太史儋，他没有完全肯定《老子》的作者就是老聃。多种古代文献的记载和现代学者们的研究告诉我们：

　　老聃是春秋末期楚国苦县厉乡曲仁里人，大约生于公元前581年。可能从早年起就在东周王朝做"守藏室之史"。他的年龄比孔子大，孔子曾经向他请教过周礼。约在中年时期，因受到迫害，逃居鲁国数年，后又复任原职。约在50多岁时，因东周王朝内战，史册典籍为他人携走，自然失去官职。他离开东周去秦国。经过函谷关时，关令尹喜请求他为自己写书，老子便写下了这部书。以后老子在秦国隐居，不为世人所知。

　　老聃的思想在春秋末年已形成，成书和传播可能在战国前期。现存最早的马王堆出土的《老子》帛书甲、乙本和韩非的《解老》、《喻老》篇表明，《老子》在先秦只分上下篇，上篇为《德》，下篇为《道》，不分章，也不称经。就《老子》文本而言，它只是一个言论集，并非前后文字内容紧密相连的一个整体。分章始于汉代，至王弼定型。分章能够明晰原文的意思，同时也有割裂原义、造成后来抄写产生文句段落次序错乱等弊病。现在通行的《老子》为5400多字，81章。前37章为《道经》，后44章为《德经》。

　　《老子》是中国哲学史上第一部具有完整哲学体系的著作。老子的哲学涵盖了宇宙观、人生观和社会政治观。

　　"道"和"德"是老子哲学思想的理论基础。"道"在书中共出现 74 次，"德"44 次，这还不包括其他的替代词。"道"是由人生论、社会论和政治论上升到本体论的高度概括，"德"则是道的显现、展开，以及在人生、社会和政治生活中具体的指导和应用。"道"和"德"是体与用之间的关系。道是指未曾渗入一丝一毫人为的自然状态，即形而上学的道，落实到人生的层面上，其所显现的特征为人类所体验、所取法，都可以说是德的范围。

　　宇宙万物的本原是道，老子在书中反复说明这一点："道……渊兮，似万物之宗。"（第 4 章）"谷神不死，是谓玄牝。玄牝之门，是谓天地根。"（第 6 章）"'道'生一，一生二，二生三，三生万物。"（第 42 章）但是，老子又说："天下万物生于'有'，'有'生于'无'。"（第 40 章）"'无'，名天地之始；'有'，名万物之母。"（第 1 章）那么究竟"有"和"无"与"道"的关系如何来确定呢？"故常'无'，欲以观其妙；常'有'，欲以观其徼。此两者，同出而异名，同谓之玄。"（第 1 章）老子虽然说道是无，但是他又承认："'道'之为物，惟恍惟惚。惚兮恍兮，其中有象；恍兮惚兮，其中有物。窈兮冥兮，其中有精；其精甚真，其中有信。"（第 21 章）老子对于道的描述的不确定性，引起后人不同的理解，也因此产生了不同的哲学派别。同时，道作为老子哲学的最高范畴，从根本上否定了天作为人格神的至上的权威，使无神论的思想理论化，这种历史的进步以及对后人的影响是巨大的。

　　"道"的含义在《老子》书中虽然主要是形而上的或是抽象的，它也指具体的规律，这种具体规律含义的"道"就同于"德"了。例如："水善利万物而不争，处众人之所恶，

故几于'道'。"（第8章）

　　"道"的含义虽然很多，但是它有两种最突出的规律：对立转化和返本复初。用对立统一的观点解释世界的构成和变化，源于原始思维的哲学观，古希腊毕达哥拉斯学派的宇宙论以及列维—布留尔在《原始思维》和列维—斯特劳斯在《野性的思维》中都有类似的描述，但是《老子》一书中不仅对立的观念十分突出，如：有无、难易、高下等有 70 对以上，而且强调将这些观念上升到矛盾普遍性的高度，"万物负阴而抱阳"（第 42 章），同时他注意强调矛盾的对立面，例如："三十辐共一毂，当其无，有车之用。埏埴以为器，当其无，有器之用。凿户牖，以为室，当其无，有室之用。"（第 11 章）他强调矛盾的平衡，"冲气以为和"（第 42 章），强调相互依存，"天下皆知美之为美，斯恶已；皆知善之为善，斯不善已。"（第 2 章）同时，世界上的万事万物不仅相反相成，而且相互转化，并且这种转化是绝对的。"故飘风不终朝，暴雨不终日"（第 23 章），不仅如此，万事万物的变化都是向其反面转化。"曲则全，枉则直，洼则盈，敝则新，少则得，多则惑。"（第 22 章）"祸兮，福之所倚；福兮，祸之所伏。"（第 58 章）同时，这种变化也是由量变而质变的。"合抱之木，生于毫末；九层之台，起于累土；千里之行，始于足下。"（第 64 章）因此做事要"图难于其易，为大于其细；天下难事，必作于易，天下大事，必作于细"（第 63 章）。"其安易持，其未兆易谋。其脆易泮，其微易散。为之于未有，治之于未乱。"（第 64 章）所谓"反者'道'之动"（第 40 章），或是返本复初，是指道表现出的一种循环运动的规律。然而，老子强调的是复初、归根、守静和复命。正如第 52 章所说："天下有始，以为天下母。既得其母，以知其子；既知其子，复守其母，没身不殆。"

　　老子对世界的认识是深刻的，但是他认识世界的方法却是隐者的方法：静观与玄览。人可以"不出户，知天下；不窥牖，见天道。其出弥远，其知弥少"（第47章）。通过主观的直觉认识，来达到"玄同"，即主客观的绝对同一。正是这种认识方法与佛教、道教等修炼方法相通，对后人产生了深远的影响。

　　以这样的宇宙观和认识论看待人生，所要遵循的原则是"'道'生之，'德'畜之，物形之，势成之。是以万物莫不尊'道'而贵'德'"（第51章）。"德"是得自于道的自然本性，"孔'德'之容，惟'道'是从。"（第21章）做人因此就应该"见素抱朴，少私寡欲，绝学无忧"（第19章）。甚至要做到"含'德'之厚，比于赤子"（第55章）。这样做人就要做到与世无争，要能够"知其雄，守其雌，为天下溪。为天下溪，常德不离，复归于婴儿。知其白，守其黑，为天下式。为天下式，常德不忒，复归于无极。知其荣，守其辱，为天下谷。为天下谷，常德乃足，复归于朴"（第28章）。做人还要有自知之明。"知不知，尚矣；不知知，病也。圣人不病，以其病病。夫唯病病，是以不病。"（第71章）"是以圣人自知不自见，自爱不自贵。"（第72章）为人做事不能躁进，"重为轻根，静为躁君。"（第26章）"企者不立；跨者不行；自见者不明；自是者不彰；自伐者无功；自矜者不长。"（第24章）同时要明白"持而盈之，不如其已；揣而锐之，不可长保。金玉满堂，莫之能守；富贵而骄，自遗其咎。功遂身退，天之道也"（第9章）。所以，"上士闻道，勤而行之。"（第41章）要能够充分理解：

　　　　明道若昧；进道若退；

　　　　夷道若纇；上德若谷；

　　　　广德若不足；建德若偷；

　　　　质真若渝；大白若辱；

大方无隅；大器晚成；

大音希声；大象无形；

"道"隐无名。（第41章）

至于养生，老子的主要观点有三：一是寡欲，"五色令人目盲；五音令人耳聋；五味令人口爽；驰骋畋猎，令人心发狂；难得之货，令人行妨。"（第12章）所以要"塞其兑，闭其门，挫其锐，解其纷，和其光，同其尘"（第56章）。二是不自益其生，"益生曰祥"（第55章），因为"物壮则老，谓之不道，不道早已"（第55章）。"人之生，动之于死地，亦十有三。夫何故？以其生生之厚。"（第50章）三是保养精气，"载营魄抱一"，并且"专气致柔"（第10章）。

老子的政治观可以用三句话来概括："以正治国，以奇用兵，以无事取天下。"（第57章）"'道'常无为而无不为。侯王若能守之，万物将自化。"（第37章）"我无为，而民自化；我好静，而民自正；我无事，而民自富；我无欲，而民自朴。"（第57章）只有"圣人处无为之事"（第2章），模仿"天地不仁，以万物为刍狗；圣人不仁，以百姓为刍狗"（第5章），任其自然发展，就能够做到"为无为，则无不治"（第3章）。从这一角度出发，老子既反对以法治国，也反对儒家的仁义礼智，他认为"法令滋彰，盗贼多有"（第57章）；"大道废，有仁义；智慧出，有大伪；六亲不和，有孝慈；国家昏乱，有忠臣"（第18章）；"故失'道'而后'德'，失'德'而后仁，失仁而后义，失义而后礼。夫礼者，忠信之薄，而乱之首。前识者，'道'之华，而愚之始"（第38章）。结合具体的历史实际来看，那个时代提倡的法制和仁义礼智不可能使百姓过着和平、安宁的生活。

老子反对战争，他认为"夫兵者，不祥之器，物或恶之，故有道者不处"（第31章），"以道佐人主者，不以兵强天下。其事好还。师之所处，荆棘生焉。大军之后，必有凶年。"（第30章）但是老子并不绝对拒绝战争，"不得已而用之，恬淡为上。"（第31章）用兵的目的在于济困救危，"善有果而已，不敢以取强。果而勿矜，果而勿伐，果而勿骄，果而不得已，果而勿强。"（第30章）如果夸示自己的兵力，以示强大，那么"而美之者，是乐杀人。夫乐杀人者，则不可得志于天下矣"（第31章）。

老子的理想社会是一幅"小国寡民"之图。"小国寡民。使有什伯之器而不用，使民重死而不远徙。虽有舟舆，无所乘之；虽有甲兵，无所陈之。使民复结绳而用之。甘其食，美其服，安其居，乐其俗，邻国相望，鸡犬之声相闻，民至老死，不相往来。"（第80章）这是一个隐居者的乌托邦，是一个原始愚昧的社会，是不可能真正达到所谓"甘食、美服、安居和乐俗"的。不过，我们从它的反面却看到了春秋末期战争不断和弱肉强食的动荡社会给老子带来的痛苦和思考。我们从老子的大量论述中能够深刻地感受到这一点：

朝甚除，田甚芜，仓甚虚；服文采，带利剑，厌饮食；财货有余，是谓盗夸。非道也哉！（第53章）

民不畏威，则大威至。无狎其所居，无厌其所生。夫唯不厌，是以不厌。（第72章）

民不畏死，奈何以死惧之？若使民常畏死，而为奇者，吾得执而杀之，孰敢？（第74章）

民之饥，以其上食税之多，是以饥。民之难治，以其上之有为，是以难治。民之轻死，以其上求生之厚，是以轻死。（第75章）

天之道，损有余而补不足。人之道，则不然，损不足以奉有余。（第77章）

唯有道者，能有余以奉天下。(第77章)

受国之垢，是谓社稷主；受国不祥，是为天下王。(第78章)

老子智慧的特征是"贵柔"，即"柔弱胜刚强"(第36章)。他以最普通的自然现象作比喻，"天下莫柔弱于水，而攻坚强者莫之能胜。"(第78章)"人之生也柔弱，其死也坚强。草木之生也柔脆，其死也枯槁。故坚强者死之徒，柔弱者生之徒。"(第76章)正是对柔弱的深刻和辩证的认识，运用到实践中，便成了一种制人之术。"将欲歙之，必固张之；将欲弱之，必固强之；将欲废之，必固兴之；将欲取之，必固与之。"(第36章)所以，老子以静、柔、弱、退、不敢、无为来达到战胜他人的目的。而这种制人之术的最佳境界便是"行无行；攘无臂；扔无敌；执无兵"(第69章)。

老子总结自己的思想，说："我有三宝，持而保之。一曰慈，二曰俭，三曰不敢为天下先。"(第67章)这可能是对"贵柔"思想的最好注解。而"柔弱胜刚强"的具体表现，即老子称赞的做法，可以从《老子》中众多含有"善"字的句子归纳如下：

23

一、"天之道，不争而善胜，不言而善应，不召而自来，繟然而善谋"(第73章)。"天道无亲，常与善人"(第79章)。"上善若水"(第8章)。

二、古之善为道者，微妙玄通，深不可识。夫唯不可识，故强为之容：

豫兮其若冬涉川；

犹兮其若畏四邻；

俨兮其若客；

涣兮其若凌释；

敦兮其若朴；

旷兮其若谷；

混兮其若浊；

（澹兮其若海；

飚兮若无止。）

孰能浊以静之徐清；

孰能安以动之徐生。

保此道者不欲盈。夫唯不盈，故能敝而新成。

（第15章）

　　三、古之善为道者，非以明民，将以愚之。民之难治，以其智多。故以智治国，国之贼；不以智治国，国之福。如此两者亦稽式。常知稽式，是谓"玄德"，"玄德"深矣，远矣，与物反矣，然后乃至大顺。（第65章）

　　四、居善地，心善渊，与善仁，言善信，政善治，事善能，动善时。（第8章）

　　五、善行无辙迹；

善言无瑕谪；

善数不用筹策；

善闭无关楗而不可开；

善结无绳约而不可解。

是以圣人常善救人，故无弃人；

常善救物，故无弃物。（第27章）

　　六、盖闻善摄生者，

陆行不遇兕虎，

入军不被甲兵；

兕无所投其角，

虎无所用其爪，

兵无所用其刃。（第50章）

　　七、善建者不拔，

善抱者不脱，

子孙以祭祀不辍。

修之于身，

其德乃真；

修之于家，

其德乃余；

修之于乡，

其德乃长；

修之于邦，

其德乃丰；

修之于天下，

其德乃普。(第54章)

八、善为士者，不武；

善战者，不怒；

善胜敌者，不与；

善用人者，为之下。

是谓不争之德，

是谓用人之力，

是谓配天古之极。(第68章)

　　老子用"善"字表达了自己的智慧和理想，教导人们如何做人，如何运用智慧指导行动，他还强调理论要联系实际。"吾言甚易知，甚易行。天下莫能知，莫能行。"(第70章)"弱之胜强，柔之胜刚，天下莫不知，莫能行。"(第78章)所以他反复强调"知和曰'常'"(第55章)、"复命曰常"(第16章)、"知常容"(第16章)、"是谓袭常"(第52章)、"知常曰'明'"(第16章和第55章)。"知常容，容乃公，公乃全，全乃天，天乃道，道乃久，没身不殆。"(第16章)也许第25章和第39章的两段话可以作为总结："人法地，地法天，天法'道'，'道'法自然。""昔之得

'一'者：天得'一'以清；地得'一'以宁；神得'一'以灵；谷得'一'以盈；万物得'一'以生；侯王得'一'以为天下正。"

老子的智慧博大精深。分析、解释、评论和批判老子思想的著作和文章很多，这里只是试图客观地描述老子思想的主要内容。

老子思想并非凭空产生，书中的"圣人云"、"用兵者有言"、"建言有之"、"古之所谓"等表明他继承了前人的思想，这种成分有多大，还有待学者们的进一步研究。

《老子》思想的形成对后世产生了巨大的影响。

首先，道家思想在战国中后期展开，形成两大流派。一派为以庄子为代表的道家，另一派为稷下黄老道家。老子在世时没有公开收徒讲学，只是以自隐为务，所以关于他的弟子的史料是很少的。据《庄子》和其他一些古籍记载，老子的弟子有关尹、庚桑楚、列御寇、杨朱等人。关尹的思想，《庄子·天下》中并列引用关尹和老子的话，以显示他们思想的一致，其中有："关尹曰'在己无居，形物自著。其动若水，其静若镜，其应若响。芴乎若亡，寂乎若清。同焉者和，得焉者失。未尝先人而常随人'。"《庄子·庚桑楚》中说："老聃之役，有庚桑楚者，偏得老聃之道。"李定生、徐慧君认为："继承和发展老子'道'的学说的，在其门人中，以庚桑楚和文子最为著名……庚桑楚这一派，实际上就是庄子学派，所以庄子称赞他'偏得老聃之道'。"庚桑楚的著作没有流传下来。1973年河北定县40号汉墓出土《文子》残篇，证明其书为先秦古籍，今传的通行本成书应在庄子著作之后。从《文子》一书中看，文子的思想特点是以道家为主，同时也吸收了儒、墨、法等家的影响。列御寇，古籍多有记载其为关尹的弟子，他的思想和老子的思想多有相同之处，其特点《吕氏春秋》称"列子贵虚"。《列子》中说："非其名也，莫如静，莫如虚。静也虚也，得其居矣；取也与也，失其所矣。事之破砀而后有舞仁义者，弗能复也。"杨朱的思想也是以道家思想为主，特点是轻物重生。庄子则是先秦道家学派的集大成者，司马迁说庄子"其学无所不窥，然其要本归于老子之言"。庄子对老子的发展在于他对作为本体论的道转化成为心灵境界，更为深广地发挥了人的自由性与自在性。

诸子学说到了战国中期以后，由各家交流趋向汇合。稷下学派、黄老学派都是融合儒、墨、名、法、阴阳各家思想而以道家为主体的学派。自田齐第二代国君桓公开创稷下学宫至襄王，历时约100多年，据《史记·田齐世家》："宣王喜文学游说之士，自如邹衍、淳于髡、田骈、接予、慎到、环渊之徒七十六人，皆赐列第为上大夫，不治而议论，是以齐稷下学士复盛，且数百千人。"稷下学宫所历时间之长，形成学派之多，其学术影响之深广是中国历史上所罕见的。稷下道家又称黄老之学，其原因在于齐国君把黄帝看作自己的祖先，老子又是齐国统治者故国的思想家，它把道家的自然哲学改造成为政治权术。其学术思想对战国后期的政治斗争产生了十分重大的影响。所以，后来《汉书·艺文志》说："道家者流，盖出于史官，历记成败、存亡、祸福、古今之道，然后知秉要执本，清虚自守，卑弱自持，此君人南面之术也。"例如宋钘和尹文以道家思想为主，又有墨家和名家思想的特征；慎到和田骈把道家思想和法家思想结合起来，形成了道法结合的思想体系。《管子》4篇、黄老帛书4篇等都是以道家思想为主，兼容其他诸家思想。

老子的思想对先秦其他各家思想均有一定程度的影响。孔子曾经向老子问礼，其思想中有老子影响的痕迹。孟子和荀子的思想中有一些明显受到老子思想影响的痕迹。法家代表人物申不害和韩非，都是本于黄老思想的。老子的思想对先秦兵家思想影响很大。唐代的王真就说过："老子之言……未尝有一章不属意于兵也。"后世兵家则认为，上篇《道经》是对兵略兵法思想给予理论上的概括并提高到宇宙观和世界观上给予论证。下篇《德经》是直接论述军事战略战术，并通过总结战争规律而引申出社会历史观和人生观。

《吕氏春秋》作为先秦时期思想的总结，是一部以老、庄与黄老为主体，同时又吸收阴阳、儒、墨、名、法各家观点的一部巨著。

黄老思想作为统治术发展的成熟，加上长期战乱的结束和人心思安的客观社会需要，西汉前、中期一直为统治者所用。经过几十年的休养生息，汉代的经济繁荣起来。后来的每一个新的封建王朝建立，差不多都吸取了汉初道家思想治世的经验，使社会由动乱转为安定，使经济得到发展。正是这样的社会实践，使得道家思想得到进一步的发展，《淮南子》和司马谈的《论六家之要指》正是这一时期道家思想的总结。"其为术也，因阴阳之大顺，采儒墨之善，撮名法之要。与时迁移，应物变化，立俗施事，无所不宜。指约而易操，事少而功多。"很清楚地说明道家思想的发展与优势。

西汉中后期和东汉时期，儒家思想虽然占上风，但严遵《老子指归》和河上公《老子河上公章句》的出现，王充、王符和仲长统等社会批判家的著作，对老子思想的传播起到了积极的作用。神化黄老、长生成仙之道由上层逐渐传播到民间，内修炼丹、符水治病为道教的建立做好铺垫，《老子想尔注》、《太平经》和《周易参同契》的出现使得借老子思想而建立的道教真正有了理论基础。

魏晋南北朝时期道家思想的影响呈现出多样化。玄学的发展是以道家思想为主的儒道合流。从王弼的"名教出于自然"，到阮籍、嵇康的"越名教而任自然"，到郭象的"名教即自然"都是如此。佛教从两汉之际传入中国后，先是依附黄老道术，后又依附于玄学，即使鸠摩罗什在翻译中努力再现印度佛学的本来面目，实际上佛学与老庄和玄学仍有诸多相似之处。同时，大批士族人物进入道教，使道教组织的阶级成分和文化水平发生了变化，东晋葛洪、北魏寇谦之、刘宋陆修静和南朝陶弘景从各自的立场、利益和实际出发，对道教从形式到内容进行了全面系统的变革，道家思想和道教信仰合为一体，作为民间宗教的道教由于理论的系统化和宗教仪规的正规化走到了官方宗教的地位，这也使道家思想得到更广泛的传播和发展。

隋唐时期，道家思想和道教的传播由于统治者的关系进入鼎盛时期，李世民的"贞观之治"就是再次显现了道家思想在封建政权治国中的作用。唐玄宗崇道，亲自注疏《道德经》，在历史上第一次纂修道藏，并采取了一系列崇道的措施。道教的理论和养生的理论与实践在隋唐五代不断得以发展和深化。

宋代以后，道家思想仍然发挥着重要的作用。统治者的提倡和道教本身发展的需要，各种不同道教宗派的产生，推动着道教理论的不断深化发展，最显著的特征之一就是宋明时期多次进行《道藏》的编修。如真宗诏令编修《宝文统录》、张君房撮其精要为《云笈七籖》，宋徽宗时的《政和万寿道藏》，明代的《正统道藏》和《万历续道藏》。这说明宋、元、明统治者对道教的重视和扶持，也说明《道藏》的重要价值。清代《白云观重修〈道藏〉记》中说："《道藏》真经为入道之门墙、修仙之法则，其间三教九流、天文地理无不全备，俾出世者有助于身心，住世者有助于家国，是非特修道者赖乎此，即治世者亦未尝弗资乎此矣。"

宋明理学和心学多方面吸收融合了道家思想。例如：周敦颐将内丹修炼的无极图改造为太极图时，其文字说明：无极→太极→阴阳→五行→四时→万物和人类，是一个道家的宇宙生成模式，正是周氏的这一模式奠定了宋明理学本体论的基石。王廷相说："老子谓道生天地，宋儒谓天地之先只有此理，此乃改易面目立论耳，与老庄之旨何殊？"邵雍的宇宙生成次序为太极→阴阳→（两仪）→四象→八卦→万物。他理解的道和太极是一个东西，同时也明确认为道或太极都是心的表现；陆九渊和王阳明正是继承了邵雍的思想，创造了陆王心学。王阳明在《传习录》中说："这心体即所谓道，心体明即是道明，更无二。"

大批的道家思想学者注释《老子》和研究道家思想著作不断出现，使得道家思想与儒释相融合，成为历史潮流。而且自宋以来，作为道教养生学的一个重要部分的内丹学，在道家思想的发展和指导下，有了很大的发展。一部《道德经》被理解成为一幅无极——太极图，道家气功的指导书，被理解成：道在天，更在人；在身，更在心。

清代以及近现代学者对于道家思想和道教的研究不断深入细致，使我们越来越认识到老子思想的博大精深。也使我们充分认识到老子思想和孔子思想一起构成中国正统传统文化思想的主流。

《老子》在中国流传 2500 年，先秦以来，研究和注释《道德经》的书籍种类繁多，确切多少，实难估计。元代人张与材序杜道坚《道德经原旨》（《道藏》本）说："《道德》八十一章，注者三千余家。"这个数字也许有些夸大。张松如《老子校读》所列引用书目只有 94 种，陈鼓应《老子注译及评介》参考书目为 262 种。一般而言，比较通行和有影响的本子大体有：

先秦至六朝：马王堆汉墓帛书《老子》、河上公《老子章句》和王弼《道德真经注》；初唐至五代：傅奕《道德经古本篇》；两宋至元代：王安石《老子注》、苏辙《老子解》、林希逸《老子口义》、范应元《老子道德经古本集注》和吴澄《道德真经注》；明代：薛蕙《老子集解》、释德清《老子道德经解》、沈一贯《老子通》和焦竑《老子翼》；清代：王念孙《老子杂志》、余樾《老子平议》、高延第《老子证义》、易顺鼎《读老札记》和刘师培《老子斠补》；民国：马叙伦《老子校诂》、奚侗《老子集解》、高亨《老子正诂》、蒋锡昌《老子校诂》、劳健《老子古本考》和严灵峰《老子章句新编》；建国以后：朱谦之《老子校释》、车载《论老子》、《哲学研究》编辑部《老子哲学讨论集》；1973年马王堆帛书公布后：张松如《老子校读》和陈鼓应《老子注释及评介》。

《老子》一书早期向国外传播的情况由于资料有限和语言的障碍，目前难以清晰描绘。综合马祖毅、任荣珍《汉籍外译史》、黄鸣奋《英语世界中国古典文学之传播》和外语教学与研究出版社汉英对照本《道德经》王岳川序言中有关《老子》在国外传播的资料，并以笔者所搜集资料为主要线索，可以大体勾勒这样一个传播的轮廓。

最晚在隋代，《道德经》一书就传到了日本。以后多种注译本的传入，丰富了日本对老子的研究。巴黎的保罗·佩里奥 1912 年在《通报》上曾撰文说，《道德经》曾在公元 7 世纪被译成梵文。

西方人开始接触《老子》应该是 18 世纪。约在 18 世纪中叶，《老子》被译成拉丁文。据说比利时籍耶稣会士卫方济（1651—1729）曾以法文译《道德经》，傅圣泽约于 1729 年用拉丁文和法文译《道德经评注》，法国汉学家雷慕萨 1732 年只译了《道德经》4 章。1842 年巴黎出版了斯坦尼斯拉·朱里安《老子道德经》法文本，1870 年莱比锡出版了维克多·施特劳斯的《老子道德经》德译本。最早的俄译本由丹尼尔·西维洛夫完成于 19 世纪上半叶，虽然至 1915 年才发表。最早的《老子》英译本出现在 19 世纪 70 年代前后。

1884 年，伦敦出版了巴尔弗的《道书》。理雅各《道书》译本 1891 年由牛津出版。1898 年美国芝加哥出版的保罗·卡鲁斯《老子道德经》译本，一般认为是质量较好的通行本。该书比较系统地介绍了老子生平和《道德经》在中国的流传。译文后还附有评论、阅读参考书目和索引，以后重印过多次。瑞典传教士艾利克·福尔基在本世纪初用瑞典文译《老子》。

本世纪初，大批《老子》译本的出现和已有译本的多次重印，从一个侧面反映了《老子》在西方的普及。例如：老沃尔特·高尔恩《老子》译本 1904 年第 1 版，1905 年通行本，1913 年第 3 版，1922 年重印。贾尔斯《老子言论集》1905 年第 1 版，以后分别于 1906、1909、1911、1917 和1922 年 5 次重印，这个集子将老子之言分为 10 类，对一般读者了解老子思想十分有益。第一次世界大战后，德国出现过"老子热"，有多种德文《道德经》译本，1921 年出版了卫礼贤《老子道德经》译本。这期间的诸多译本是难以确切统计的。

1934 年伦敦出版的亚瑟·韦利英译本《道和德〈道德经〉及其在中国思想中的地位研究》对《老子》在西方的传播有较大的影响，重印过多次。该书比较系统地叙述了中国先秦哲学和老子思想的地位，译文注意表达老子的哲学思想。

老子思想对西方的影响是多方面的。德国哲学家海德格尔译过《老子》，他的晚年深受老子思想的影响。俄国伟大的作家列夫·托尔斯泰翻译过《老子》。美国伟大的戏剧家尤金·奥尼尔在其作品中显示了老子对他的影响。同时，我们还看到许多有关老子思想对国外物理学家、音乐家、诗人、政治家等的影响以及国外学者从语言学、美学等多角度研究《老子》的记述。

从现有的资料看，第一个英译《道德经》的中国人是胡泽龄，他的译本 1936 年在成都出版。吴经熊的《道德经》译文1939 和 1940 年发表在《天下》月刊 9、10 两期上。林语堂1948 年纽约出版的《老子智慧》和 1959 年伦敦出版的初大告《道德经》译本在西方有一定的影响。第一个用法文翻译《道德经》的中国人是刘嘉槐。四五十年代开始，港、台和海外华人学者对于《老子》在西方的普及做出了很大的贡献。

50 年代后，荷兰、匈牙利、罗马利亚、波兰、西班牙、捷克、希腊等国相继都有《道德经》译本问世。林振述在《老子〈道德经〉和王弼注英译》序言中说：各种外文译本已有七八十种之多。而且至少是世界上每一种语言有一种译本。又据陈荣捷《老子之道》："《道德经》已 44 次被译成英文。特别是在过去的 20 年里（自 1963 年往前推算），几乎每隔一年都有一种新译本出版，其中这些译本的半数是在美国出版的。"

自 1963 年以来，特别是 1973 年长沙马王堆汉墓出土的帛书《老子》甲、乙本出版后，海外掀起一阵老子研究热、东方文化研究热。研究老子其人其书、帛书《老子》各种注本以及新英译本大量出现。笔者所读到的帛书《老子》英译本有三：刘殿爵《老子道德经》，香港中文大学，1989 年，后来又在美国和加拿大重版；韩禄伯《老子德道经》，麦克米兰公司，1989 年和梅维恒 1990 年帛书《老子》译本。应该指出的是，帛书虽是迄今为止最古老的本子，对于我们研究先秦哲学和文化有重要的价值，但却不是最好的文本。一般来讲，学者们研究和翻译仍以王弼本为主。

自 1978 年中国大陆实行改革开放政策以来，对外交流的扩大，也促进了国内学者英译和校注已有的英译本，90 年代以来，几乎每年国内外都有《老子》新译问世。

《道德经》译本众多，难以统计。其中译文质量较好且有影响的英译本还有：1963 年纽约出版的陈荣捷《老子之道》、1963 年企鹅丛书刘殿爵译《道德经》、1977 年密执安大学出版的林振述《老子道德经及王弼注英译》、1977 年台湾出版的杨有维和罗杰·艾米斯合译陈鼓应《老子注译及评介》和 1989 年麦克米兰公司出版的韩禄伯《老子德道经——最新发现马王堆帛书新译》。

在西方，除《圣经》外，《老子》译本种类最多。这毫无疑问地证明，博大精深的老子思想不仅是中国人民宝贵的遗产，同样也是世界人民宝贵的文化遗产。

西方学者为什么对《老子》一书如此迷恋，为什么英译本不断出现，贾尔斯博士在为初大告英译本写的序言中一段话也许使我们能够窥见一斑。他认为《道德经》是一本警句集，尽管有如此多的译本，似乎没有一个译本与原作能够完全一致。如同一面镜子，译文从不同的层面折射出老子的思想，但是老子的话仍然深奥难懂。"原作的用词十分深刻、简洁。可以肯定：从来没有一本书内容如此丰富而篇幅又如此短小。宇宙间分布着一定数量的'白矮星'。它们通常体积很小，但是原子堆积非常紧凑，相对体积而言，其重量是巨大的，因此也需要放射更多的热量，其表面温度远高于太阳的表面温度。将《道德经》比作哲学著作中的'白矮星'是恰当的，因为它分量十分厚重、结构非常紧凑和内涵特别丰富，不断放射出思想的白矮星光。"

笔者所阅读过的近 20 种《道德经》译本中，韦利先生的译本应该算是上乘译作之一。其文字浅显、流畅，对原文的理解比较细微、精确。加上韦利先生精通中国先秦典籍，所采用的底本为王弼本，同时也参照多家注本，并在少数地方加以自己的考证和诠释。对于他自己的译文，韦利先生说过下面一番话："依我看来，如果将译作的文字优美放在重要的位置，同时又要重视原文在译文中的质量，译者就得准备牺牲大量精确的细节。这种翻译，我把它叫做'文学翻译'，相对应的是'文字翻译'。我要表明的是，这本《道德经》译文不是'文学翻译'。理由很简单，原文的重要性并不存在于其文学质量，而是它所要表达的哲理。我的一个目的就是要在细节上精确地表达原文的意思。"该译文由著名英国文学家贾尔斯博士审校。

本书的汉语原文与今译选用陈鼓应教授的《老子注译及评介》。英译选用英国著名汉学家亚瑟·韦利先生的《道德经》译本。

笔者所做的工作有以下几点：

一、调整字、句次序。陈鼓应教授说："《老子》一书，错简（指文句段落颠倒）、衍文（指误增）、脱字及误字不少，今依王弼本为蓝本，参看帛书本及傅奕本等古本，根据历代校诂学者可取的见解，加以订正。"韦氏所依底本亦是王弼本，从整体上来说，字、词次序的调整数量不大。

二、注解不同的字、句和理解有歧义的字、句。对于两种本子出现的少量不同的字、句，说明出处和原因，对于两种本子字句有不同理解的，一般以陈本为主，并引用其他译本符合陈本意思的词句作为参考。

三、填补漏缺、改正错误。少数错、漏之处，或其中一个本子多出的字句，我都反复阅读陈本以及各种注释，并参照其他多种比较可靠的本子，如张松如《老子校读》等，保持原文不动，在注中说明如何改动、删减、增添。个别译文，笔者认为不妥的，择其他较好的译文附录于注释中供参考。

还有一点要说明的是，陈鼓应教授的今译因在时间上作于韦利先生英译之后，两种本子之间理解和表达上的一些差别，只好任其自然，不宜加注。

笔者学识有限，错误难免，敬请读者赐教。

傅惠生
1999 年春于华东师大

35

INTRODUCTION

The book of *Laozi* or *Dao De Jing* was written by Lao Dan.

There has been long in history a doubt whether there once existed such a Lao Dan, and whether he is the author of the book. This is mainly because Sima Qian, the first person in history to write the biography of Laozi in *Records of the Historian*, mentioned three men named "Laozi," i. e. Lao Dan, Lao Laizi and Historian Dan. He did not confirm that the author of the book of *Laozi* was Lao Dan. Many books written in the pre-Qin times and studies of modern scholars tell us:

Lao Dan (c. 581 — 500 B. C.) was a native from Quren Village, Li District, Hu County (now in Henan Province) in the State of Chu in the later Spring and Autumn Period. Possibly he began his career as the librarian and archivist at the royal court of the Eastern Zhou dynasty when young. He was much older than Confucius, and Confucius once sought advice from him about rites of the Zhou dynasty. At about middle age, he escaped to the State of Lu for some years because of persecution at home, then he returned and resumed his work. At about fifty, when war broke out within the Empire, all his books and documents were looted away, and he naturally lost his position. He left then for the State of Qin. When he arrived at the Hangu Pass, the pass keeper Yin Xi asked him to write a book for Xi, thus Lao Dan wrote this book. After then, Lao Dan lived as a recluse in the State of Qin, and no one knew anything about him thereafter.

The thought of Laozi took shape possibly in the later years of the Spring and Autumn Period, but the book was written down and circulated

in the early years of the Warring States Period. The earliest texts exca-
vated from Mawangdui, *Exposition on Laozi* and *Understanding of Laozi in Stories* in the book of *Han Fei* indicate that in the pre-Qin times, the book was divided only in two parts, *De* for Volume 1, and *Dao* for Volume 2, and there was no such a word *Jing* (classic) for the name. The text is an anthology, and not a cohesive and coherent whole. It was divided into chapters in the Han dynasties, and became fixed when Wang Bi (226-249) commented on the book. Division of the text into chapters brought clearer the meaning of sentences and paragraphs, and at the same time, caused misplacement of sentences and paragraphs, and mis-understanding of the original meaning in the text. The popular edition of *Laozi* now is divided into 81 chapters with over 54,000 words, the first thirty-seven chapters is *Dao Jing*, and the second forty-four *De Jing*.

The book of *Laozi* is the first with comprehensive philosophical sys-
tem in the history of Chinese philosophy. The philosophy of Laozi is first about the universe, then human life and next, politics.

"Dao" as the metaphysical core appears for seventy-four times and "De" as a key concept forty-four times in the text, exclusive of different substitutes and pronouns. Dao derives from the perspicacious generali-zation from human life, society, politics to ontology; while De is the rev-elation and expansion of Dao, the application of Dao to give guidance to social, political and human life. The relation between Dao and De is that between a body and its function. Dao refers to the natural state without any sign of man's interference, i. e. the metaphysical Dao, when it is applied to the human or social life, its unfolded characteristics emulated and experienced by human beings are all that can be regarded within the scope of De. The origin of the universe and myriad things comes from Dao. Laozi reiterates in the book, "The Way(Dao)... is bottomless, the very progenitor of all the things in the world. " (Ch. 4) "The Valley Spirit (Dao) never dies, it is named the Mysterious Female. " (Ch. 6) "Tao (Dao) gave birth to the One, the One gave birth successively to two things, three things, up to ten thousand. " (Ch. 42) Laozi also expresses the thought in another way that "All creatures under heaven are the products of Being, Being itself is the product of Non-being. " (Ch. 40) "It was from the Nameless that Heaven and Earth sprang; The named is but the mother that rears the ten thousand creatures, each after its kind (Non-being names the beginning of Heaven and Earth; Being names the mother of the myriad things). " (Ch. 1) But what about the relation between Dao and Being and Non-being? "Only he that rids himself forever of desire can see the Secret Essences; He that has never rid himself of desire can see only the Outcomes (Constantly from the angle of non-being, we can perceive the mysteries of Dao; from the angle of being, we can perceive its boundaries. These two are of the same origin with different names, so it can only be called the Mystery). " (Ch. 1) Although Laozi holds Dao is non-being, he also admits, "For the Way (Dao) is a thing impalpable, incommensurable. Incommensurable, impalpable, yet latent in it are forms; impalpable, incommensurable, yet within it are entities. Shadowy it is and dim; yet within it there is a force (essence), a force (the essence) that though rarefied is none the less efficacious. " (Ch. 21) The ambiguous description of Dao in the book derived different interpretations in the later generations and also brought into existence of different philosophical schools. Dao as the core of Laozi's philosophy denies the absolute and divine power of heaven, and theorizes the atheistic thoughts, this historic progress produces profound influence on later generations.

The meaning of Dao in the book is mainly metaphysical or abstract, but it also refers to the concrete laws, in such a sense, Dao has the meaning same or similar to De, for example, "The goodness of water is that it benefits the ten thousand creatures; yet itself does not scramble, but is content with the places that all men disdain. It is this that makes water so near to the Way (Dao). " (Ch. 8)

Although there are multiple meanings for Dao, the two most outstanding laws are: unity of opposites and return to the root. The theory of unity of opposites in exposition of the universe and its change derives from the primitive thought. We can read many similar descriptions, for instance, in *Les fonctions mentals dans les sociétés inferieures* by Lucien Levy-Brühl, in *La Pensée sauvage* by Claude Lévi-Strauss and in the description of the universe by the Pythagorean School. However, not only the pairs of opposites are overwhelming in the book numbered over seventy, for example, being and non-being, difficulty and easiness, height and low, and so on, but also universality of the concept is emphasized, "these ten thousand creatures cannot turn their backs to the shade without having the sun on their bellies (the myriad things shoulder the *yin* and embrace the *yang*). " (Ch. 42)

At the same time, he lays tight hold on the opposite side of the contradiction, for instance, "We put thirty spokes together and call it a wheel; but it is on the space where there is nothing that the usefulness of the wheel depends. We turn clay to make a vessel; but it is on the space where there is nothing that the usefulness of the vessel depends. We pierce doors and windows to make a house; and it is on these spaces where there is nothing that the usefulness of the house depends (Thirty spokes converge at one hub, but only when there is non-being does the function of carriage exist. We mould clay to make a vessel, only when there is non-being does the function of the vessel exist. We bore out doors and windows to make a house, only when there is non-being does

大中华文库

the function of the house exist). " (Ch. 11) He emphasizes the balance and harmony of contradictions, "it is on this blending of the breaths that their harmony depends (Through coalescing of *yin* and *yang*, they attain a state of harmony). " (Ch. 42) He also emphasizes interdependence of the opposites. "It is because every one under Heaven recognizes beauty as beauty, that the idea of ugliness exists. And equally if every one recognized virtue (goodness) as virtue(goodness), this would merely create fresh conceptions of wickedness. " (Ch. 2) At the same time, the myriad things under Heaven are not only opposite and interdependent but also mutually changeable, and the change is definite to take place. "A hurricane never lasts a whole morning, nor a rainstorm all day. " (Ch. 23) Furthermore, every change moves towards its opposite side, "To remain whole, be twisted! To become straight, let yourself be bent. To become full, be hollow. Be tattered, that you may be renewed. Those that have little, may get more; those that have much, are but perplexed. " (Ch. 22) "It is upon bad fortune that good fortune leans, upon good fortune that bad fortune rests. " (Ch. 58) And the change is usually gradual from quantity to quality. "The tree big as a man's embrace began as a tiny sprout, the tower nine storeys high began with a heap of earth, the journey of a thousand leagues began with what was under feet. "(Ch. 64) Therefore, "Deals with the hard while it is still easy, with the great while it is still small. "(Ch. 63) "What stays still is easy to hold; before there has been an omen it is easy to lay plans. What is tender is easily torn, what is minute is easy to scatter. Deal with things in their state of not-yet-being, put them in order before they have got into confusion. " (Ch. 64) Another important characteristic is that "In Tao (Dao) the only motion is returning. " (Ch. 40) Or return to the root and the beginning is another law of circular movement manifested by Dao. However, what Laozi emphasizes is to go back to the root and return to the beginning, to remain tranquility and submit to the fate. As he explains in the fifty-second chapter: "That which was the beginning of all things under heaven we may speak of as the 'mother' of all things. He who apprehends the mother thereby knows the sons. And he who has known the sons, will hold all the tighter to the mother, and to the end of his days suffer no harm. "

Although Laozi has a profound understanding of the universe, his epistemological approach is one that a recluse usually holds: observation by quiescence and reflection of the mysterious mirror. A man can "knows everything under heaven without leaving his door and all the ways of heaven without looking out of his window. For the further one travels, the less one knows. " (Ch. 47) Through this subjective intuitive understanding, he reaches the state of "mysterious sameness," i. e. absolute subjective and objective sameness. It is because of this approach similar or identical to that of Buddhism and Taoism that it extends a far-reaching influence of generations through ages.

With such an outlook of universe and epistemological approach, a man should follow the principle that "Tao gave them (myriad things) birth, the power of Tao (De) reared them, shaped them according to their kinds, perfected them, giving to each its strength. Therefore, of the ten thousand things (myriad things), there is not one that does not worship Tao (Dao) and do homage to its power (De). " (Ch. 51) De is the revelation of Dao in nature. "Such the scope of the All-pervading Power. That it alone can act through the Way (The nature of great De is to follow Dao only). " (Ch. 21) Therefore, the guiding principle for a man in his conduct is to "give them Simplicity to look at, the Uncarved Block to hold, give them selflessness and fewness of desires. Banish learning, and there will be no more grieving (anxiety). " (Ch. 19) Even he should "maintain an

41

abundance of De comparable to that of an infant. " (A. Waley translated this sentence as : The impunity of things fraught with the "power" may be likened to that of an infant. Ch. 55) He should contend with no one and "he who knows the male, yet cleaves to what is female becomes like a ravine, receiving all things under heaven. And being such a ravine he knows all the time a power that he never calls upon in vain. This is returning to the state of infancy. He who knows the white, yet cleaves to the black becomes the standard by which all things are tested; and being such a standard he has all the time a power that never errs, he returns to the Limitless. He who knows glory, yet cleaves to ignominy becomes like a valley that receives into it all things under heaven. And being such a valley he has all the time a power that suffices; he returns to the state of the Uncarved Block."(Ch. 28) He should also know himself. "To know when one does not know is best. To think one knows when one does not know is a dire disease. Only he who recognizes this disease as a disease can cure himself of the disease. The sage's way of curing disease also consists in making people recognize their diseases as diseases and thus ceasing to be diseased." (Ch. 71) "The Sage knows himself but does not show himself. Knows his own value, but does not put himself on high. " (Ch. 72) Still, in dealing with people and handling affairs, he should not be rash and restless, "the heavy must be the foundation of the light, so quietness is lord and master of activity. " (Ch. 26) "He who stands on tip-toe, does not stand firm; he who takes the longest strides, does not walk the fastest. He who does his own looking sees little; he who defines himself is not therefore distinct. He who boasts of what he will do succeeds in nothing; he who is proud of his work, achieves nothing that endures." (Ch. 24) At the same time, you should understand that "stretch a bow to the very full, and you will wish you had stopped in time; temper a sword-edge to its very sharpest, and you will find it soon grows dull. When bronze and jade fill your hall, it can no longer be guarded. Wealth and place breed insolence, that brings ruin in its train. When your work is done, then withdraw! Such is the Heaven's Way. " (Ch. 9) Therefore, "when the man of highest capacities hears Tao, he does his best to put it into practice. " (Ch. 41) He should have such an insight:

The way out into the light often looks dark,

The way that goes ahead often looks as if it went back.

The way that is least hilly often looks as if it went up and down,

The "power" that is really loftiest looks like an abyss,

What is sheerest white looks blurred.

The "power" that is most sufficing looks inadequate,

The "power" that stands firmest looks flimsy.

What is in its natural, pure state looks faded;

The largest square has no corners,

The greatest vessel takes the longest to finish,

Great music has the faintest notes,

The Great Form is without shape.

For Tao is hidden and nameless. (Ch. 41)

As to preservation of life, the main ideas in Laozi are three: the first is few desires, for "the five colours confuse the eye, the five sounds dull the ear, the five tastes spoil the palate. Excess of hunting and chasing makes mind go mad. " (Ch. 12) Thus he should "block the passages, shut the doors, let all sharpness be blunted, all tangles untied, all glare tempered, all dust smoothed. " (Ch. 56) The second is no addition to one's vitality. "To fill life to the brim is to invite omens, " (Ch. 55) because "Whatever has a time of vigour also has a time of decay. Such things are against Tao, and whatever is against Tao is soon destroyed. "

(Ch. 55) "How is it that the death-spots in man's life and activity are also thirteen? (Those who could have lived long but walk into death of their own accord also number about three-tenths. Why?) It is because men feed life too grossly. " (Ch. 50) The third is to keep vital *qi*. A man should always "keep the unquiet physical-soul from straying, hold fast to the Unity (keep the spiritual and sentient souls united) " and "concentrate your breath make it soft (concentrate the vital *qi* to attain a state of pliancy) . " (Ch. 10)

The political views in the book of *Laozi* can be mainly expressed in three sentences: "Kingdoms can only be governed if rules are kept, battles can only be won if rules are broken. But the adherence of all under heaven can only be won by letting-alone. " (Ch. 57) "Tao never does, yet through it all things are done. If the barons and kings would but possess themselves of it, the ten thousand creatures would at once be transformed (of their own accord). " (Ch. 37) "So long as I do nothing, the people will of themselves be transformed. So long as I love quietude, the people will of themselves go straight. So long as I act only by inactivity the people will of themselves become prosperous. So long as I have no wants the people will of themselves return to the 'state of the Uncarved Block. '" (Ch. 57) Therefore, "the Sage relies on actionless activity, " (Ch. 2) and emulates heaven and earth. Because "Heaven and Earth are ruthless. To them the ten thousand things are but as straw dogs. The Sage too is ruthless. To him the people are but as straw dogs. " (Ch. 5) Let everything develop by itself, he then can see " through his actionless activity all things are duly regulated. " (Ch. 3) Because of this, Laozi opposes to rule a country with laws, as well as with benevolence, righteousness, rites and intelligence. He holds that "the more laws promulgated, the more thieves and bandits there will be. " (Ch. 57) "It was when the Great Way

(Dao) declined that human kindness and morality (benevolence and righteousness) arose; it was when intelligence and knowledge appeared that the Great Artifice began (there was great hypocrisy). It was when the six near ones were no longer at peace that there was talk of dutiful sons (filial piety and parental affection). Nor till fatherland was dark with strife did we hear of loyal slaves (loyal ministers). " (Ch. 18) "After Tao (Dao) was lost, then came the power (De); after the power was lost, then came human kindness (benevolence); after human kindness (benevolence) was lost, then came morality (righteousness); after morality (righteousness) was lost, then came ritual (rites). Now ritual (rites) is the mere husk of loyalty and promise-keeping, and is indeed the first step towards brawling (chaos). "(Ch. 38) Taking into consideration of laws, benevolence, righteousness, rites and intellegence prevailing in that time, we can see they could not bring a peaceful life to people.

Laozi opposes wars. He believes that "fine weapons are none the less ill-omened things. People despise them, therefore, those in possession of the Tao (Dao) do not depend on them. "(Ch. 31) "He who by Tao purposes to help a ruler of men will oppose all conquest by force of arms; for such things are wont to rebound. Where armies are, thorn and brambles grow. The raising of a great host is followed by a year of dearth. " (Ch. 30) Weapons and armies can only be used for avoidance and relief from dissolution of dangers and calamities. "Therefore a good general effects his purpose and then stops; he does not take further advantage of his victory. Fulfils his purpose and does not glory in what he has done; fulfils his purpose and does not boast of what he has done; fulfils his purpose, but takes no pride in what he has done; fulfils his purpose, but only as a step that could not be avoided; fulfils his purpose, but without violence. " (Ch. 30) If he makes a show of his army and his strength and "delights in them, and to delight in them means to delight in the slaughter of men. And he who delights in the slaughter of men will never get what he looks for out of those that dwell under heaven. " (Ch.31)

The ideal society that Laozi describes is a picture of "a small country with few inhabitants (a small population)." In such a country, "he could bring it about that though there should be among the people contrivances requiring ten times, a hundred times less labour, they would not use them. He could bring it about that the people would be ready to lay down their lives and lay them down again in defence of their homes, rather than emigrate. There might still be boats and carriages, but no one would go in them; there might still be weapons of war but no one would drill with them. He could bring it about that "the people should have no use for any form of writing save knotted ropes, should be contented with their food, pleased with their clothing, satisfied with their homes, should take pleasure in their rustic tasks. The next place might be so near at hand that one could hear the cocks crowing in it, the dogs barking; but the people would grow old and die without ever having been there." (Ch. 80) This is a Uopia for a recluse, a primitive society, people cannot, in a true sense, "be contented with their food, pleased with their clothing, satisfied with their homes and happy in the way they live." On the contrary, we can see the constant wars and chaos and calamities ensued in the late Spring and Autumn Period which made Laozi feel painful and angry. Many quotations can be cited from the book:

So long as the Court is in order, they are content to let their fields run to weed, and their granaries stand empty. They wear patterns and embroideries, carry sharp swords, glut themselves with drink and food, have more possessions than they can use. These are the riotous ways of brigandage; they are not the Highway. (Ch. 53)

Never mind if the people are not intimidated by your authority. A Mightier Authority will deal with them in the end. Do not narrow their dwellings or harass their lives; and for the very reason that you do not harass them, they will cease to turn from you. (Ch. 72)

The people are not frightened of death. What then is the use of trying to intimate them with the death-penalty? And even supposing people were generally frightened of death and did not regard it as an everyday thing, which of us would dare to seize them and slay them?(Ch. 74)

The people starve because those above them eat too much tax-grain. That is the only reason why they starve. The people are difficult to keep in order because those above them interfere. That is the only reason why they are so difficult to keep in order. The people attach no importance to death, because those above them are too grossly absorbed in the pursuit of life. That is why they attach no importance to death. (Ch.75)

So too does Heaven take away from those who have too much, and give to those that have not enough. But if it is Heaven's way to take from those who have too much and give to those who have not enough, this is far from being man's way. He takes away from those that have not enough in order to make offering to those who already have too much. (Ch. 77)

Only the possessor of Dao can "afford to make offerings to all under heaven. " "Only he who has accepted the dirt of the country can be lord of its soil-shrines; only he who takes upon himself the evils of the country can become a king among those what dwell under heaven. "(Chs. 77&78)

The characteristic of Laozi's wisdom is that "emphasis on softness," i. e. "the soft and weak overcomes the hard and strong. " (Ch. 36) He took the simile of an ordinary natural phenomenon as an example, "Noth-

47

ing under heaven is softer or more yielding than water." (Ch. 78) "When he is born, man is soft and weak; in death he becomes stiff and hard. The ten thousand creatures and all plants and trees while they are alive are supple and soft, but when they are dead they become brittle and dry. Truly, what is stiff and hard is a companion of death; what is soft and weak is a companion of life. " (Ch. 76) It is because of his profound and dialectical understanding of the soft and weak that in actual life, this thought becomes an art of control and conquest of others. "What is in the end to be shrunk must first be stretched. Whatever is to be weakened must begin by being made strong. What is to be overthrown must begin by being set up. He who would be a taker must begin as a giver. " (Ch. 36) Therefore, Laozi fulfils his purpose of victory by the means of quietude, softness, weakness, withdrawal, timidity and no-action. The best way of applying this art of conquest is that "to march without moving, to roll the sleeve, but present no bare arm, the hand that seems to hold, yet had no weapon in it, a host that can confront, yet presents no battlefront." (Ch. 69)

Laozi clearly states the essence of his thought: "Here are my three treasures. Guard and keep them! The first is pity; the second, frugality; the third, refusal to be foremost of all things under heaven. " (Ch. 67) This is probably the best explanation to his emphasis on softness. To be specific, sentences with the word "goodness" in the book of *Laozi* tell us what should a man in possession of Dao be:

1. It is the way of Heaven not to strive but none the less to conquer, not to speak, but none the less to get an answer; not to beckon, yet things come to it of themselves. Heaven is like one who says little, yet none the less has laid his plans. (Ch. 73) Heaven's way, without distinction of persons, to keep the good perpetually supplied. (Ch. 79) The highest good

is like that of water. (Ch. 8)

2. Of old those that were the best officers of Court had inner natures subtle, abstruse, mysterious, penetrating, too deep to be understood. And because such men could not be understood I can but tell of them as they appeared to the world: Circumspect they seemed, like one who in winter crosses a stream; watchful, as one who must meet danger on every side. Ceremonious, as one who pays a visit; yet yielding, as ice when it begins to melt. Blank, as a piece of uncarved wood; yet receptive as a hollow in the hills. Murky, as a troubled stream —Tranquil, as the vast reaches of the sea, drifting, as the wind with no stop. Which of you can assume such murkiness, to become in the end still and clear? Which of you can make yourself inert, to become in the end full of life and stir? Those who possess this Tao do not try to fill themselves to the brim, and because they do not try to fill themselves to the brim, they are like a garment that endures all wear and need never be renewed. (Ch. 15)

3. In the days of old those who practised Tao with success did not, by means of it, enlighten the people, but on the contrary sought to make them ignorant. The more knowledge people have, the harder they are to rule. Those who seek to rule by giving knowledge are like bandits preying on the land. Those who rule without giving knowledge bring a stock of good fortune to the land. To have understood the difference between these two things is to have a test and standard. To be always able to apply this test and standard is called the mysterious "power," the mysterious "power," so deep-penetrating, so far-reaching, that can follow things back —All the way back to the Great Concordance.(Ch. 65)

4. And if men think the ground the best place for building a house upon, if among thoughts they value those that are profound, if in friendship they value gentleness, in words, truth; in government, good order; in deeds,

effectiveness; in actions, timeliness — (Ch. 8)

5. Perfect activity leaves no track behind it; perfect speech is like a jade-worker whose tool leaves no mark. The perfect reckoner needs no counting-slips; the perfect door has neither bolt nor bar, yet cannot be opened. The perfect knot needs neither rope nor twine, yet cannot be untied. Therefore, the Sage is all the time in the most perfect way helping men, he certainly does not turn his back on men; is all the time in the most perfect way helping creatures, he certainly does not turn his back on creatures. (Ch. 27) The good man does not prove by argument. (Ch. 81)

6. It is said that he who has a true hold on life, when he walks on land does not meet tigers or wild buffaloes; in battle he is not touched by weapons of war. Indeed, a buffalo that attacked him would find nothing for its horns to butt, a tiger would find nothing for its claws to tear, a weapon would find no place for its point to enter in.(Ch. 50)

7. What Tao plants cannot be plucked, what Tao clasps, cannot slip. By its virtue alone can one generation after another carry on the ancestral sacrifice. Apply it to yourself and by its power you will be freed from dross. Apply it to your household and your household shall thereby have abundance. Apply it to the village, and the village will be made secure. Apply it to the kingdom, and the kingdom shall thereby be made to flourish. Apply it to an empire, and the empire shall thereby be extended. (Ch. 54)

8. The best charioteers do not rush ahead; the best fighters do not make displays of wrath; the greatest conqueror wins without joining issue; the best user of men acts as though he were their inferior. This is called the power that comes of not contending, is called the capacity to use men, the secret of being mated to heaven, to what was of old (to nature). (Ch. 68)

The word goodness or perfection in the book expresses the wisdom and ideal of Laozi. He teaches people how to conduct and guide their actions with wisdom. At the same time, he lays emphasis on practice. "My words are very easy to understand and very easy to put into practice. Yet no one under heaven understands them; no one puts them into practice. " (Ch. 70) "That the yielding conquers the resistant and the soft conquers the hard is a fact known by all men, yet utilized by none. " (Ch. 78) Therefore, he emphasizes repeatedly "to understand such harmony is to understand the always-so (constancy). " (Ch. 55) "What has submitted to Fate has become part of the always-so (constancy). " (Ch. 16) "This is called resorting to the always-so (constancy). " (Ch. 52) "To understand the always-so (constancy) is to be illumined. " (Chs. 16&55) "He who knows the always-so (constancy) has room in him for everything; he who has room in him for everything is without prejudice. To be without prejudice it to be kingly (complete); to be kingly (complete) is to be of (in accord with) heaven. To be of heaven is to be in Tao. Tao is forever and he that possesses it, though his body ceases, is not destroyed." (Ch. 16) We may bring the conclusion of the account of main points of Laozi's thought by citing two paragraphs from Chapters 25 and 39 respectively: "The ways of men are conditioned by those of earth. The ways of earth, by those of heaven. The ways of heaven by those of Tao, and the ways of Tao by the Self-so. " "As for the things that from of old have understood the Whole (One) —The sky (heaven) through such understanding remains limpid, earth remains steady, the spirits keep their holiness, the abyss is replenished, the ten thousand (myriad) creatures bear their kind, barons and princes direct their people. " The wisdom of Laozi is so profound that numerous books and essays have been written in analysis, exposition, commentary and criticism on it, here it is only a

51

tentative and objective description of the main points of the thought in the book of *Laozi*. Laozi also inherited some of the thoughts from the past, the sentences in the book prove this, such as: the sage says, the strategists have the sayings, the proverb has it, the ancient saying is, and so on. But to what extent that he inherited the thoughts of ancient people, this needs further study by scholars.

The thought of Laozi has influenced Chinese people profoundly through the ages.

Firstly, after the mid-Warring States Period, Taoism developed into two major branches: one was the School of Zhuangzi; another was the Jixia Taoism in the State of Qi. Laozi did not openly take on any disciple when he was alive as other famous scholars at that time, therefore, only a little has been known about his disciples. In the book of *Zhuangzi* and some other ancient books, we can learn that some of Laozi's disciples are Guan Yin, Gengsang Chu, Lie Yukou, Yang Zhu. As for the thought of Guan Yin, the quotations of Laozi and Guan Yin in parallel in the book of *Zhuangzi* indicate the obvious similarities between them. Guan Yin says, "If a man does not look at things with prejudice, the things will become clear themselves. Therefore, he takes action like flowing water, keeps still as a mirror, responds to others like an echo. He can keep him in a state that nothing seems to exist, and keep himself as tranquil as limpid water. He feels harmonious in embracing himself with universe but loses himself in satisfying his desires. He should follow, instead of leading others. " In the Chapter of Gengsang Chu in *Zhuangzi*, it says, "Gengsang Chu, among the disciples of Laozi, is one who truly understands the Taoism of Laozi. " Li Dingsheng and Xu Huijun held, "Among the disciples of Laozi, Gengsang Chu and Wenzi are most well known to have understood truly Taoism. The School of Gengsang Chu, in fact, is the School of Zhuangzi, that is why Zhuangzi praised Gengsang Chu as the disciple who also got the true essence of Laozi's Taoism. " Gengsang Chu's works have been long lost. In 1973, in the No. 40 Han Tomb in the Ding County, Hebei Province, some remnantal pages of the book of *Wenzi* were excavated and proved to be one of the books written in the pre-Qin times, the popular edition of *Wenzi* must have been written after the book of *Zhuangzi*. The characteristics of Wenzi, based on the book, show that Taoism is dominant, meanwhile with obvious influence from Confucianism, Mohism, Legalism and so on. Lie Yukou was regarded as a disciple of Guan Yin in some ancient books. There are similarities between his thought and that of Laozi. *The Lü's Spring and Autumn Annals* comments on the characteristic of Liezi's thought as that "Liezi shows his preference for void. " In the book of *Liezi*, it says, "The Dao exists with no name, rather it is tranquil and void. With tranquility and void, a man can truly hold himself; with desires to give or take, he loses control of himself. After destruction and ruin, no one can restore the previous state with advocation of benevolence and righteousness. " Yang Zhu's philosophy is mainly Taoism, and the characteristic is the emphasis on life instead of wealth. Zhuangzi is held as the greatest successor of Taoism in the pre-Qin times. Sima Qian made the comment on Zhuangzi that "His philosophy reflects the absorption of every different school, however, the core of his thought comes from what Laozi said. " Zhuangzi developed Laozi's thought in changing the ontological Dao into a spiritual conception of mind, and emancipated man in even more depth and extension of freedom.

Different schools and theories gradually tended to converge after the mid-Warring States Period from exchange and contention. The Jixia Academy and Yellow-Emperor-and-Laozi School both kept Taoism as the main

53

body of the thoughts, and at the same time, tried to absorb thoughts from different schools, such as Confucianism, Mohism, Logician School, Legalism, *Yin* and *Yang* School, and so on. Since Duke Huan of Qi started the Jixia Academy to its end by the reign of Duke Xiang, it lasted over one hundred years. In "Hereditary House of Tian in the Qi State" in the *Records of the Historian*, it says, "King Xuan showed his favour for the scholars and orators, such as Zou Yan, Chunyu Kun, Tian Pian, Jie Zi, Shen Dao, Huan Yuan and so on, there were seventy six altogether, all were given the title of senior royal officials, they did not manage affairs but gave comments, advice and criticism. That is why scholars assemblied at Jixia Academy again, with the number over several hundred or a thousand." It is a rare phenomenon that in Chinese history the Jixia Academy lasted so long, so many schools came into existence, so far-reaching for its academic influence. Jixia Taoist School is also called the Yellow-Emperor-and-Laozi School, the reason came that the kings of the Qi State believed Yellow Emperor was their ancestor. Laozi was a famous philosopher from the same native land as the rulers of Qi. His thought played an important role in the political struggle in the late Warring States Period. That is why later *The Records of Literature and Arts* in the *History of Han Dynasty* says, "The school of Taoism probably came out of historians. They recorded success and failure, survival and peril, happiness and disaster, and the Dao of the past and the present in history, then they knew to hold firmly to the root and basis, to keep void and tranquil and to appear soft and weak, these are the arts of rulers. " Song Jian and Yin Wen both adhered to Taoism but absorbed Mohist and Logician thoughts, Shen Dao and Tian Pian combined Taoism with Legalism, brought into existence a system of Taoism and Legalism. The book of *Guanzi* and the Four Yellow-Emperor-and-Laozi Silk Writings all manifested clearly that Taoism was the backbone, but mixed with thoughts of different schools.

Laozi's thought extended influence to a certain degree on other different schools in the pre-Qin times. Confucius once paid visits to Laozi and asked instruction about rites of Zhou. We can also see his influence on Mencius and Xunzi. The legalists Shen Buhai and Han Fei based their thoughts on Yellow-Emperor-and-Laozi School. Laozi's thought also influenced the militarists. Wang Zhen of the Tang dynasty once said, "Not a chapter in the book of *Laozi* that does not give concern about war. " The strategists and militarists held that the first part of *Dao Jing* was a theoretical generalization of military thoughts, and then they were raised to the level of outlooks of the universe and human life. The second part of *De Jing* expounded clearly military strategy and tacticism, brew out and established outlooks towards social history and human life through the summation of laws of war.

The book of *Lü's Spring and Autumn Annals* is a comprehensive philosophic work with the thoughts of Laozi, Zhuangzi and Yellow-Emperor-and-Laozi School as its main body and also with combination of miscellaneous thoughts of *Yin* and *Yang* School, Confucianism, Mohism, Logician School and Legalism as the summation of thoughts of the pre-Qin times.

In the beginning and middle period of the Western Han dynasty, Taoism was accepted by the rulers as the guiding thought. The Yellow-Emperor-and-Laozi thought grew to be a mature art of ruling, it met the social needs and the demands of peace from people. Through several decades of development and peaceful life, the Han dynasty became prosperous. Since then, when a new dynasty was founded, almost all the rulers drew the good experiences from this period. They maintained the social stability and kept the economic development. Just because of such social practice, Taoism got the chances to develop. *Huai Nan* and *On Gists of Six Schools* by Sima Tan are the summation of this period. "As an art of ruling, it includes the follow of the natural course of *Yin* and *Yang*, goodness of Confucianism and Mohism, the key concepts of logician and legalist schools. Taoists make changes as time and things change, establish customs and handle everything in proper way. The main ideas are concise, and easy to put into practice. And accomplishments are many but with only a few actions. " This comment gives a high praise of the development and advantages of Taoism.

In the middle and late Western Han dynasty and the Eastern Han dynasty, although Confucian thought took the dominant position for the rulers, but the circulation of *The Gist of Laozi* by Yan Zun, *Interpretation of Chapters and Sentences in Laozi* by Heshang Gong, the works of social critics, such as that by Wang Chong, Wang Fu and Zhong Changtong, played an active role in spreading the thought of Laozi, the deification of Yellow-Emperor-and-Laozi Taoism, the spread of ways of longevity and immortality in the upper class, inner cultivation and production of elixir, treatment of diseases with magic water, and so on, paved the way for the founding of Taoist religion. Circulation of books, such as *Annotations on Laozi* by Xianger, *The Great Peace Canon* and *The Concordance of Changes, Taoism and Elixir Making* laid the real theoretic foundation for the establishment of Taoist religion.

In the Wei, Jin and Six dynasties, the influence of Taoist thought appeared in many respects. The development of metaphysical school is a trend of convergence of Confucianism and Taoism but with Taoism as the main body. From Wang Bi's advocation that "Confucian ethical code came out of nature," to Ruan Ji and Ji Kang's slogan that "transcendence of Confucian ethical code and return to nature," to Guo Xiang's compromise proposal that "Confucian ethical code is identical to nature." Buddhism was introduced into China between the Han dynasties. It first attached itself to Yellow-Emperor-and-Laozi School, then to the Metaphysical school. Even after Kumarajiva tried his best in his translation to give a true picture of Indian Buddhism, in fact, there still existed many similarities between Buddhism and Lao-Zhuang and Metaphysical schools. During this period, many upper class intellectuals converted to Taoist religion, caused the change of the Taoist organizations in their components and cultural levels. Ge Hong in the Eastern Jin, Kou Qianzhi in the Northern Wei, Lu Xiujing in the Liu Song and Tao Hongjing in the Southern dynasty based on their own stands, interests and reality, reformed the Taoist religion systematically on the whole from form to content. Taoist thought and Taoist religious beliefs were then combined into one. As a result of systematization of religious theories and formalization of religious rites and rituals, the folk religion became an official religion, all this promoted Taoist thought for further spread and development.

In the Sui and Tang dynasties, with the preference of the rulers, Taoist thought and religion went in full flourish. Peace and prosperity in the years of Zhenguan under the rule of Li Shimin proved again in history the usefulness of Taoist thought in governing the feudal empire. Xuan Zong of the Tang dynasty himself annotated and expounded *Dao De Jing*, and for the first time in history, he gave the order for the compilation of the *Taoist Canon*, and took a series of measures for raising the social position of Taoist thought and religion. Taoist religious theories and health preservation theories and practice in the Sui, Tang and Five dynasties won the chance and time for further development.

After the Song dynasty, Taoist thought still played an important role.

The advocation by the rulers and the needs of development of the Taoist religion itself and emergence of different Taoist religious schools promoted the development of Taoist religious theories. For several times, the Taoist canons were compiled in the Song, Yuan and Ming dynasties. For instance, Zhen Zong gave the order to the compilation of *The Complete Records of Precious Writings*, Zhang Junfang abridged it as *Seven Lots of the Bookbag of the Clouds*, Hui Zong of the Song gave the order to complete the *Taoist Canon of Longevity of the Zhenghe Reign*, the *Taoist Canon of the Zhengtong Reign* in the Ming dynasty, and the *Supplement to Taoist Canon of the Wanli Reign*. All these indeed tell us that the rulers in the Song, Yuan and Ming dynasties paid great attention to it and also gave their support for the work. This from another respect proved the important value of the *Taoist Canon*. *The Account of Re-editing the Taoist Canon at the White Cloud Temple* in the Qing dynasty says, "The true scriptures in the *Taoist Canon* are the basic knowledge for us to understand the Taoist religion and the rules of cultivation to be immortals, as well as knowledge including the other two religions and nine schools of thought, astronomy and geography and so on. It is beneficial to the Taoist disciples in cultivating their minds and bodies, for non-religious people, it will benefit their families and the country. It is not just the Taoist disciples who depend on it for their cultivation of Dao, and even the rulers can benefit from reading it. "

Neo-Confucianism developed in the Song and Ming dynasties absorbed and mixed in many respects with Taoist thought. For example, Zhou Dunyi reformed the diagram of *Wuji* for inner pellet cultivation into the diagram of the Supreme Ultimate with written explanation as: the Ultimateless→ the Supreme Ultimate→*Yin* and *Yang*→Five Elements and Four Seasons →Myriad Creatures and Man. This is a Taoist model or pattern how the universe came into being. It is right on this model the School of Principle based its ontology. Wang Tingxiang, a famous philosopher in the Ming dynasty, said, "Laozi said Dao gave birth to Heaven and Earth, the Neo-Confucian scholars in the Song dynasty said that before the birth of heaven and earth, there was only the principle. They simply changed a word, and I can see no difference of it from the thoughts of Laozi and Zhuangzi. " The order of birth of universe described by Shao Yong is: the Supreme Ultimate → (two extremes) → four seasons → eight trigrams → myriad creatures. He thought Dao was identical with the Supreme Ultimate, and at the same time, he expressed clearly Dao or the Supreme Ultimate was the expression of the mind. It is the thought of Shao Yong that Lu Jiuyuan and Wang Yangming inherited from to have created the School of Mind. In the *Records of Instructions*, Wang Yangming said, "The mind is just the so-called Dao, a thorough understanding of mind is a real understanding of Dao, they are identical. "

Constant study of Taoist thought and annotations on the book of *Laozi* showed a historical trend of combination of Taoist thought with Confucianism and Buddhism. Moreover, since the Song dynasty, the theories and practice of the inner elixir cultivation, as an important part of health preservation in Taoist religion, made great progress in improvement under the guidance of Taoist thought. The book of *Dao De Jing* is understood as a picture of the Ultimateless — the Supreme Ultimate, as a book of guidance for Taoist Qigong; as that Dao exists in heaven, even more in man; it exists in man's body and even more in his mind.

Scholars in the Qing dynasty and modern times made even more detailed and careful studies on Taoist thought and religion, which, made us realize more and more the profoundity of the thought of Laozi. The thoughts of Laozi and Confucius constitute the mainstream of Chinese orthodoxical traditional cultural thoughts.

The book of *Laozi* has been handed down in China for about 2500 years now. Since the pre-Qin times, there have been so many books of annotation and study on *Dao De Jing* that it is quite difficult to give an exact number of them. Zhang Yucai of the Yuan dynasty in his foreword to *The True Thought of Dao De Jing* by Du Daojian (in the *Taoist Canon*) said, "The book of *Dao* and *De* with eighty-one chapters had been annotated by over three thousand people." It is probably an exaggeration for the number. Zhang Songru in his *A Collation of Laozi with Textual Study* lists ninety-four reference books, Chen Guying in his *Annotations on Laozi with Contemporary Chinese Translation* two hundred sixty-two reference books. Generally speaking, more influential and popular ones are as the following:

From the pre-Qin times to the Six Dynasties: the Silk Texts of *Laozi* excavated from the Han Tomb at Mawangdui of Changsha in Hunan Province, Heshang Gong *Interpretation of Chapters and Sentences of Laozi* and Wang Bi *Commentary on the Genuine Scripture of Dao and De*; from Early Tang to Five dynasties: Fu Yi *Ancient Text of Dao De Jing*; from the Song to Yuan dynasties: Wang Anshi *Annotations on Laozi*, Su Zhe *An Exposition of Laozi*, Lin Xiyi *Exposition of Laozi in Easy Language*, Fan Yingyuan *A Collection of Ancient Annotations on Laozi Dao De Jing* and Wu Cheng *Annotations on the Genuine Scripture of Dao and De*; Ming dynasty: Xue Hui *Collected Expositions of Laozi*, Deqing, A Buddhist *An Exposition of Laozi Dao De Jing*, Shen Yiguan *The Understanding of Laozi* and Jiao Hong *Wings to Laozi*; Qing dynasty: Wang Niansun *Miscellaneous Notes on Reading Laozi* and Liu Shipei *Collected Notes for Supplementary Explanation of Laozi*; the Republic of China: Ma Xulun *A Collation of Laozi with Explanations*, Xi Dong *Collected Explanations of Laozi*, Gao Heng

A Collation and Textual Study of Laozi, Lao Jian *An Inquiry into the Ancient Texts of Laozi* and Yan Lingfeng *A New Arrangement of Laozi Text*; New China: Zhu Qianzhi *A Collation of Laozi with Explanation*, Che Zai *On Laozi*, Editing Board of Philosophy Study *Collected Essays on the Philosophy of Laozi*; Since 1973, after the publication of Mawangdui Silk Texts: Zhang Songru *A Collation of Laozi with Textual Study* and Chen Guying *Annotations on Laozi with Contemporary Chinese Translation.*

It is very difficult to give a detailed description at present about the spread of the book of *Laozi* abroad because of limited materials and language barriers. With reference of *A History of Translations of Chinese Books into Foreign Languages* by Ma Zuyi and Ren Rongzhen, *Classical Chinese Literature in the English World* by Huang Mingfen and the Introduction to *Tao Te Ching* published by Foreign Languages Teaching and Study Press by Wang Yuechuan, at the same time, with my collection of materials as the main part, we can roughly give an outline of spread of *Laozi* abroad:

Possibly before the Sui dynasty, *Dao De Jing* was brought to Japan, after that, many annotated books on *Laozi* helped Japanese understand and study Taoism. Paul Pelliot of Paris said in his article in *Tong P'ao* in 1912 that *Dao De Jing* was once translated into Sanskrit in the seventh century.

The westerners began to know about the book of *Laozi* in eighteenth century. In about the middle of the eighteenth century, *Laozi* was translated into Latin. It is said that Belgian Jesuit Francois Noel (1651-1729) translated *Dao De Jing* into French, Jean Francois Foucquet translated *Annotations on Dao De Jing* into Latin and French in 1729. French Sinologist Abel Remusat translated only four chapters of *Dao De Jing* into French. Stanislas Julien in 1842 translated *Lao Tseu Tao Te King en Francais*. In 1870, Leipzig published the first German translation of *Lao Zi Dao De Jing* by Victor Strauβ. Although Russian translation of Laozi was done at about the middle of nineteenth century by Данил Щивелов, it was published in 1915. The first English translation of *Laozi* appeared in about 1870. F. H. Balfour's translation of *Laozi* was published in London in 1884. James Legge's translation of *Texts of Taoism* in Oxford in 1891. Paul Carus' translation of *Lao Tze's Tao-Teh-King* published in Chicago in 1898 was quite popular at that time. Besides the translation, it gives a biography of Laozi, a brief introduction of study of *Laozi* in China with comments, bibliography and index. It was reprinted many times. Swedish missionary Erick Follce at the beginning of this century translated *Laozi* into Swedish.

The appearance of many translations and reprints of existed translations of *Laozi* at the beginning of this century in the West from one respect shows the popularity of the book of *Dao De Jing*. For instance, Walter Gorn Old's translation first came out in 1904, popular edition in 1905, the third edition in 1913, and reprint in 1922. Lionel Giles' *The Sayings of Laozi* was first published in London in 1905, reprinted in 1906, 1909, 1911, 1917 and 1922 respectively. This book divides Laozi's sayings into ten parts and is quite helpful to readers in their understanding of its thought. After World War I, there appeared a craze of studying Laozi in Germany, there were many translations of *Laozi* at that time. Richard Wilhelm's German translation of *Laotse vom Sinn and Leben* was published in 1921.

Arthur Waley's English translation of *The Way and Its power, A Study of the Tao Te Ching and Its Place in Chinese Thought* published in London in 1934 played an important role in spreading of Laozi's thought in the West. The translation which was reprinted for several times gives a more systematic introduction to the Chinese philosophy in the pre-Qin times and the place of Laozi's thought. In his translation, Mr. Waley paid attention to the expression of the subtle meanings.

The influence of Laozi's thought on the West can be traced in many respects. Heidegger, German philosopher once translated *Laozi* and liked to read it in his late years. The great Russian writer Lev Tolstoy rendered *Laozi* into Russian. The great American dramatist Eugene O'neil in his works showed his fondness of Laozi. We, too, have read many stories that physicists, musicians, poets, statesmen, and so on throughout the world liked to read *Laozi* and scholars studied *Laozi* from the perspectives of not only philosophy, politics, but also linguistics, esthetics, and so on.

From the sources available now, Hu Zeling is the first Chinese who translated *Lao Tsu Tao Teh Ching* into English and his translation was published in Chengdu in 1936. John C. H. Wu's translation of *The Tao and Its Virtue* was published in *Tien-Hsia Monthly* Nos. 9 and 10 in 1939 and 1940. Lin Yutang's *The Wisdom of Laotse* published in New York in 1948 and Chu Dagao's translation of *Tao Te Ching* published in London in 1959 did make their contributions to the spread of the thought of Laozi in the West. Liu Jiahuai is the first Chinese to have translated *Laozi* into French. From about 1940s, Chinese scholars in Hong Kong, Taiwan and throughout the world made great contributions to the spread of Laozi's thought.

Since 1950s, translations of *Dao De Jing* was successively published in Holland, Hungary, Romania, Poland, Spain, Czech, Greece and so on. Paul Lin in the *Introduction to A Translation of Lao Tzu's Tao Te Ching and Wang Pi's Commentary* said, "There are now over seventy or eighty translations of *Lao Tzu's Tao Te Ching*, most of which are based on Wang Pi's edition of the *Lao Tzu*. "Chan Wing-tsit in his *The Way of Lao Tzu* also told us that translations have been done in so many different languages that every language has at least one version. The *Tao Te Ching* has, for example, already been translated into English forty-four times. A new version has appeared about every other year during the last twenty years (before 1963), with half of them in the United States. Since 1963, especially since the publication of Mawangdui Silk Texts in 1973, there have been eager and earnest studies of Laozi and oriental cultures. Publications of annotations and translations of *Laozi*, Mawangdui Silk Texts and Taoism have appeared in great number. I have read three English translations of Silk Texts: Dim Cheuk Lau *Lao Tzu Tao Te Ching*, Hong Kong Chinese University, 1989; Robert Henricks *Lao Zi De Dao Jing*, Macmillan Co., 1989 and Victor Mair *Lao Zi*, 1990. Although the Silk Texts are the earliest texts we have found by now, they are of important value in our study of philosophy and culture in the pre-Qin times, it is not the best as far as the text is concerned. Generally speaking, scholars still take *Dao De Jing* annotated and commented by Wang Bi as the best text in their study and translation.

Since 1978, the reform and opening drive on the mainland China, with the promotion of cultural exchange with the outside world, scholars at home also have translated and annotated *Laozi*. Since 1990, almost every year, we can read new books about *Laozi* and Taoism both at home and abroad.

Of so many English translations it is quite difficult to give an exact number. However, more influential ones with better translation quality can also be found in Chan Wing-tsit's *The Way of Laotse*, Bobbs-Merrill Co. 1963; Dim Cheuk Lau *Lao Tzu Tao Te Ching*, Penguin Books, 1963;

Paul Lin *A Translation of Lao Tzu's Tao Te Ching and Wang Bi's Commentary*, Michigan University Press, 1977; Rhett Young and Roger Ames *Lao Tzu Text, Notes and Comments*, Chinese Materials Center, Taiwan, 1977 and Robert Henricks *Lao Tze Te-Tao Ching A New Translation Based on the Recently Discovered Ma-wang-tui Texts*, Macmillan, 1989.

In the West, the translations of *Laozi* are only next to that of the Bible in number. This, from one aspect, undoubtedly proves that the profound thought of Laozi is the precious cultural heritage not only for the Chinese but also for the people of all the world.

Why have western scholars been so fascinated about *Laozi*? Why has the book of *Laozi* been translated time and again? Dr. Giles' foreword to Chu Dagao's English translation of *Dao De Jing* may give us a hint: He thought *Dao De Jing* was only a collection of epigrams, although there were many translations, none was identical to the original. Just as a mirror, different translations only reflected the original from different perspectives and layers, still what Laozi said was most baffling obscure. "The wording of the original is extraordinarily vigorous and terse: never, surely, has so much thought been compressed into a small space. Throughout the universe there are scattered a certain number of stars belonging to a class known as ' white dwarfs.' They are usually very small, yet the atoms of which they consist are crushed together so closely that their weight is enormous in relation to their size, and this entails the radiation of so much energy that the surface is kept at a temperature vastly hotter than that of the sun. The *Tao Te Ching* may fitly be called a 'white dwarf 'of philosophical literature, so weighty is it , so compact, and so suggestive of a mind radiating thought at a white heat. "

Of about twenty English translations I have read, Mr. Waley's translation is one of the best with its simple and fluent language, and subtle and accurate understanding of the original. Mr. Waley is familiar with the classical Chinese Literature in the pre-Qin times, and his translation is based on the Wang Bi's text, with the reference of many other editions, at the same time, with some of his own textual study. As for his own translation, he said, "It seems to me that when the main importance of a work is its beauty, the translator must be prepared to sacrifice a great deal in the way of detailed accuracy in order to preserve in the translation the quality which gives the original its importance. Such a translation I call 'literary'; as opposed to 'philological.' I want to make it clear that this translation of the *Tao Te Ching* is not 'literary'; for the simple reason that the importance of the original lies not in its literary quality but in the things it says, and it has been my one aim to reproduce what the original says with detailed accuracy. " Moreover, the famous English sinologist Dr. Giles did the proofreading.

The Chinese text and modern Chinese translation in this book are selected from the book of *Annotations on Laozi with Contemporary Chinese Translation* by Prof . Chen Guying (China Book Company, 1984). English translation is selected from *The Way and Its Power, A Study of the Tao Te Ching and Its Place in Chinese Thought* by Mr. Arthur Waley, a quite famous English sinologist (George Allen and Unwin, Ltd., London, 1934).

What I have done for this book is as the following:

Firstly, adjustment of the word and sentence order. Prof. Chen Guying tells us, "The book of *Laozi* has many misplacements of bamboo slips (disorder of words, sentences and even paragraphs), redundancy of miscopying (unnecessary additions), wrong words and omissions. Now I revise the text by using Wang Bi's text as the basis, with the reference of the Silk, Fu Yi and other ancient texts, useful annotations by scholars through the ages. " On the whole, there are not many differences between Chen and Waley's texts, so it does not cause too much trouble to match the two.

Secondly, annotations on the different words, sentences, and different understanding between the two texts. Generally speaking, I take Chen's text as the basis, try to give out the reasons why such differences exist, and also quote from other translations the appropriate words and sentences for reference.

Thirdly, supplement of the omissions, and correction of the mistakes. If I find mistakes and omissions, or sentences only appear in one text, I first read carefully the Chen's text and his annotations with the reference of several reliable annotated texts of Zhang Songru, Gao Heng, Ma Xunlun and Wang Bi. I usually mark out the places in the texts, then explain why and how to do correction, deletion and addition in the notes.

The modern Chinese translation of the original text was done by Prof. Chen Guying long after Mr. Waley's English translation, so some of the differences between them are kept intact of understanding and expression of the original text.

The limitation of my knowledge and ability may result in mistakes in the book. I sincerely welcome criticism from the readers.

Fu Huisheng

At the East China Teachers University

April 20, 1999

目　录

CONTENTS

老子(约前 581—约前 500 年)
Laozi (c.581 — 500 B.C.)

第一章

【原文】

道可道，非常"道"；名可名，非常"名"。

"无"，名天地之始；"有"，名万物之母。

故常"无"，欲以观其妙；

常"有"，欲以观其徼。

此两者，同出而异名，同谓之玄。

玄之又玄，众妙之门。

【今译】

可以用言词表达的道，就不是常"道"；可以说得出来的名，就不是常"名"。

"无"，是天地的本始；"有"，是万物的根源。

所以常从"无"中，去观照"道"的奥妙；常从"有"中，去观照"道"的端倪。

"无"和"有"这两者，同一来源而不同名称，都可说是深远莫测的，从有形的深远境界到达无形的深远境界，这就是一切变化的总门径。

Chapter 1

The Way that can be told of is not an Unvarying Way;

The names that can be named are not unvarying names.

It was from the Nameless that Heaven and Earth sprang;

The named is but the mother that rears the ten thousand creatures, each after its kind.[1]

Truly, "Only he that rids himself forever of desire can see the Secret Essences";

He that has never rid himself of desire can see only the Outcomes.[2]

These two things issued from the same mould, but nevertheless are different in name.

This "same mould" we can but call the Mystery,

Or rather the "Darker than any Mystery, "[3]

The Doorway whence issued all Secret Essences.[4]

3

第二章

【原文】

天下皆知美之为美，斯恶已；皆知善之为善，斯不善已。

有无相生，难易相成，长短相形，高下相盈，音声相和，前后相随，恒也。

是以圣人处无为之事，行不言之教；万物作而弗始，生而弗有，为而弗恃，功成而弗居。夫唯弗居，是以不去。

【今译】

天下都知道美之所以为美，丑的观念也就产生了；都知道善之所以为善，不善的观念也就产生了。

有和无互相生成，难和易互相完成，长和短互相形成，高和下互相包含，音和声互相和调，前和后在对立中互相区分，这是永远如此的。

所以有道的人以"无为"的态度来处理世事，实行"不言"的教导；让万物兴起而不加倡导；生养万物而不据为己有；作育万物而不自恃己能；功业成就而不自我夸耀。正因他不自我夸耀，所以他的功绩不会泯没。

Chapter 2

It is because every one under Heaven recognizes beauty as beauty, that the idea of ugliness exists.[1]

And equally if every one recognized virtue[2] as virtue, this would merely create fresh conceptions of wickedness.

For truly, Being and Not-being grow out of one another;

Difficult and easy complete one another.

Long and short test one another;

High and low determine one another.

Pitch and mode give harmony to one another.

Front and back give sequence to one another.

Therefore[3] the Sage relies on actionless activity,[4]

Carries on wordless teaching,

But the myriad creatures are worked upon by him; he does not disown them.[5]

5

He rears them, but does not lay claim to them,

Controls them, but does not lean upon them.

Achieves his aim, but does not call attention to what he does;

And for the very reason that he does not call attention to what he does.

He is not ejected from fruition of what he has done.

第三章

【原文】

不尚贤，使民不争；不贵难得之货，使民不盗；不见可欲，使民心不乱。

是以圣人之治，虚其心，实其腹，弱其志，强其骨。常使民无知无欲。使夫智者不敢为也。为无为，则无不治。

【今译】

不标榜贤才异能，使人民不争功名；不珍贵难得的财货，使人民不做盗贼；不显耀可贪的事物，使人民不被惑乱。

所以有道的人治理政事，要净化人民的心思，满足人民的安饱，减损人民的心志，增强人民的体魄。常使人民没有(伪诈的)心智，没有(争盗的)欲念。使一些自作聪明的人不敢妄为。以"无为"的态度去处理事务，就没有不上轨道的。

大中华文库

6

Chapter 3

If we stop looking for "persons of superior morality" (hien)[1] to put in power, there will be no more jealousies among the people. If we cease to set store by products that are hard to get, there will be no more thieves. If the people never see such things as excite desire, their hearts will remain placid and undisturbed. Therefore the Sage rules

By emptying their hearts[2]

And filling their bellies,

Weakening their intelligence

And toughening their sinews

Ever striving to make the people knowledgeless and desireless.

Indeed he sees to it that if there be any who have knowledge, they dare not interfere.

Yet through his actionless activity all things are duly regulated.

第四章

【原文】

道冲，而用之或不盈。

渊兮，似万物之宗；

（挫其锐，解其纷；

和其光，同其尘；）

湛兮，似或存。

吾不知谁之子，象帝之先。

【今译】

"道"体是虚空的，

然而作用却不穷竭。

渊深啊！它好像是万物的主宰；

（不露锋芒，消解纷扰；

含敛光耀，混同尘世；）

幽隐啊！似亡而又实存。

我不知道它是从哪里产生的，

似乎在有天地以前就有了它。

Chapter 4

The Way is like an empty vessel

That yet may be drawn from

Without ever needing to be filled.

It is bottomless; the very progenitor of all things in the world.[1]

(In it all sharpness is blunted,

All tangles untied,

All glare tempered,

All dust soothed.)[2]

It is like a deep pool that never dries.[3]

Was it too the child of something else? We cannot tell.

But as a substanceless image it existed before the Ancestor.[4]

第五章

【原文】

　　天地不仁，以万物为刍狗；圣人不仁，以百姓为刍狗。

　　天地之间，其犹橐籥乎！虚而不屈，动而愈出。

　　多言数穷，不如守中。

【今译】

　　天地无所偏爱，任凭万物自然生长；"圣人"无所偏爱，任凭百姓自己发展。

　　天地之间，岂不像个风箱吗？空虚但不会穷竭，发动起来而生生不息。

　　议论太多，反而加速败亡，不如持守虚静。

Chapter 5

Heaven and Earth are ruthless;[1]

To them the Ten Thousand Things are but as straw dogs.[2]

The Sage too is ruthless;[3]

To him the people are but as straw dogs.

Yet Heaven and Earth and all that lies between

Is like a bellows

In that it is empty, but gives a supply that never fails.

Work it, and more comes out.

Whereas the force of words is soon spent.

Far better is it to keep what is in the heart.[4]

11

第六章

【原文】

谷神不死，是谓玄牝。

玄牝之门，是谓天地根。

绵绵若存，用之不勤。

【今译】

虚空的变化是永不停竭的，这就是微妙的母性。

微妙的母性之门，是天地的根源。

它连绵不绝地永存着，愈用愈出，无穷无尽。

Chapter 6

The Valley Spirit never dies.[1]

It is named the Mysterious Female.[2]

And the Doorway of the Mysterious Female

Is the base from which Heaven and Earth sprang.

It is there within us all the while;

Draw upon it as you will, it never runs dry.[3]

13

第七章

大中华文库

【原文】

　　天长地久。天地所以能长且久者，以其不自生，故能长生。

　　是以圣人后其身而身先；外其身而身存。非以其无私邪？故能成其私。

【今译】

　　天地是长久存在的。天地所以能够长久，乃是因为它们的一切运作都不是为了自己，所以能够长久。

　　所以有道的人把自己放在后面，反而能赢得爱戴；把自己生命置于度外，反而能保全生命。不正是由于他不自私吗？反而能达到自私的目的。

Chapter 7

Heaven is eternal, the Earth everlasting.

How come they to be so? It is because they do not foster their own lives;[1]

That is why they live so long.[2]

Therefore the Sage

Puts himself in the background; but is always to the fore.

Remains outside; but is always there.[3]

It is not just because he does not strive for any personal end

That all his personal ends are fulfilled?[4]

15

第八章

大中华文库

【原文】

上善若水。水善利万物而不争，处众人之所恶，故几于"道"。居善地，心善渊，与善仁，言善信，政善治，事善能，动善时。夫唯不争，故无尤。

【今译】

最善的人好像水一样。水善于滋润万物而不和万物相争，停留在大家所不愿处的地方，所以最接近于"道"。

居处善于选择地方，心胸善于保持沉静，待人善于真诚相爱，说话善于遵守信用，为政善于精简处理，处事善于发挥所长，行动善于掌握时机。

只因为有不争的美德，所以没有过错。

Chapter 8

The highest good is like that of water.[1] The goodness of water is that it benefits the ten thousand creatures; yet itself does not scramble, but is content with the places that all men disdain. It is this that makes water so near to the Way.

And if men think the ground the best place for building a house upon,

If among thoughts they value those that are profound,

If in friendship they value gentleness,

In words, truth; in government, good order;

In deeds, effectiveness; in actions, timeliness—[2]

In each case it is because they prefer what does not lead to strife,

And therefore does not go amiss.

17

第九章

【原文】

> 持而盈之，不如其已；
> 揣而锐之，不可长保。
> 金玉满堂，莫之能守；
> 富贵而骄，自遗其咎。
> 功遂身退，天之道也。

【今译】

> 执持盈满，不如适时停止；
> 显露锋芒，锐势难保长久。
> 金玉满堂，无法守藏；
> 富贵而骄，自取祸患。
> 功业完成，含藏收敛，
> 是合于自然的道理。

Chapter 9

Stretch a bow[1] to the very full,

And you will wish you had stopped in time;

Temper a sword-edge to its very sharpest,

And you will find it soon grows dull.

When bronze[2] and jade fill your hall.

It can no longer be guarded.

Wealth and place breed insolence.

That brings ruin in its train.

When your work is done, then withdraw![3]

Such is Heaven's Way.[4]

19

大中华文库

20

第十章

【原文】

载营魄抱一，能无离乎？

专气致柔，能婴儿乎？

涤除玄览，能无疵乎？

爱民治国，能无为乎？

天门开阖，能为雌乎？

明白四达，能无知乎？

（生之畜之。生而不有，为而不恃，

长而不宰，是谓"玄德"。）

【今译】

精神和形体合一，能不分离吗？

结聚精气以致柔顺，能像无欲的婴儿吧？

洗清杂念而深入观照，能没有瑕疵吗？

爱民治国，能自然无为吗？

感官和外界接触，能守静吗？

通晓四方，能不用心机吗？

（生长万物，养育万物。生长而不占有，畜养而不依恃，导引而不主宰，这就是最深的"德"。）

Chapter 10

Can you keep the unquiet physical-soul[1] from straying, hold fast to the Unity, and never quit it?

Can you, when concentrating your breath, make it soft like that of a little child?

Can you wipe and cleanse your vision of the Mystery[2] till all is without blur?

Can you love the people and rule the land, yet remain unknown?[3]

Can you in opening and shutting the heavenly gates play always the female part?

Can your mind penetrate every corner of the land, but you yourself never interfere?

(Rear them, then, feed them,

Rear them, but do not lay claim to them.

Control them, but never lean upon them;

Be chief among them, but do not manage them.

This is called the Mysterious Power.)[4]

第十一章

大中华文库

22

【原文】

　　三十辐共一毂，

　　当其无，有车之用。

　　埏埴以为器，

　　当其无，有器之用。

　　凿户牖，以为室，

　　当其无，有室之用。

　　故有之以为利，

　　无之以为用。

【今译】

　　三十根辐条汇集到一个毂当中，车毂中有了空的地方，才有车的作用。

　　糅合陶土做成器具，器皿中有了空的地方，才有器皿的作用。

　　开凿门窗建造房屋，门窗四壁中有了空的地方，才有房屋的作用。

　　所以"有"给人便利，须靠"无"发挥作用。

Chapter 11

We put thirty spokes together and call it a wheel;[1]

But it is on the space where there is nothing that the usefulness of the wheel depends.

We turn clay to make a vessel;

But it is on the space where there is nothing that the usefulness of the vessel depends.

We pierce doors and windows to make a house;

And it is on these spaces where there is nothing that the usefulness of the house depends.

Therefore just as we take advantage of what is, we should recognize the usefulness of what is not.[2]

23

第十二章

【原文】

　　五色令人目盲；

　　五音令人耳聋；

　　五味令人口爽；

　　驰骋畋猎，令人心发狂；

　　难得之货，令人行妨。

　　是以圣人为腹不为目，

　　故去彼取此。

【今译】

　　缤纷的色彩使人眼花缭乱；

　　纷杂的音调使人听觉不敏；

　　饮食餍饫会使人舌不知味；

　　纵情狩猎使人心放荡；

　　稀有物品使人行为不轨；

　　因此圣人但求安饱而不逐声色之娱，所以摒弃物欲的诱惑而保持安足的生活。

Chapter 12

The five colours confuse the eye,

The five sounds dull the ear,

The five tastes spoil the palate.

Excess of hunting and chasing

Makes minds go mad.[1]

Products that are hard to get

Impede their owner's movements.

Therefore the Sage

Considers the belly not the eye,

Truly, "he rejects that but takes this."[2]

25

第十三章

【原文】

　　宠辱若惊，贵大患若身。

　　何谓宠辱若惊？宠为下，得之若惊，失之若惊，是谓宠辱若惊。

　　何谓贵大患若身？吾所以有大患者，为吾有身，及吾无身，吾有何患？

　　故贵以身为天下，若可寄天下；爱以身为天下，若可托天下。

【今译】

　　得宠和受辱都使人感到惊慌失措，重视身体好像重视大患一样。

　　什么叫做得宠和受辱感到惊慌失措？得宠仍是下等的，得到恩惠感到心惊不安，失去恩惠也觉惊恐慌乱，这就叫做得宠和受辱感到惊慌失措。

　　什么叫做重视身体像重视大患一样？我所以有大患，乃是因为我有这个身体，如果没有这个身体，我会有什么大患呢？

　　所以能够以贵身的态度去为天下，才可以把天下寄托给他；以爱身的态度去爱天下，才可以把天下委托给他。

大中华文库

Chapter 13

"Favour and disgrace goad as it were to madness; high rank hurts keenly as our bodies hurt."[1]

What does it mean to say that favour and disgrace goad as it were to madness? It means that when a ruler's subjects get it they turn distraught,[2] when they lose it they turn distraught. That is what is meant by saying favour and disgrace goad as it were to madness. What does it mean to say that high rank hurts keenly as our bodies hurt? The only reason that we suffer hurt is that we have bodies; if we had no bodies, how could we suffer?

Therefore we may accept the saying: "He who in dealing with the empire regards his high rank as though it were his body[3] is the best person to be entrusted with rule; he who in dealing with the empire loves his subjects as one should love one's body is the best person to whom one can commit the empire."

第十四章

【原文】

视之不见，名曰"夷"；听之不闻，名曰"希"；搏之不得，名曰"微"。此三者不可致诘，故混而为一。

其上不皦，其下不昧。绳绳兮不可名，复归于无物。是谓无状之状，无物之象，是谓惚恍。迎之不见其首；随之不见其后。

执古之道，以御今之有。能知古始，是谓道纪。

【今译】

看它看不见，名叫"夷"；听它听不到，名叫"希"；摸它摸不着，名叫"微"。这三者的形象无从推问，它是浑然一体的。

它上面不显得光亮，它下面也不显得阴暗，它绵绵不绝而不可名状，一切的运动都会还回到不见物体的状态。这是没有形状的形状，不见物体的形象，叫它做"惚恍"。迎着它，看不见它的前头；随着它却看不见它的后面。

把握着早已存在的"道"，来驾驭现在的具体事物。能够了解宇宙的原始，叫做"道"的规律。

Chapter 14

Because the eye gazes but can catch no glimpse of it,

It is called elusive.

Because the ear listens but cannot hear it,

It is called the rarefied.

Because the hand feels for it but cannot find it,

It is called the infinitesimal.

These three, because they cannot be further scrutinized,

Blend into one.

Its rising brings no light;

Its sinking, no darkness.[1]

Endless the series of things without name

On the way back to where there is nothing.

They are called shapeless shapes;

Forms without form;

Are called vague semblances.

Go towards them, and you can see no front;

Go after them, and you see no rear.

Yet by seizing on the Way that was

You can ride[2] the things that are now.

For to know what once there was,[3] in the Beginning,

This is called the essence[4] of the Way.[5]

第十五章

【原文】

　　古之善为道者，微妙玄通，深不可识。夫唯不可识，故强为之容：

　　豫兮其若冬涉川；犹兮其若畏四邻；

　　俨兮其若客；涣兮其若凌释；

　　敦兮其若朴；旷兮其若谷；

　　混兮其若浊；

　　（澹兮其若海；飂兮若无止。）

　　孰能浊以静之徐清；孰能安以动之徐生。

　　保此道者不欲盈。夫唯不盈，故能敝而新成。

【今译】

　　古时善于行道的人，精妙通达，深刻而难以认识。正因为难以认识，所以勉强对他进行描绘：

　　小心审慎啊，像冬天涉足江河；

　　警觉戒惕啊，像提防四周的围攻；

　　拘谨严肃啊，像作宾客；

　　融和可亲啊，像冰柱消融；

　　淳厚朴质啊，像未经雕琢的素材；

　　空豁开广啊，像深山的幽谷；

　　浑朴淳厚啊，像浊水的样子；

　　（沉静恬淡啊，好像湛深的大海；

　　飘逸无系啊，好像无有止境。）

　　谁能在动荡中安静下来而慢慢地澄清？

　　谁能在安定中变动起来而慢慢地趋进？

　　保持这些道理的人不肯自满。只因为他不自满，所以能去故更新。

Chapter 15

Of old those that were the best officers of Court[1]

Had inner natures subtle, abstruse, mysterious, penetrating,

Too deep to be understood.

And because such men could not be understood

I can but tell of them as they appeared to the world:

Circumspect they seemed, like one who in winter crosses a stream;

Watchful, as one who must meet danger on every side.

Ceremonious, as one who pays a visit;

Yet yielding, as ice when it begins to melt.

Blank, as a piece of uncarved wood;

Yet receptive as a hollow in the hills.

Murky, as a troubled stream —

(Tranquil, as the vast reaches of the sea,

Drifting, as the wind with no stop.)[2]

Which of you can assume such murkiness, to become in the end still and clear?

Which of you can make yourself inert, to become in the end full of life and stir?

Those who possess this Tao do not try to fill themselves to the brim,

And because they do not try to fill themselves to the brim,

They are like a garment that endures all wear and need never be renewed.[3]

第十六章

【原文】

> 致虚极，守静笃。
>
> 万物并作，吾以观其复。
>
> 夫物芸芸，各复归其根。
>
> 归根曰静，静曰复命。
>
> 复命曰常，知常曰明。
>
> 不知常，妄作凶。
>
> 知常容，容乃公，
>
> 公乃全，全乃天，
>
> 天乃道，道乃久，
>
> 没身不殆。

【今译】

致虚和守静的功夫，做到极笃的境地。

万物蓬勃生长，我看出往复循环的道理。

万物纷纷纭纭，各自返回到它的本根。返回本根叫做静，静叫做复命。复命叫做常，了解常叫做明。不了解常，轻举妄动就会出现乱子。

了解常道的人是无所不包的，无所不包就能坦然大公，坦然大公才能无不周遍，无不周遍才能符合自然，符合自然才能符合于道，体道而行才能长久，终身可免于危殆。

Chapter 16

Push far enough towards the Void,

Hold fast enough to Quietness,

And of the ten thousand things none but can be worked on by you.

I have beheld them, whither they go back.

See, all things howsoever they flourish

Return to the root from which they grew.

This return to the root is called Quietness;

Quietness is called submission to Fate;

What has submitted to Fate has become part of the always-so.

To know the always-so is to be illumined;

Not to know it, means to go blindly to disaster.

He who knows the always-so has room in him for everything;

He who has room in him for everything is without prejudice.

To be without prejudice is to be kingly;[1]

To be kingly is to be of heaven;[2]

To be of heaven is to be in Tao.

Tao is forever and he that possesses it,

Though his body ceases, is not destroyed.[3]

第十七章

【原文】

太上，不知有之；
其次，亲而誉之；
其次，畏之；
其次，侮之。
信不足焉，有不信焉。
悠兮其贵言。
功成事遂，
百姓皆谓："我自然。"

【今译】

最好的世代，人民根本不感到统治者的存在；其次，人民亲近而赞美他；再其次的，人民畏惧他；更其次的，人民轻侮他。

统治者的诚信不足，人民自然不相信他。

(最好的统治者)却是悠然而不轻于发号施令。事情办成功了，百姓都说："我们本来是这样的。"

Chapter 17

Of the highest the people merely know[1] that such a one exists;

The next they draw near to and praise.

The next they shrink from, intimated; but revile.

Truly, "It is by not believing people that you turn them into liars."[2]

But from the Sage it is so hard at any price to get a single word

That when his task is accomplished, his work done,

Throughout the country everyone says, "It happened of its own accord."

第十八章

【原文】

大道废，有仁义；
智慧出，有大伪；
六亲不和，有孝慈；
国家昏乱，有忠臣。

【今译】

大道废弃，才提倡仁义；
智巧出现，才产生伪诈；
家庭纠纷，才显出孝慈；
国家昏乱，才见出忠臣。

Chapter 18

It was when the Great Way declined

That human kindness and morality[1] arose;

It was when intelligence and knowledge appeared

That the Great Artifice began.

It was when the six near ones[2] were no longer at peace

That there was talk of "dutiful sons"; [3]

Nor till fatherland was dark with strife

Did we hear of "loyal slaves."[4]

第十九章

【原文】

绝圣弃智，民利百倍；
绝仁弃义，民复孝慈；
绝巧弃利，盗贼无有。
此三者以为文不足。
故令有所属：
见素抱朴，少私寡欲，绝学无忧。

【今译】

抛弃聪明和智巧，人民可以得到百倍的好处；
抛弃仁和义，人民可以恢复孝慈的天性；
抛弃巧诈和私利，盗贼就自然会消失。
（圣智、仁义、巧利）这三者全是巧饰的，
不足以治理天下。
所以要使人有所归属：保持淳朴，减少私欲，抛弃（圣智礼法的）学问，没有忧虑。

Chapter 19

Banish wisdom, discard knowledge,

And the people will be benefited a hundredfold.

Banish human kindness, discard morality,

And the people will be dutiful and compassionate.

Banish skill, discard profit,

And thieves and robbers will disappear.

If when these three things are done they find life too plain and un-

adorned,

Then let them have accessories;

Give them Simplicity to look at,

The Uncarved Block to hold,

Give them selflessness and fewness of desires.

Banish learning, and there will be no more grieving.[1]

39

第二十章

【原文】

　　唯之与阿，相去几何？美之与恶，相去若何？人之所畏，不可不畏。
　　荒兮，其未央哉！
　　众人熙熙，如享太牢，如春登台。
　　我独泊兮，其未兆；沌沌兮，如婴儿之未孩；累累兮，若无所归。
　　众人皆有余，而我独若遗。
　　我愚人之心也哉！
　　俗人昭昭，我独昏昏。俗人察察，我独闷闷。
　　（澹兮其若海，飂兮若无止。）
　　众人皆有以，而我独顽且鄙。我独异于人，而贵食母。

【今译】

40

　　应诺和呵声，相差好多？所谓美好和丑恶相差好多？人们所畏惧的，也不必去触犯。
　　精神领域开阔啊，好像没有尽头的样子！
　　众人兴高采烈，好像参加丰盛的筵席，又像春天登台眺望景色。
　　而我独个儿淡泊宁静啊，不炫耀自己；浑浑沌沌啊，好像不知嬉笑的婴儿；闲闲散散啊，好像无家可归。
　　众人都有多余，惟独我好像不足的样子。
　　我真是"愚人"的心肠啊！
　　世人都光耀自炫，惟独我昏昏昧昧的样子。
　　世人都精明灵巧，惟独我无所识别的样子。
　　沉静恬淡啊，好像湛深的大海，飘逸无奈啊，好像没有止境。
　　众人都好像很有作为，惟独我愚昧而笨拙。
　　我和世人不同，而重视进"道"的生活。

Chapter 20

Between wei and o[1]

What after all is the difference?

Can it be compared to the difference between good and bad?

The saying "what others avoid I too must avoid"

How false and superficial it is![2]

All men, indeed, are wreathed in smiles,

As though feasting after the Great Sacrifice,

As though going up to the Spring Carnival.

I alone am inert, like a child that has not yet given sign;

Like an infant that has not yet smile.

I droop and drift, as though I belonged nowhere.

All men have enough and to spare;

I alone seem to have lost everything.[3]

Mine is indeed the mind of a very idiot,

So dull am I.

The world is full of people that shine;

I alone am dark.

They look lively and self-assured;

I alone depressed.

(I seem unsettled as the ocean;

Blown adrift, never brought to a stop.)[4]

All men can be put to some use;

I alone am intractable and boorish.

But wherein I most am different from men

Is that I prize no sustenance that comes not from the Mother's[5] breast.

第二十一章

【原文】

孔"德"之容，惟"道"是从。

"道"之为物，惟恍惟惚。

惚兮恍兮，其中有象；

恍兮惚兮，其中有物。

窈兮冥兮，其中有精。

其精甚真，其中有信。

自今及古，其名不去，

以阅众甫。

吾何以知众甫之状哉！

以此。

42

【今译】

大"德"的样态，随着"道"而转移。

"道"这个东西是恍恍惚惚的。那样地惚惚恍恍，其中却有形象；那样地恍恍惚惚，其中却有实物。那样地深远暗昧，其中却有精质；这精质是非常真实的，这精质是可信验的。

从当今上溯到古代，它的名字永远不能消去，依据它才能认识万物的本始。我怎么知道万物本始的情形呢！从"道"认识的。

Chapter 21

Such the scope of the All-pervading Power.

That it alone can act through the Way.

For the Way is a thing impalpable, incommensurable.

Incommensurable, impalpable.

Yet latent in it are forms;

Impalpable, incommensurable

Yet within it are entities.

Shadowy it is and dim;

Yet within it there is a force,[1]

A force that though rarefied

Is none the less efficacious.

From the time of old till now

Its charge has not departed

But cheers onward the many warriors.

How do I know that the many warriors are so?

Through this.[2]

43

第二十二章

【原文】

曲则全，枉则直，

洼则盈，敝则新，

少则得，多则惑。

是以圣人抱一为天下式。

不自见，故明；

不自是，故彰；

不自伐，故有功；

不自矜，故长。

夫唯不争，故天下莫能与之争。

古之所谓"曲则全"者，

岂虚言哉！

诚全而归之。

【今译】

委曲反能保全，屈就反能伸展，低洼反能充盈，敝旧反能生新，少取反能多得，贪多反而迷惑。

所以有道的人坚守这一原则作为天下事理的范式。不自我表扬，反能显明；不自以为是，反能彰显；不自己夸耀，反能见功；不自我矜持，反能长久。

正因为不跟人争，所以天下没有人和他争。古人所说的"委曲可以保全"等话，怎么会是空话呢！它实实在在能够达到的。

Chapter 22

"To remain whole, be twisted!"

To become straight, let yourself be bent.

To become full, be hollow.

Be tattered, that you may be renewed.

Those that have little, may get more,

Those that have much, are but perplexed.

Therefore the Sage

Clasps the Primal Unity,

Testing by it everything under heaven.

He does not show himself; therefore he is seen everywhere.

He does not define himself, therefore he is distinct.

He does not boast of what he will do, therefore he succeeds.

He is not proud of his work, and therefore it endures.

He does not contend,

And for that very reason no one under heaven can contend with him.

So then we see that the ancient saying "To remain whole, be twisted!"

was no idle word; for true wholeness can only be achieved by return.[1]

大中华文库

46

第二十三章

【原文】

希言自然。

故飘风不终朝，骤雨不终日。孰为此者？天地。天地尚不能久，而况于人乎？

故从事于"道"者，同于"道"；"德"者同于"德"；失者，同于失。同于"道"者，"道"亦乐得之；同于"德"者，"德"亦乐得之；同于失者，失亦乐得之。

信不足焉，有不信焉。

【今译】

不言教令是合于自然的。

所以狂风刮不到一早晨，暴雨下不了一整天。谁使他这样的？是天地。天地的狂暴都不能持久，何况人呢？

所以从事于"道"的，就同于"道"；从事"德"的，就同于"德"；表现失"道"失"德"的，行为就是暴戾恣肆。同于"道"的人，"道"也乐于得到他；同于"德"的，"德"也乐于得到他；同于失"道"失"德"的，就会得到失"道"失"德"的后果。

统治者的诚信不足，人民自然不相信他。

Chapter 23

To be always talking is against nature.

For the same reason a hurricane never lasts a whole morning, nor a rainstorm all day. Who is it that makes the wind and rain? It is Heaven-and-Earth.[1]

And if even Heaven-and-Earth cannot blow or pour for long, how much less in his utterance should man?

Truly, if one uses the Way as one's instrument, the results will be like the Way; if one uses the "power" as one's instrument, the results will be like the "power." If one uses what is the reverse of the "power,"[2] the results will be the reverse of the "power."

For to those who have conformed themselves to the Way, the Way readily lends its power. To those who have conformed themselves to the power, the power readily lends more power. While to those who conform themselves to inefficacy, inefficacy readily lends its ineffectiveness.

"It is by not believing in people that your turn them into liars." [3]

47

第二十四章

【原文】

企者不立；

跨者不行；

自见者不明；

自是者不彰；

自伐者无功；

自矜者不长。

其在道也，

曰：余食赘形。

物或恶之，

故有道者不处。

【今译】

踮起脚跟，是站不牢的；跨步前进，是走不远的；自逞己见的，反而不得自明；自以为是的，反而不得彰显；自己夸耀的，反而不得见功；自我矜持的，反而不得长久。

从"道"的观点来看，这些急躁炫耀的行为，可说都是剩饭赘瘤。惹人厌恶，所以有"道"的人不这样做。

Chapter 24

"He who stands on tip-toe, does not stand firm;

He who takes the longest strides, does not walk the fastest."

He who does his own looking sees little,[1]

He who defines himself is not therefore distinct.

He who boasts of what he will do succeeds in nothing;

He who is proud of his work, achieves nothing that endures.

Of these, from the standpoint of the Way, it is said,

"Pass round superfluous dishes to those that have already had enough,

And no creature but will reject them in disgust."

That is why he that possesses Tao does not linger.[2]

49

第二十五章

【原文】

有物混成，先天地生。

寂兮寥兮，

独立而不改，

周行而不殆，

可以为天地母。

吾不知其名，

强字之曰"道"，

强为之名曰"大"。

大曰逝，逝曰远，远曰反。

故"道"大，

天大，地大，人亦大。

域中有四大，

而人居其一焉。

人法地，地法天，天法"道"，"道"法自然。

【今译】

有一个浑然一体的东西，在天地形成以前就存在。听不见它的声音也看不着它的形体，它独立长存而永不衰竭，循环运行而生生不息，可以为天地万物的根源。我不知道它的名字，勉强叫它做"道"，再勉强给它起个名字叫做"大"。它广大无边而周流不息，周流不息而伸展遥远，伸展遥远而返回本源。

所以说，"道"大，天大，地大，人也大。宇宙间有四大，而人是四大之一。

人取法地，地取法天，天取法"道"，"道"纯任自然。

Chapter 25

There was something formless yet complete,

That existed before heaven and earth;

Without sound, without substance,

Dependent on nothing, unchanging,

All pervading, unfailing.

One may think of it as the mother of all things under heaven.

Its true name we do not know;

"Way" is the by-name that we give it.

Were I forced to say to what class of things it belongs

I should call it Great (ta) .

Now ta also means passing on,

And passing on means going far away

And going far away means returning.[1]

Thus just as Tao[2] has "this greatness" and as earth has it and as heaven has it, so may the ruler[3] also have it.

Thus "within the realm there are four portions of greatness," and one belongs to the king.

The ways of men are conditioned by those of earth.

The ways of earth, by those of heaven.

The ways of heaven, by those of Tao, and the ways of Tao, by the Self-so.[4]

第二十六章

【原文】

　　重为轻根，
　　静为躁君。
　　是以君子终日行不离辎重。
　　虽有荣观，燕处超然。
　　奈何万乘之主，
　　而以身轻天下？
　　轻则失根，
　　躁则失君。

【今译】

　　厚重是轻浮的根本，静定是躁动的主帅。

　　因此君子整天行走不离开载重的车辆。虽然有华丽的生活，却安居泰然。为什么身为大国的君主，反而把自身看得比天下社稷还轻微呢？

　　轻率就失去了根本，躁动就失去了主体的地位。

Chapter 26

As the heavy must be the foundation of the light,

So quietness is lord and master of activity.

Truly, "A man of consequence though he travels all day

Will not let himself be separated from his baggage-wagon,

However magnificent the view,[1] he sits quiet and dispassionate."

How much less, then, must be the lord of ten thousand chariots

Allow himself to be lighter[2] than these he rules!

If he is light, the foundation is lost;

If he is active, the lord and master[3] is lost.[4]

53

第二十七章

【原文】

善行无辙迹；

善言无瑕谪；

善数不用筹策；

善闭无关楗而不可开；

善结无绳约而不可解。

是以圣人常善救人，故无弃人；

常善救物，故无弃物。

是谓袭明。

故善人者，不善人之师；

不善人者，善人之资。

不贵其师，

不爱其资，

虽智大迷。

是故要妙。

【今译】

　　善于行走的，不留痕迹；善于言谈的，言辞没有差错；善于计算的，不用筹码；善于关闭的，不用栓销却使人不能开；善于捆缚的，不用绳索却使人不能解。

　　因此，有道的人经常善于做到人尽其才，所以没有被遗弃的人；经常善于做到物尽其用，所以没有被废弃的物。这就叫做保持明境。

　　所以善人可以做为不善人的老师，不善人为善人的借鉴。不尊重他的老师，不珍惜他的借鉴，虽然自以为聪明，其实是大迷糊。这真是个精要深奥的道理。

Chapter 27

Perfect activity[1] leaves no track behind it;

Perfect speech is like a jade-worker whose tool leaves no mark.

The perfect reckoner needs no counting-slips;[2]

The perfect door has neither bolt nor bar,

Yet cannot be opened.

The perfect knot needs neither rope nor twine,

Yet cannot be untied.

Therefore the Sage,

Is all the time in the most perfect way helping men,

He certainly does not turn his back on men;

Is all the time in the most perfect way helping creatures,

He certainly does not turn his back on creatures.

This is called resorting to the Light.[3]

Truly, "the perfect man is the teacher of the imperfect;

But the imperfect is the stock-in-trade of the perfect man."[4]

He who does not respect his teacher,

He who does not take care of his stock-in-trade,

Much learning though he may possess, is far astray.

This[5] is the essential secret.

55

第二十八章

【原文】

　　知其雄，守其雌，

　　为天下溪。

　　为天下溪，常德不离，

　　复归于婴儿。

　　知其白，（守其黑，

　　为天下式。

　　为天下式，常德不忒，

　　复归于无极。

　　知其荣，）守其辱，

　　为天下谷。

　　为天下谷，常德乃足，

　　复归于朴。

　　朴散则为器，圣人用之，

　　则为官长，

　　故大制不割。

【今译】

　　深知雄强，却安于雌柔，作为天下的溪涧。作为天下的溪涧，常"德"就不会离失，而回复到婴儿的状态。

　　深知明亮，（却坚守黑暗，作为检验万物的准则。坚持这一准则，常"德"就不会出错，而回归到无限的状况。深知荣耀，）却安于暗昧，作为天下的川谷。作为天下的川谷，常"德"才可以充足，而回复到真朴的状态。

　　真朴的"道"分散成万物，有道的人沿用真朴，则为百官的首长。所以完善的政治是不割裂的。

Chapter 28

"He who knows the male, yet cleaves to what is female

Becomes like a ravine, receiving all things under heaven,"

And being such a ravine

He knows all the time a power that he never calls upon in vain.

This is returning to the state of infancy.

He who knows the white, (yet cleaves to the black

Becomes the standard by which all things are tested;

And being such a standard

He has all the time a power that never errs,

He returns to the Limitless.

He who knows glory,)[1] yet cleaves to ignominy

Becomes like a valley that receives into it all things under heaven,

And being such a valley

He has all the time a power that suffices;

He returns to the state of the Uncarved Block.

Now when a block is sawed up it is made into implements;[2]

But when the Sage uses it, it becomes Chief of all Ministers.

Truly, "The greatest carver[3] does the least cutting."

57

第二十九章

【原文】

　　将欲取天下而为之，
　　吾见其不得已。
　　天下神器，
　　不可为也，
　　（不可执也。）
　　为者败之，
　　执者失之。
　　（是以圣人无为，故无败；无执，故无失。）
　　夫物或行或随；
　　或歔或吹；
　　或强或羸；
　　或载或隳。
　　是以圣人去甚，
　　去奢，去泰。

【今译】

　　想要治理天下却用强力去做，我看他不能达到目的了。"天下"是神圣的东西，不能出于强力，（不能加以把持。）出于强力的，一定会失败；加以把持的，一定会失去。（因此圣人不妄为，所以不会失败；不把持，所以不会失去。）

　　世人（秉性不一）有前行，有后随，有呴暖，有吹寒；有刚强，有羸弱；有安定，有危险。

　　因此圣人要去除极端的、奢侈的、过度的措施。

Chapter 29

Those that would gain what is under heaven by tampering with it — I have seen that they do not succeed.

For that which is under heaven is like a holy vessel,[1] dangerous to tamper with.

(And impossible to grab at.)[2]

Those that tamper with it, harm it.

Those that grab at it, lose it.

(Therefore the Sage does not act,

And as a result, he doesn't ruin things;

He does not hold on to things,

And as a result, he doesn't lose things.)[3]

For among the creatures of the world[4] some go in front, some follow;

Some blow hot when others would be blowing cold.

Some are feeling vigorous just when others are worn out.

Some are loading just when others would be tilting out.

Therefore the Sage "discards the absolute, the all-inclusive, the extreme."[5]

59

大中华文库

第三十章

【原文】

以道佐人主者，不以兵强天下。其事好还。师之所处，荆棘生焉。大军之后，必有凶年。

善有果而已，不敢以取强。果而勿矜，果而勿伐，果而勿骄，果而不得已，果而勿强。

物壮则老，是谓不道，不道早已。

【今译】

用道辅助君主的人，不靠兵力逞强于天下。用兵这件事一定会得到还报。军队所到的地方，荆棘就长满了。大战过后，一定会变成荒年。

善用兵的只求达到救济危难的目的就是了，不敢用兵来逞强。达到目的却不矜持，达到目的却不夸耀，达到目的却不骄傲，达到目的却出于不得已，达到目的却不逞强。

凡是气势壮盛的就会趋于衰败，这是不合于道的，不合于道很快就会消逝。

Chapter 30

He who by Tao purposes to help a ruler of men

Will oppose all conquest by force of arms;

For such things are wont to rebound.[1]

Where armies are, thorn and brambles grow.

The raising of a great host

Is followed by a year of dearth.

Therefore a good general effects his purpose and then stops; he does not take further advantage of his victory.

Fulfils his purpose and does not glory in what he has done;

Fulfils his purpose and does not boast of what he has done;

Fulfils his purpose, but takes no pride in what he has done;

Fulfils his purpose, but only as a step that could not be avoided.

Fulfils his purpose, but without violence;

For what has a time of vigour also has a time of decay.

This is against Tao,

And what is against Tao will soon perish.

第三十一章

【原文】

夫兵者，不祥之器，物或恶之，故有道者不处。

君子居则贵左，用兵则贵右。兵者不祥之器，非君子之器，不得已而用之，恬淡为上。胜而不美，而美之者，是乐杀人。夫乐杀人者，则不可得志于天下矣。

吉事尚左，凶事尚右。偏将军居左，上将军居右。言以丧礼处之。杀人之众，以悲哀泣之，战胜以丧礼处之。

【今译】

兵革是不祥的东西，大家都厌恶它，所以有道的人不使用它。

君子平时以左方为贵，用兵时以右方为贵。兵革是不祥的东西，不是君子所使用的东西。万不得已而使用它，最好要淡然处之。胜利了也不要得意洋洋，如果得意洋洋，就是喜欢杀人。喜欢杀人的，就不能实现统治天下的愿望啦。

吉庆的事情以左方为上，凶丧的事情以右方为上。偏将军在左边，上将军在右边，这是说出兵打仗用丧礼的仪式来处理。杀人众多，带着哀痛的心情去参加，打了胜仗要用丧礼的仪式去处理。

Chapter 31

Fine weapons[1] are none the less ill-omened things. (People despise them, therefore, those in possession of the Tao do not depend on them.)[2] That is why, among people of good birth, in peace the left-hand side is the place of honour, but in war this is reversed and the right-hand side is the place of honour. (Weapons are ill-omened things, which the superior man should not depend on. When he has no choice but to use them, the best attitude is to remain tranquil and peaceful.)[3] The Quietist, even when he conquers, does not regard weapons as lovely things. For to think them lovely means to delight in them, and to delight in them means to delight in the slaughter of men. And he who delights in the slaughter of men will never get what he looks for out of those that dwell under heaven. (Thus in happy events, the left-hand is the place of honour, in grief and mourning, the right-hand is the place of honour. The lieutenant general stands on the left, while the supreme general stands on the right, which is arranged on the rites of mourning.)[4] A host that has slain men is received with grief and mourning; he that has conquered in battle is received with rites of mourning.

63

第三十二章

【原文】

　　"道"常无名、朴。
　　虽小，天下莫能臣。
　　侯王若能守之，
　　万物将自宾。
　　天地相合，
　　以降甘露，
　　民莫之令而自均。
　　始制有名，
　　名亦既有，
　　夫亦将知止，
　　知止可以不殆。
　　譬"道"之在天下，
　　犹川谷之于江海。

【今译】

　　"道"永远是无名而又好像未经雕琢的素材。(它的呈现)虽然幽微(不可见)，天下却没有人能臣服它。侯王如果能守住它，万物将会自然地归从。

　　天地间(阴阳之气)相合，就降下甘露，人们不须指使它而自然均匀。万物兴作就产生了各种名称，各种名称已经制定了，就知道有个限度，知道有所限度，就可以避免危险。

　　"道"存在于天下，有如江海为河川所流注一样。

Chapter 32

Tao is eternal, but has no fame (name);

The Uncarved Block, though seemingly of small account,

Is greater than anything that is under heaven.[1]

If kings and barons would but possess themselves of it,

The ten thousand creatures would flock to do them homage;

Heaven-and-Earth would conspire

To send Sweet Dew,

Without law or compulsion, men would dwell in harmony.[2]

Once the block is carved, there will be names,

And so soon as there are names

Know that it is time to stop.

Only by knowing when it is time to stop can danger be avoided.

To Tao[3] all under heaven will come

As streams and torrents flow into a great river or sea.

65

第三十三章

【原文】

知人者智，自知者明。

胜人者有力，自胜者强。

知足者富。

强行者有志。

不失其所者久。

死而不亡者寿。

【今译】

认识别人的是机智，了解自己的才算高明。

战胜别人的是有力，克服自己的才算刚强。

知道满足的就是富有。

努力不懈的就是有志。

不迷失本性的就能长久。

身死而不被遗忘的是真正的长寿。

Chapter 33

To understand others is to have knowledge;

To understand oneself is to be illumined.

To conquer others needs strength;

To conquer oneself is harder still.

To be content with what one has is to be rich.

He that works through violence[1] may get his way;

But only what stays in its place

Can endure.

When one dies one is not lost, there is no other longevity.

第三十四章

【原文】

大道氾兮，其可左右。
万物恃之以生而不辞，
功成而不有。
衣养万物而不为主，
（常无欲，）可名为小；
万物归焉而不为主，
可名为大。
以其终不自为大，
故能成其大。

【今译】

大道广泛流行，无所不到。万物依赖它生长而不推辞，有所成就而不自以为有功。养育万物而不自以为主，可以称它为"小"；万物归附而不自以为主宰，可以称它为"大"。由于它不自以为伟大，所以才能成就它的伟大。

Chapter 34

Great Tao is like a boat that drifts;

It can go this way; it can go that.[1]

The ten thousand creatures owe their existence to it and it does not disown them;

Yet having produced them, it does not take possession of them.

Tao, though it covers the ten thousand things like a garment,[2]

Makes no claim to be master over them,

(And asks for nothing from them.)[3]

Therefore it may be called the Lowly.

The ten thousand creatures obey it,

Though they know not that they have a master;

Therefore it is called the Great.

So too the Sage just because he never at any time makes a show of greatness in fact achieves greatness.

第三十五章

大中华文库

【原文】

执大象，天下往。

往而不害，安平太。

乐与饵，过客止。

"道"之出口，淡乎其无味，

视之不足见，听之不足闻，

用之不足既。

【今译】

执守大"道"，天下人都会归附他。会归附他而不互相伤害，于是大家都平和安泰。

音乐和美食，能使过路的人停步。而"道"的表述，却淡得没有味道，看它却看不见，听它却听不着，用它却用不完。

Chapter 35

He who holding the Great Form[1] goes about his work in the empire

Can go about his work, yet do no harm.

All is peace, quietness and security.[2]

Sound of music, smell of good dishes

Will make the passing stranger pause.

How different the words that Tao gives forth!

So thin, so flavourless!

If one looks for Tao, there is nothing solid to see;

If one listens for it, there is nothing loud enough to hear.

Yet if one uses it, it is inexhaustible.

71

第三十六章

【原文】

将欲歙之，必固张之；

将欲弱之，必固强之；

将欲废之，必固兴之；

将欲取之，必固与之。

是谓微明。

柔弱胜刚强。

鱼不可脱于渊，

国之利器不可以示人。

【今译】

将要收敛的，必先扩张；将要削弱的，必先加强；将要废弃的，必先兴举；将要夺取的，必先给予。这就是深沉的预见。

柔弱胜过刚强。鱼不能离开深渊，国家的"利器"不可以随便耀示于人。

Chapter 36

What is in the end to be shrunk

Must first be stretched.

Whatever is to be weakened

Must begin by being made strong.

What is to be overthrown

Must begin by being set up.

He who would be a taker

Must begin as a giver.

This is called "dimming" one's light.[1]

It is thus that the soft overcomes the hard

And the weak, the strong.

"It is best to leave the fish down in his pool;

Best to leave the State's sharpest weapons[2] where none can see

them."[3]

73

大中华文库

第三十七章

【原文】

"道"常无为而无不为。

侯王若能守之，

万物将自化。

化而欲作，

吾将镇之以无名之朴。

镇之以无名之朴，

夫将不欲。

不欲以静，

天下将自正。

【今译】

　　"道"永远是顺任自然的，然而没有一件事不是它所为。侯王如果能够持守它，万物就会自生自长。自生自长而至贪欲萌作时，我就用"道"的真朴来镇住它。用"道"的真朴来镇住它，就不会起贪欲。不起贪欲而归于安静，天下自然走上正常的轨道。

Chapter 37

Tao never does;

Yet through it all things are done.

If the barons and kings would but possess themselves of it,

The ten thousand creatures would at once be transformed.[1]

And if having been transformed they should desire to act,

We must restrain them by the blankness[2] of the Unnamed.

The blankness of the Unnamed[3]

Brings dispassion;[4]

To be dispassionate is to be still.

And so,[5] of itself, the whole empire will be at rest.

75

第三十八章

【原文】

　　上"德"不德，是以有"德"；

　　下"德"不失德，是以无"德"。

　　上"德"无为而无以为；下"德"无为而有以为。

　　上仁为之而无以为；上义为之而有以为。

　　上礼为之而莫之应，则攘臂而扔之。

　　故失"道"而后"德"，失"德"而后仁，

　　失仁而后义，失义而后礼。

　　夫礼者，忠信之薄，而乱之首。

　　前识者，"道"之华，而愚之始。

【今译】

　　上"德"的人不自恃有德，所以真正是有"德"；下"德"的人自以为不离失德，所以没有达到"德"。

　　上"德"的人顺任自然而无心作为；下"德"的人顺任自然而有心作为。

　　上仁的人有所作为却出于无意；上义的人有所作为且出于有意。

　　上礼的人有所作为而得不到回应，于是就扬着胳膊使人强从。

　　所以失去了"道"而后才有"德"，失去了"德"而后才有仁，失去了仁而后才有义，失去了义而后才有礼。

　　礼是忠信的不足，而祸乱的开端。

　　所谓"先知"，不过是"道"的虚华，是愚昧的开始。

Chapter 38

The man of highest "power" does not reveal himself as a possessor of "power";

Therefore he keeps his "power."

The man of inferior "power" cannot rid it of the appearance of "power";

Therefore he is in truth without "power."

The man of highest "power" neither acts[1] nor is there any who so regards him;[2]

The man of inferior "power" both acts and is so regarded.

The man of highest humanity, though he acts, is not so regarded;

Whereas a man of even the highest morality both acts and is so regarded;

While even he who is best versed in ritual not merely acts, but if people fail to respond

Then he will pull up his sleeves and advance upon them.

That is why it is said,

"After Tao was lost, then came the 'power';

After the 'power' was lost, then came human kindness.

After human kindness was lost, then came morality,

After morality was lost, then came ritual.

Now ritual is the mere husk of loyalty and promise-keeping

And is indeed the first step towards brawling."[3]

Foreknowledge may be the "flower of doctrine,"

But it is the beginning of folly.

【原文】

是以大丈夫处其厚，

不居其薄；

处其实，不居其华。

故去彼取此。

【今译】

因此大丈夫立身敦厚，而不居于浇薄；存心笃实，而不居于虚华。所以舍弃薄华而采取厚实。

Therefore the full-grown man[4] takes his stand upon the solid substance and not upon the mere husk,

Upon the fruit and not upon the flower.

Truly, "he rejects that and takes this."

大中华文库

第三十九章

【原文】

　　昔之得"一"者：

　　天得"一"以清；地得"一"以宁；

　　神得"一"以灵；谷得"一"以盈；

　　万物得"一"以生；侯王得"一"以为天下正。

　　其致之也，谓天无以清，将恐裂；

　　地无以宁，将恐废；神无以灵，将恐歇；

　　谷无以盈，将恐竭；万物无以生，将恐灭；

　　侯王无以正，将恐蹶。

　　故贵以贱为本，高以下为基。

　　是以侯王自称孤、寡、不穀。

　　此非以贱为本邪？非乎？故至誉无誉。

　　是故不欲琭琭如玉，珞珞如石。

【今译】

　　从来凡是得到"一"的——天得到"一"而清明；地得到"一"而宁静；神得到"一"而灵妙；河谷得到"一"而充盈；万物得到"一"而生长；侯王得到"一"而使得天下安定。

　　推而言之，天不能保持清明，难免要崩裂；地不能保持宁静，难免要震溃；神不能保持灵妙，难免要消失；河谷不能保持充盈，难免要涸竭；万物不能保持生长，难免要绝灭；侯王不能保持清静，难免要颠覆。

　　所以贵以贱为根本，高以下为基础。

　　因此侯王自称为"孤"、"寡"、"不穀"。这不是把低贱当作根本吗？岂不是吗？所以最高的称誉是无须夸誉的。因此不愿像玉的华丽，宁可如石块般的坚实。

Chapter 39

As for the things that from of old have understood the Whole —

The sky through such understanding remains limpid,

Earth remains steady,

The spirits keep their holiness,

The abyss is replenished,

The ten thousand creatures bear their kind,

Barons and princes direct their people.

It is the Whole that causes it.

Were it not so limpid, the sky would soon get torn,

Were it not for steadiness, the earth would soon tip over,

Were it not for their holiness, the spirits would soon wither away,

Were it not for this replenishment, the abyss would soon go dry,

Were it not that the ten thousand creatures can bear their kind,

They would soon become extinct.

Were the barons and princes no longer directors of their people and for that reason honoured and exalted, they would soon be overthrown.

Truly, "the humble is the stem upon which the mighty grows, the low is the foundation upon which the high is laid."

That is why barons and princes refer to themselves as "The Orphan," "The Needy," "The Ill-provided."[1]

Is this not indeed a case of might rooting itself upon humility?

True indeed are the sayings:

"Enumerate the parts of a carriage, and you still have not explained what a carriage is, "[2] and "They[3] did not want themselves to tinkle like jade-bells, while others resounded like stonechimes." [4]

81

第四十章

大中华文库

【原文】

　　反者"道"之动；

　　弱者"道"之用。

　　天下万物生于"有"，

　　"有"生于"无"。

【今译】

　　"道"的运动是循环的；"道"的作用是柔弱的。

　　天下万物生于"有"，"有"生于"无"。

Chapter 40

In Tao the only motion is returning;

The only useful quality, weakness.

For though all creatures under heaven are the products of Being,

Being itself is the product of Not-being.[1]

83

第四十一章

【原文】

上士闻道，勤而行之；中士闻道，若存若亡；下士闻道，大笑之。

不笑不足以为道。

故建言有之：

明道若昧；进道若退；

夷道若纇；上德若谷；

广德若不足；建德若偷；

质真若渝；大白若辱；

大方无隅；大器晚成；

大音希声；大象无形；

"道"隐无名。

夫唯"道"，善贷且成。

【今译】

上等士人听了"道"，努力去实行；中等士人听了"道"，将信将疑；下等士人听了"道"，哈哈大笑。——不被嘲笑，那就不足以成为"道"！所以古时候立言的人说过这样的话：

光明的道好似暗昧；前进的道好似后退；

平坦的道好似崎岖；崇高的德好似低下的川谷；

广大的德好似不足；刚健的德好似懈怠的样子；

质朴而纯真好似浑浊的样子；最洁白的好像含垢的样子；

最方正的反而没有棱角；贵重的器物总是最后完成；

最大的乐声反而听来无音响；

最大的形象反而看不见形迹；

"道"幽隐而没有名称。

只有"道"，善于辅助万物。

Chapter 41

When the man of highest capacities hears Tao

He does his best to put it into practice.

When the man of middling capacity hears Tao

He is in two minds about it.

When the man of low capacity hears Tao

He laughs loudly at it.

If he did not laugh, it would not be worth the name of Tao.

Therefore the proverb has it:

"The way[1] out into the light often looks dark,

The way that goes ahead often looks as if it went back."

The way that is least hilly often looks as if it went up and down,

The "power" that is really loftiest looks like an abyss,

What is sheerest white looks blurred.[2]

The "power" that is most sufficing looks inadequate,

The "power" that stands firmest looks flimsy.

What is in its natural, pure state looks faded;

The largest square has no corners,

The greatest vessel takes the longest to finish,

Great music has the faintest notes,

The Great Form is without shape.

For Tao is hidden and nameless.

Yet Tao alone supports all things and brings them to fulfilment.

第四十二章

【原文】

　　"道"生一，
　　一生二，
　　二生三，
　　三生万物。
　　万物负阴而抱阳，
　　冲气以为和。
　　（人之所恶，
　　唯孤、寡、不穀，
　　而王公以为称。
　　故物或损之而益，
　　或益之而损。
　　人之所教，
　　我亦教之。
　　强梁者不得其死，
　　吾将以为教父。）

【今译】

　　"道"是独一无偶的，独一无偶的"道"禀负阴阳两气，阴阳两气相交而成一种适匀的状态，万物都在这种状态中产生的。万物背阴而向阳，阴阳两气互相激荡而成新的和谐体。

　　（人所厌恶的就是"孤"、"寡"、"不穀"，但是王公却用来称呼自己。所以一切事物，减损它有时反而得到增加，增加它有时反而受到减损。别人教导我的，我也用来教导人。强暴的人不得好死，我把它当作施教的根本。）

Chapter 42

Tao gave birth to the One; the One gave birth successively to two things, three things, up to ten thousand.[1] These ten thousand creatures cannot turn their backs to the shade without having the sun on their bellies,[2] and it is on this blending of the breaths that their harmony depends.

(To be orphaned, needy, ill-provided[3] is what men most hate; yet princes and dukes style themselves so. Truly, "things are often increased by seeking to diminish them and diminished by seeking to increase them." The maxims that others use in their teaching I too will use in mine. Show me a man of violence that came to a good end, and I will take him for my teacher.)[4]

第四十三章

【原文】

天下之至柔，

驰骋天下之至坚。

无有入无间，

吾是以知无为之有益。

不言之教，

无为之益，

天下希及之。

大中华文库

88

【今译】

天下最柔软的东西，能战胜天下最坚硬的东西。无形的力量能穿透没有间隙的东西，我因此知道"无为"的益处。

"不言"的教导，"无为"的益处，天下很少能够做得到的。

Chapter 43

What is of all things most yielding

Can overwhelm that which is of all things most hard.

Being substanceless it can enter even where there is no space;

That is how I know the value of action that is actionless.

But that there can be teaching without words,

Value in action that is actionless,

Few indeed can understand.

第四十四章

大中华文库

【原文】

名与身孰亲?
身与货孰多?
得与亡孰病?
甚爱必大费;
多藏必厚亡。
故知足不辱,
知止不殆,
可以长久。

【今译】

　　声名和生命比起来哪一样亲切?生命和财富比起来哪一样贵重?得到名利和丧失生命哪一样更有害?

　　过分的爱名就必定要付出重大的耗费;丰富的藏货就必定会招致惨重的损失。

　　所以知道满足就不会受到屈辱,知道适可而止就不会带来危险,这样才可以保持长久。

Chapter 44

Fame or one's own self, which matters to one most?

One's own self or things bought, which should count most?

In the getting or the losing, Which is worse?[1]

Hence he who grudges expense pays dearest in the end;[2]

He who has hoarded most will suffer the heaviest loss.

Be content with what you have and are, and no one can despoil you;

Who stops in time nothing can harm.

He is forever safe and secure.

91

第四十五章

【原文】

大成若缺，其用不敝。

大盈若冲，其用不穷。

大直若屈，大巧若拙，

大辩若讷。

静胜躁，寒胜热。

清净为天下正。

【今译】

最完满的东西好像有欠缺一样，但是它的作用是不会衰竭的。

最充盈的东西好像是空虚一样，但是它的作用是不会穷尽的。

最正直的东西好像是弯曲一样，

最灵巧的东西好像是笨拙一样，

最卓越的辩才好像是口讷一样。

清净克服扰动，寒冷克服暑热。清净无为可以做人民的模范。

Chapter 45

What is most perfect seems to have something missing;

Yet its use is unimpaired.

What is most full seems empty;

Yet its use will never fail.

What is most straight seems crooked;

The greatest skill seems like clumsiness,

The greatest eloquence like stuttering.

Movement overcomes cold;

But staying still overcomes heat.[1]

So he by his limpid calm

Puts right everything under heaven.[2]

93

第四十六章

【原文】

天下有道，
却走马以粪。
天下无道，
戎马生于郊。
（罪莫大于可欲。）
祸莫大于不知足；
咎莫大于欲得。
故知足之足，
常足矣。

【今译】

国家政治清平，把战马还给农夫用来耕种。国家政治混乱，连怀胎的母马也要用来作战。

（罪过没有比诱人贪求更大的了。）

祸患没有过于不知足的了；罪过没有过于贪得无厌的了。所以知道满足为止的人，永远是满足的。

Chapter 46

When there is Tao in the empire

The galloping steeds are turned back to fertilize the ground by their droppings.

When there is not Tao in the empire

War horses will be reared even on the sacred mounds below the city walls.

(No lure is greater than to possess what others want,)[1]

No disaster greater than not to be content with what one has,

No presage of evil greater than that men should be wanting to get more.

Truly: "He who has once known the contentment that comes simply through being content, will never again be otherwise than contented."

95

第四十七章

【原文】

不出户，知天下；

不窥牖，见天道。

其出弥远，

其知弥少。

是以圣人不行而知，

不见而明，不为而成。

【今译】

不出门外，能够推知天下的事理；不望窗外，能够了解自然变化的规律。他越向外奔逐，而他所知的理也越少。

所以有道的人不必经历就能知情，不必眼见，就能心明，不必作为却能成功。

Chapter 47

Without leaving his door

He knows everything under heaven.

Without looking out of his window

He knows all the ways of heaven.

For the further one travels[1]

The less one knows.

Therefore the Sage arrives without going,

Sees all without looking,

Does nothing, yet achieves everything.

第四十八章

【原文】

为学日益，

为道日损。

损之又损，

以至于无为。

取天下常以无事，

及其有事，

不足以取天下。

【今译】

求学一天比一天增加(知见)，求道一天比一天减少(情欲)。减少又减少，一直到"无为"的境地。

如能不妄为那就没有什么事情做不成的了。治理国家要常清静不扰攘，一旦生事时，就不配治理国家了。

Chapter 48

Learning consists in adding to one's stock day by day;

The practice of Tao consists in "substracting day by day,

Substracting and yet again substracting

Till one has reached inactivity.[1]

But by this very inactivity

Everything can be activated."

Those who of old won the adherence of all who live under heaven

All did so by not interfering.

Had they interfered,

They would never have won this adherence.

第四十九章

【原文】

> 圣人常无心，
> 以百姓心为心。
> 善者，吾善之；
> 不善者，吾亦善之；
> 德善。
> 信者，吾信之；
> 不信者，吾亦信之；
> 德信。
> 圣人在天下，歙歙焉，
> 为天下浑其心，
> 百姓皆注其耳目，
> 圣人皆孩之。

【今译】

> 有道的人没有私心，以百姓的心为心。
> 善良的人，我善待他；不善良的人，我也善待他；这样可使人人向善。
> 守信的人，我信任他；不守信的人，我也信任他；这样可使人人守信。
> 有道的人在位，收敛自己的意欲，使人心思化归于浑厚淳朴，百姓都专注他们自己的耳目，有道的人使他们都回复到婴孩般(真纯)的状态。

Chapter 49

The Sage has no heart[1] of his own;

He uses the heart of the people as his heart.

Of the good man I approve,

But of the bad I also approve,

And thus he gets goodness.

The truthful man I believe, but the liar I also believe,

And thus he gets truthfulness.

The Sage, in his dealings with the world, seems like one dazed with fright;

For the world's sake he dulls his wits.

The Hundred Families[2] all the time strain their eyes and ears,

The Sage all the time sees and hears no more than an infant sees and hears.[3]

101

第五十章

【原文】

出生入死。

生之徒，十有三；

死之徒，十有三；

人之生，动之于死地，

亦十有三。

夫何故？

以其生生之厚。

盖闻善摄生者，

陆行不遇兕虎，

入军不被甲兵；

兕无所投其角，

虎无所用其爪，

兵无所用其刃。

夫何故，以其无死地。

【今译】

人出世为"生"，入地为"死"。属于长寿的，占十分之三；属于短命的，占十分之三；本来可以活得长久，却自己走向死路的，也占了十分之三。为什么呢？因为他们迫切要求生存，反而达不到目的。听说善于养护生命的人，在陆地上行走不会遇到犀牛和老虎，在战争中不会受到杀伤；犀牛用不上它的角，老虎用不上它的爪，兵器用不上它的刃。为什么呢？因为他没有进入死亡的范围。

Chapter 50

He who aims at life achieves death.[1]

If the "companions of life" are thirteen,[2] so likewise are the "companions of death" thirteen.

How is it that the "death-spots" in man's life and activity are also thirteen?[3]

It is because men feed life too grossly.

It is said that he who has a true hold on life, when he walks on land does not meet tigers or wild buffaloes;[4] in battle he is not touched by weapons of war.

Indeed, a buffalo that attacked him would find nothing for its horns to butt, a tiger would find nothing for its claws to tear, a weapon would find no place for its point to enter in.

And why?

Because such men have no "death-spots" in them.

LIBRARY OF CHINESE CLASSICS

103

第五十一章

【原文】

"道"生之，"德"畜之，物形之，势成之。

是以万物莫不尊"道"而贵"德"。

"道"之尊，"德"之贵，夫莫之命而常自然。

故"道"生之，"德"畜之；长之育之；亭之毒之；养之覆之。生而不有，为而不恃，长而不宰。是为"玄德"。

【今译】

"道"生成万物，"德"畜养万物，万物呈现各种形态，环境使万物成长。

所以万物没有不尊崇"道"而珍贵"德"的。

"道"之所以受尊崇，"德"之所以被珍贵，就在于对它不加干涉，而顺任自然。

所以"道"生成万物，"德"畜养万物；使万物成长发育；使万物成熟结果；对万物抚养调护。生长万物却不据为己有，兴作万物却不自恃己能，使万物滋长而不加以主宰。这就是最深的"德"。

Chapter 51

Tao gave them birth;

The "power" of Tao reared them,

Shaped them according to their kinds,

Perfected them, giving to each its strength.[1]

Therefore of the ten thousand things there is not one that does not worship Tao and do homage to its "power." No mandate even went forth that accorded to Tao the right to be worshipped, nor to its "power" the right to be worshipped, nor to its "power" the right to receive homage.

It was always and of itself so.

Therefore as Tao bore them and the "power" of Tao reared them, made them grow, fostered them, harboured them, brewed[2] for them, so you must

"Rear them, but not lay claim to them,

Control them,[3] but never lean upon them,

Be chief among them, but not manage them.

This is called the mysterious power."[4]

105

第五十二章

【原文】

天下有始，以为天下母。既得其母，以知其子；既知其子，复守其母，没身不殆。

塞其兑，闭其门，终身不勤。开其兑，济其事，终身不救。

见小曰明，守柔曰强。用其光，复归其明，无遗身殃；是为袭常。

【今译】

天地万物都有本始，作为天地万物的根源。如果得知根源，就能认识万物；如果认识万物，又持守着万物的根源，终身都没有危险。

塞住嗜欲的孔窍，闭起嗜欲的门径，终身都没有劳扰的事。打开嗜欲的孔窍，增添纷杂的事件，终身都不可救治。

能察见细微的叫做"明"，能持守柔弱的叫做"强"。运用智慧的光，返照内在的"明"，不给自己带来灾殃；这叫做永续不绝的常"道"。

Chapter 52

That which was the beginning of all things under heaven

We may speak of as the "mother" of all things.

He who apprehends the mother[1]

Thereby knows the sons.[2]

And he who has known the sons,

Will hold all the tighter to the mother,

And to the end of his days suffer no harm:

"Block the passages, shut the doors,

And till the end your strength shall not fail.

Open up the passages, increase your doings,

And till your last day no help shall come to you."

As good sight means seeing what is very small

So strength means holding on to what is weak.[3]

He who having used the outer-light can return to the inner-light

Is thereby preserved from all harm.

This is called resorting to the always-so.

第五十三章

【原文】

　　使我介然有知，行于大道。

　　唯施是畏。

　　大道甚夷，

　　而人好径。

　　朝甚除，

　　田甚芜，

　　仓甚虚；

　　服文采，

　　带利剑，厌饮食，财货有余；

　　是谓盗夸。非道也哉！

108

【今译】

　　假使我稍微有些认识，在大道上行走，担心惟恐走入了邪路。

　　大道很平坦，但是人君却喜欢走险僻的小路。宫殿十分整洁，农田非常荒芜，仓库十分空虚；还穿着锦绣的衣服，佩带锋利的宝剑，饱足精美的饮食，搜括足余的财货；这就叫做强盗头子。多么的无道啊！

Chapter 53

He who has the least scrap of sense, once he has got started on the great highway has nothing to fear so long as he avoids turning. For great highways are safe and easy.

But men love by-paths.[1]

So long as the Court is in order[2]

They are content to let their fields run to weed

And their granaries stand empty.

They wear patterns and embroideries,

Carry sharp swords, glut themselves with drink and food, have more possessions than they can use.

These are the riotous ways of brigandage; they are not the Highway.

第五十四章

【原文】

善建者不拔，善抱者不脱，子孙以祭祀不辍。

修之于身，其德乃真；

修之于家，其德乃余；

修之于乡，其德乃长；

修之于邦，其德乃丰；

修之于天下，其德乃普。

故以身观身，以家观家，

以乡观乡，以邦观邦，

以天下观天下。

吾何以知天下然哉？

以此。

【今译】

善于建树的不会中途动摇，善于保持的不会脱落，如果子孙能遵行这个道理，则世世代代的祭祀不会断绝。

拿这个道理贯彻到个人，他的"德"是会真实的；贯彻到一家，他的"德"可以有余；贯彻到一乡，他的"德"能受尊崇；贯彻到一国，他的"德"就会昌盛；贯彻到天下，他的"德"就会普遍。

所以要从（我）个人观照（其他的）个人，从（我）家观照（其他人的）家，从（我的）乡观照（其他的）乡，从（我的）国观照（其他的）国，从（我的）天下观照（其他的）天下。我怎么知道天下的情况呢？就是用这种道理。

Chapter 54

What Tao[1] plants cannot be plucked,

What Tao clasps, cannot slip.

By its virtue alone can one generation after another carry on the ancestral sacrifice.[2]

Apply it to yourself and by its power you will be freed from dross.

Apply it to your household and your household shall thereby have abundance.

Apply it to the village, and the village will be made secure.

Apply it to the kingdom, and the kingdom shall thereby be made to flourish.

Apply it to an empire, and the empire shall thereby be extended.

Therefore just as through[3] oneself one may contemplate Oneself,

So through the household one may contemplate the Household[4],

And through the village, one may contemplate the Village,

And through the kingdom, one may contemplate the Kingdom,

And through the empire, one may contemplate the Empire.

How do I know that the empire is so?

By this.

大中华文库

第五十五章

【原文】

含"德"之厚，比于赤子。

毒虫不螫，猛兽不据，

攫鸟不搏。

骨弱筋柔而握固。

未知牝牡之合而朘作，

精之至也。

终日号而不嗄，

和之至也。

知和曰"常"，

知常曰"明"。

益生曰祥。

心使气曰强。

物壮则老，

谓之不道，

不道早已。

【今译】

含"德"深厚的人，比得上初生的婴儿。毒虫不刺伤他，猛兽不伤害他，凶鸟不搏击他。他筋骨柔弱，拳头却握得很牢固。他还不知道男女交合但小生殖器却常常勃起，这是精气充足的缘故。他整天号哭，但是他的喉咙却不会沙哑，这是元气醇和的缘故。

认识醇和的道理叫做"常"，认识"常"叫做"明"。贪生纵欲就会灾殃，欲念主使和气就是逞强。过分的强壮就趋于衰老，这叫做不合于"道"，不合于"道"很快就会死亡。

Chapter 55

The impunity of things[1] fraught with the "power"

May be likened to that of an infant.

Poisonous insects do not sting it,

Nor fierce beasts seize it,

Nor clawing birds maul it.

Its bones are soft, its sinews weak; but its grip is strong.

Not yet to have known the union of male and female, but to be completely formed,

Means that the vital force is at its height;

To be able to scream all day without getting hoarse

Means that the harmony is at its perfection.

To understand such harmony is to understand the always-so.

To understand the always-so is to be illumined[2]

But to fill life to the brim is to invite omens.

If the heart makes calls upon the life-breath, rigidity follows.

Whatever has a time of vigour also has a time of decay.

Such things are against Tao,

And whatever is against Tao is soon destroyed.

第五十六章

【原文】

知者不言，

言者不知。

（塞其兑，

闭其门；）

挫其锐，

解其纷，

和其光，

同其尘，

是为"玄同"。

故不可得而亲，

不可得而疏；

不可得而利，

不可得而害；

不可得而贵，

不可得而贱。

故为天下贵。

【今译】

智者是不会夸夸其谈的，夸夸其谈的人就不是智者。

（塞住嗜欲的孔窍，闭起嗜欲的门径；）不露锋芒，消解纷扰，含敛光耀，混同尘世，这就是玄妙齐同的境界。这样就不分亲，不分疏；不分利，不分害；不分贵，不分贱。所以为天下人所尊贵。

Chapter 56

Those who know do not speak;

Those who speak do not know.

(Block the passages,

Shut the doors,)[1]

Let all sharpness be blunted,

All tangles untied,

All glare tempered.

All dust smoothed.

This is called the mysterious levelling.[2]

He who has achieved it cannot either be drawn into friendship or

repelled,

Cannot be benefited, cannot be harmed,

Cannot either be raised or humbled,

And for that very reason is highest of all creatures under heaven.

115

第五十七章

【原文】

　　以正治国，以奇用兵，以无事取天下。

　　吾何以知其然哉？

　　以此：

　　天下多忌讳，而民弥贫；

　　人多利器，国家滋昏；

　　人多伎巧，奇物滋起；

　　法令滋彰，盗贼多有。

　　故圣人云："我无为，

　　而民自化；

　　我好静，而民自正；

　　我无事，而民自富；

　　我无欲，而民自朴。"

【今译】

　　以正大光明的方法治国，以诡奇的方法用兵，以不搅扰人民来治理天下。我怎么知道是这样的？从下面这些事端上可以看出：

　　天下的禁忌越多，人民越陷于贫困；人间的利器越多，国家越陷于昏乱；人们的技巧越多，邪恶的事情就连连发生；法令越森严，盗贼反而不断地增加。

　　所以有道的人说："我无为，人民就自然顺化；我好静，人民就自然上轨道；我不搅扰，人民就自然富足；我没有贪欲，人民就自然朴实。"

Chapter 57

"Kingdoms can only be governed if rules are kept;

Battles can only be won if rules are broken."[1]

But the adherence of all under heaven can only be won by letting-alone.

How do I know that it is so?

By this.[2]

The more prohibition there are, the more ritual avoidances,

The poorer the people will be.

The more "sharp weapons" there are,

The more benighted will the whole land grow.

The more cunning craftsmen there are,

The more pernicious contrivances will be invented.

The more laws are promulgated,

The more thieves and bandits there will be.

Therefore a sage has said:

So long as I "do nothing" the people will of themselves be transformed.

So long as I love quietude, the people will of themselves go straight.

So long as I act only by inactivity the people will of themselves become prosperous.

So long as I have no wants the people will of themselves return to the "state of the Uncarved Block."

117

第五十八章

【原文】

其政闷闷，其民淳淳；

其政察察，其民缺缺。

祸兮，福之所倚；

福兮，祸之所伏。

孰知其极？其无正也。

正复为奇，善复为妖。

人之迷，其日固久。

是以圣人方而不割，

廉而不刿，

直而不肆，

光而不耀。

【今译】

政治宽厚，人民就纯朴；政治严苛，人民就狡黠。

灾祸啊，幸福倚傍在它里面；幸福啊，灾祸藏伏在它之中。谁知道它们的究竟？它们并没有一个定准！正忽而转变为邪，善忽而转变为恶。人们的迷惑，已经有长久的时日了。

因而有道的人方正而不割人，锐利而不伤人，直率而不放肆，光亮而不耀目。

Chapter 58

When the ruler looks depressed the people will be happy and satisfied;[1]

When the ruler looks lively and self-assured the people will be carping and discontented.

"It is upon bad fortune that good fortune leans, upon good fortune that bad fortune rests."

But though few know it, there is a bourn where there is neither right nor wrong;

In a realm where every straight is doubled by a crooked, and every good by an ill, surely mankind has gone long enough astray?

Therefore the Sage

Squares without cutting,

Shapes the corners without lopping,

Straightens without stretching,

Gives forth light without shining.[2]

第五十九章

【原文】

> 治人事天，莫若啬。
> 夫唯啬，是谓早服；
> 早服谓之重积德；
> 重积德则无不克；
> 无不克则莫知其极；
> 莫知其极，
> 可以有国；
> 有国之母，可以长久；
> 是谓深根固柢，
> 长生久视之道。

120

【今译】

治理国家，养护身心，没有比爱惜精力更重要。

爱惜精力，乃是早作准备；早作准备就是不断地积"德"；不断地积德就没有什么不能胜任的；没有什么不能胜任就无法估计他的力量；无法估计他的力量，就可以担负保护国家的责任；掌握治理国家的道理，就可以长久维持；这就是根深柢固、"长生久视"的道理。

Chapter 59

You cannot rule men nor serve heaven[1] unless you have laid up a store;[2]

This "laying up a store" means quickly absorbing,

And "quickly absorbing" means doubling one's garnered "power".

Double your garnered power and it acquires a strength that nothing can overcome.

If there is nothing it cannot overcome, it knows no bounds,

And only what knows no bounds is huge enough to keep a whole kingdom in its grasp.

But only he who having the kingdom goes to the Mother can keep it long.

This[3] is called the art of making the roots strike deep by fencing the trunk, of making life long by fixed staring.[4]

121

第六十章

【原文】

　　治大国，若烹小鲜。

　　以道莅天下，其鬼不神；

　　非其鬼不神，其神不伤人；

　　非其神不伤人，圣人亦不伤人。

　　夫两不相伤，故德交归焉。

【今译】

　　治理大国，好像煎小鱼。

　　用"道"治理天下，鬼怪起不了作用；不但鬼怪起不了作用，神祇也不侵越人；不但神祇不侵越人，圣人也不侵越人。鬼神和有道者都不侵越人，所以彼此能相安无事。

Chapter 60

Ruling a large kingdom is indeed like cooking small fish.

They who by Tao ruled all that is under heaven did not let an evil spirit within them display its powers. Nay, it was not only that the evil spirit did not display its powers; neither was the Sage's good[1] spirit used to the hurt of other men. Nor was it only that his good spirit was not used to harm other men, the Sage himself was thus saved from harm.[2] And so, each being saved from harm, their "powers" could converge towards a common end.

123

第六十一章

【原文】

　　大邦者下流，
　　天下之牝，
　　天下之交也。
　　牝常以静胜牡，
　　以静为下。
　　故大邦以下小邦，
　　则取小邦；
　　小邦以下大邦，
　　则取大邦。
　　故或下以取，
　　或下而取。
　　大邦不过欲兼畜人，
　　小邦不过欲入事人。
　　夫两者各得所欲，
　　大者宜为下。

【今译】

　　大国要像居于江河的下流，处在天下雌柔的位置，是天下交汇的地方。雌柔常以静定而胜过雄强，因为静定而又能处下的缘故。

　　所以大国对小国谦下，就可以汇聚小国；小国对大国谦下，就可以见容（于大国）。所以有时（大国）谦下以汇聚（小国），有时（小国）谦下而见容于大国。大国不过要聚养小国，小国不过要求见容于大国。这样大国小国都可以达到愿望。大国尤其应该谦下。

Chapter 61

A large kingdom must be like the low ground towards which all streams flow down. It must be a point towards which all things under heaven converge. Its part must be that of the female in its dealings with all things under heaven.[1]

The female by quiescence conquers the male; by quiescence gets underneath. If a large kingdom can in the same way succeed in getting underneath a small kingdom then it will win the adherence of the small kingdom; and it is because small kingdoms are by nature in this way underneath large kingdoms that they win the adherence[2] of large kingdoms. The one must get underneath in order to do it; the other is underneath and therefore does it. (What large countries really need is more inhabitants; and what small countries need is some place where their surplus inhabitants can go and get employment.)[3] Thus each gets what it needs. That is why I say the large kingdom must "get underneath."

125

第六十二章

【原文】

道者万物之奥。
善人之保，
不善人之所保。
美言可以市尊，
美行可以加人。
人之不善，
何弃之有？
故立天子，
置三公，
虽有拱璧以先驷马，
不如坐进此道。古之所以贵此道者何？
不曰求以得，
有罪以免邪？
故为天下贵。

【今译】

　　"道"是万物的归宿。善人珍贵它，不善的人也处处保住它。

　　(得"道"的善人)嘉美的言词可以博人尊敬，良好的行为可以见重于人。不善的人，怎能把"道"舍弃呢？所以立位天子，设置三公，虽然敬奉拱璧在先、驷马在后的礼仪，还不如用"道"来作为献礼。

　　古时候重视"道"的原因是什么呢？岂不是说有求的就可以得到，有罪的就可以免除吗？所以被天下人所贵重。

Chapter 62

Tao in the Universe is like the southwest corner in the house.[1]

It is the treasure of the good man,

The support of the bad.

There is a traffic in speakers of fine words;

Persons of grave demeanour are accepted as gifts;

Even the bad let slip no opportunity to acquire them.

Therefore on the day of an Emperor's enthronement

Or at the installation of the three officers[2] of State

Rather than send a team of four horses, preceded by a disc of jade,

Better were it, as can be done without moving from one's seat, to send this Tao.

For what did the ancients say of this Tao, how did they prize it? Did they not say of those that have it "Pursuing, they shall catch; pursued, they shall escape"? They thought it, indeed, most precious of all things under heaven.

第六十三章

【原文】

为无为，事无事，味无味。

大小多少，（报怨以德。）图难于其易，为大于其细；天下难事，必作于易，天下大事，必作于细。是以圣人终不为大，故能成其大。

夫轻诺必寡信，多易必多难。是以圣人犹难之，故终无难矣。

【今译】

以无为的态度去作为，以不搅扰的方式去作事，以恬淡无味当作味。

大生于小，多起于少，（用德来报答怨恨。）处理困难要从容易的入手，实现远大要从细微的入手；天下的难事，必定从容易的做起；天下的大事，必定从细微的做起。所以有道的人始终不自以为大，因此能成就大的事情。

轻易允诺的信用一定不足；把事情看得太容易时遭遇的困难一定更多。所以有道的人遇见事情总是把它看得艰难，因此终究没有困难了。

Chapter 63

It acts without action, does without doing, finds flavour in what is flavourless,

Can make the small great and the few many,[1]

(Requites injuries with good deeds,)[2]

Deals with the hard while it is still easy,

With the great while it is still small.

In the governance of empire everything difficult must be dealt with while it is still easy,

Everything great must be dealt with while it is still small.

Therefore the Sage never has to deal with the great; and so achieves greatness.

But again "Light assent inspires little confidence

And 'many easies' means many a hard."

Therefore the Sage knows too how to make the easy difficult, and by doing so avoid all difficulties!

第六十四章

大中华文库

【原文】

其安易持，其未兆易谋。其脆易泮，其微易散。

为之于未有，治之于未乱。

合抱之木，生于毫末；

九层之台，起于累土；

千里之行，始于足下。

（为者败之，执者失之。

是以圣人无为故无败；无执故无失。）

民之从事，常于几成而败之。

慎终如始，则无败事。

（是以圣人欲不欲，不贵难得之货；

学不学，复众人之所过，以辅万物之自然而不敢为。）

【今译】

局面安稳时容易持守，事变没有迹象时容易图谋。事物脆弱时容易消解，事物微细时容易散失。要在事情没有发生以前就处理妥当，要在祸乱没有产生以前就早作准备。

合抱的大木，是从细小的萌芽生长起来的；九层的高台，是从一堆泥土建筑起来的；千里的远行，是从脚下举步开始走出来的。

（出于强力的，一定会失败；加以把持的，一定会失去。因此圣人不妄为，所以不会失败；不把持，所以不会失去。）

人们做事情，常常在快要成功的时候就失败了。事情要完成的时候也能像开始的时候一样的谨慎，那就不会败事了。

（所以有道的人意欲别人所不意欲的，不珍贵难得的货品；有道的人学别人所不学的，挽救众人的过错，以辅助万物的自然发展而不加以干预。）

Chapter 64

What stays still is easy to hold;

Before there has been an omen it is easy to lay plans.

What is tender is easily torn,

What is minute is easy to scatter.

Deal with things in their state of not-yet-being,

Put them in order before they have got into confusion.

For "the tree big as a man's embrace began as a tiny sprout,

The tower nine storeys high began with a heap of earth,

The journey of a thousand leagues began with what was under the feet."

(He who acts, harms; he who grabs, lets slip.

Therefore the Sage does not act, and so does not harm;

Does not grab, and so does not let slip.)[1]

Whereas the people of the world, at their tasks,

Constantly spoil things when within an ace of completing them.

Heed the end no less than the beginning,

And your work will not be spoiled.

(Therefore the Sage wants only things that are unwanted,

Sets no store by products difficult to get,

And so teaches things untaught,

Turning all men back to the things they have left behind,

That the ten thousand creatures may be restored to their Self-so.

This he does; but dare not act.)[2]

131

第六十五章

132

【原文】

古之善为道者，
非以明民，
将以愚之。
民之难治，
以其智多。
故以智治国，
国之贼；
不以智治国，
国之福。
如此两者亦稽式。
常知稽式，
是谓"玄德"，
"玄德"深矣，远矣，
与物反矣，
然后乃至大顺。

【今译】

从前善于行道的人，不是教人民精巧，而是使人民淳朴。

人民所以难治，乃是因为他们使用太多的智巧心机。所以用智巧去治理国家，是国家的灾祸；不用智巧去治理国家，是国家的幸福。

了解这两种治国方式的差别就是一个法则。经常认识这个法则，就是"玄德"，"玄德"好深好远啊！和事物复归到真朴，然后顺应于自然。

Chapter 65

In the days of old those who practised Tao with success did not, by means of it, enlighten the people, but on the contrary sought to make them ignorant.

The more knowledge people have, the harder they are to rule.

Those who seek to rule by giving knowledge

Are like bandits preying on the land.

Those who rule without giving knowledge

Bring a stock of good fortune to the land.

To have understood the difference between these two things is to have a test and standard[1]

To be always able to apply this test and standard

Is called the mysterious "power,"

The mysterious "power," so deep-penetrating,

So far-reaching,

That can follow things back —

All the way back to the Great Concordance.

第六十六章

【原文】

江海之所以能为百谷王者，
以其善下之，
故能为百谷王。
是以圣人欲上民，
必以言下之；
欲先民，
必以身后之。
是以圣人处上而民不重，
处前而民不害。
是以天下乐推而不厌。
以其不争，
故天下莫能与之争。

【今译】

江海所以能成为许多河流汇往的地方，因为它善于处在低下的地位，所以能成为许多河流所汇往。

所以"圣人"要成为人民的领导，必须心口一致地对他们谦下；要作为人民的表率，必须把自己的利益放在人民的后面。所以"圣人"居于上位而人民不感到负累；居于前面而人民不感到受害。所以天下人民乐于推戴而不厌弃。因为他不跟人争，所以天下没有人能和他争。

Chapter 66

How did the great rivers and seas get their kingship over the hundred lesser streams?

Through the merit of being lower than they; that was how they got their kingship.

Therefore the Sage

In order to be above the people

Must speak as though he were lower than the people.

In order to guide them

He must put himself behind them.

Only thus can the Sage be on top and the people not be crushed by his weight.

Only thus can he guide, and the people not be led into harm.

Indeed in this way everything under heaven will be glad to be pushed by him[1] and will not find his guidance irksome. This he does by not striving; and because he does not strive, none can contend with him.

135

第六十七章

【原文】

（天下皆谓我："'道'大，似不肖。"夫唯大，故似不肖。若肖，久矣其细也夫！）

我有三宝，持而保之。一曰慈，二曰俭，三曰不敢为天下先。

慈故能勇；俭故能广；不敢为天下先，故能成器长。

今舍慈且勇；舍俭且广；舍后且先；死矣！

夫慈，以战则胜，以守则固。天将救之，以慈卫之。

【今译】

（天下人都对我说："'道'广大，却不像任何具体的东西。"正因为它的广大，所以不像任何具体的东西。如果它像的话，早就渺小了。）

我有三种宝贝，持守而保全着。第一种叫做慈爱，第二种叫做俭啬，第三种叫做不敢居于天下人的前面。

慈爱所以能勇武；俭啬所以能宽广；不敢居于天下人的前面，所以能成为万物的首长。

现在舍弃慈爱而求取勇武；舍弃俭啬而求取宽广；舍弃退让而求取争先，是走向死路！

慈爱，用来征战就能胜利，用来守卫就能巩固。天要救助谁，就用慈爱来卫护他。

Chapter 67

(Every one under heaven says that our Way is greatly like folly. But it is just because it is great, that it seems like folly. As for things that do not seem like folly — well, there can be no question about their smallness!)[1]

Here are my three treasures.[2] Guard and keep them! The first is pity; the second, frugality; the third, refusal to be "foremost of all things under heaven."

For only he that pities is truly able to be brave;

Only he that is frugal is truly able to be profuse.

Only he that refuses to be foremost of all things

Is truly able to become chief of all Ministers.[3]

At present your bravery is not based on pity, nor your profusion on frugality, nor your vanguard on your rear; and this is death. But pity cannot fight without conquering or guard without saving. Heaven arms with pity those whom it would not see destroyed.[4]

137

大中华文库

138

第六十八章

【原文】

善为士者，不武；
善战者，不怒；
善胜敌者，不与；
善用人者，为之下。
是谓不争之德，
是谓用人之力，
是谓配天古之极。

【今译】

善作将帅的，不逞勇武；善于作战的，不轻易激怒；善于战胜敌人的，不用对斗；善于用人的，对人谦下。这叫做不争的"德"，这叫做运用别人的能力，这叫做符合于自然的道理。

Chapter 68

The best charioteers do not rush ahead;[1]

The best fighters do not make displays of wrath.

The greatest conqueror wins without joining issue;

The best user of men acts as though he were their inferior.

This is called the power that comes of not contending,

Is called the capacity to use men,

The secret of being mated to heaven, to what was of old.

139

第六十九章

【原文】

　　用兵有言：

　　"吾不敢为主，而为客；

　　不敢进寸而退尺。"

　　是谓行无行；攘无臂；

　　扔无敌；执无兵。

　　祸莫大于轻敌，

　　轻敌几丧吾宝。

　　故抗兵相若，

　　哀者胜矣。

【今译】

　　用兵的曾说："我不敢进犯，而采取守势；不敢前进一寸，而要后退一尺。"这就是说：虽然有阵势，却像没有阵势可摆；虽然要奋臂，却像没有臂膀可举；虽然面临敌人，却像没有敌人可赴；虽然有兵器，却像没有兵器可持。

　　祸患没有再比轻敌更大的了，轻敌几乎丧失了我的"三宝"。

　　所以，两军对阵兵力相当的时候，悲哀的一方可获得胜利。

Chapter 69

The strategists have the sayings: "When you doubt[1] your ability to meet the enemy's attack, take the offensive yourself, " and "If you doubt[2] your ability to advance an inch, then retreat a foot."

This latter is what we call to march without moving,

To roll the sleeve, but present no bare arm,[3]

The hand that seems to hold, yet had no weapon in it,

A host that can confront, yet presents no battle-front.[4]

Now the greatest of all calamities is to attack and find no enemy.

I can have no enemy only at the price of losing my treasure.[5]

Therefore when armies are raised and issues joined it is he who does not delight in war that wins.

第七十章

【原文】

　　吾言甚易知，甚易行。

　　天下莫能知，莫能行。

　　言有宗，事有君。

　　夫唯无知，是以不我知。

　　知我者希，则我者贵。

　　是以圣人被褐而怀玉。

【今译】

　　我的话很容易了解，很容易实行。大家却不能明白，不能实行。

　　言论有主旨，行事有根据。正由于不了解这个道理，所以不了解我。

　　了解我的人越少，取法我的人就很难得了。因而有道的圣人穿着粗衣而内怀美玉。

Chapter 70

My words are very easy to understand and very easy to put into practice. Yet no one under heaven understands them; no one puts them into practice. But my words have an ancestry, my deeds have a lord;[1] and it is precisely because men do not understand this that they are unable to understand me.

Few then understand me; but it is upon this very fact that my value depends.[2] It is indeed in this sense that "the Sage wears hair-cloth[3] on top, but carries jade underneath his dress."

第七十一章

【原文】

　　知不知，尚矣；

　　不知知，病也。

　　圣人不病，

　　以其病病。

　　夫唯病病，

　　是以不病。

【今译】

　　知道自己有所不知道，最好；不知道却自以为知道，这是缺点。有道的人没有缺点，因为他把缺点当作缺点。正因为他把缺点当作缺点，所以他是没有缺点的。

Chapter 71

To know when one does not know is best.

To think one knows when one does not know is a dire disease.

"Only he who recognizes this disease as a disease[1]

Can cure himself of the disease."[2]

The sage's way of curing disease

Also consists in making people recognize their diseases as diseases

and thus ceasing to be diseased.

145

大中华文库

第七十二章

【原文】

　　民不畏威，则大威至。
　　无狎其所居，无厌其所生。
　　夫唯不厌，是以不厌。
　　是以圣人自知不自见；
　　自爱不自贵。故去彼取此。

【今译】

　　人民不畏惧统治者的威压，那么更大的祸乱就要发生了。
　　不要逼使人民不得安居，不要压榨人民的生活。只有不压榨人民，人民才不厌恶(统治者)。
　　因此，有道的人但求自知而不自我表扬；但求自爱而不显高贵。所以舍去后者而取前者。

Chapter 72

Never mind if the people are not intimidated by your authority. A Mightier Authority[1] will deal with them in the end.[2] Do not narrow their dwellings or harass their lives;[3] and for the very reason that you do not harass them, they will cease to turn from you. Therefore the Sage knows himself but does not show himself. Knows his own value, but does not put himself on high. Truly, "he rejects that but takes this."

147

第七十三章

【原文】

　　勇于敢则杀，勇于不敢则活。

　　此两者，或利或害。

　　天之所恶，孰知其故？

　　（是以圣人犹难之。）

　　天之道，不争而善胜，

　　不言而善应，

　　不召而自来，

　　繟然而善谋。

　　天网恢恢，疏而不失。

【今译】

　　勇于坚强就会死，勇于柔弱就可活。这两种勇的结果，有的得利，有的遭害。天道所厌恶的，谁知道是什么缘故？

　　（圣人对此也难以了解。）

　　自然的规律，是不争让而善于得胜，不说话而善于回应，不召唤而自动来到，宽缓而善于筹策。自然的范围广大无边，稀疏而不会有一点漏失。

Chapter 73

He whose braveness lies in daring, slays.

He whose braveness lies in not daring, gives life.

Of these two, either may be profitable or unprofitable.[1]

But "Heaven hates what it hates;

None can know the reason why."

(Wherefore the Sage, too, disallows it.)[2]

For it is the way of Heaven not to strive but none the less to conquer,

Not to speak, but none the less to get an answer,

Not to beckon; yet things come to it of themselves.

Heaven is like one who says little, yet none the less has laid his plans.

Heaven's net is wide;

Coarse are the meshes, yet nothing slips through.

149

第七十四章

【原文】

民不畏死，奈何以死惧之？
若使民常畏死，而为奇者，
吾得执而杀之，孰敢？
常有司杀者杀。
夫代司杀者杀，
是谓代大匠斫。
夫代大匠斫者，
希有不伤其手矣。

【今译】

人民不畏惧死亡，为什么用死亡来恐吓他？如果使人民真的畏惧死亡，对于为邪作恶的人，我们就可以把他抓来杀掉，谁还敢为非作歹？

经常有专管杀人的去执行杀的任务。那代替专管杀人的去执行杀的任务，这就如同代替木匠去砍木头一样。那代替木匠砍木头的，很少有不砍伤自己手的。

Chapter 74

The people are not frightened of death. What then is the use of trying to intimate them with the death-penalty?

And even supposing people were generally frightened of death and did not regard it as an everyday thing,[1] which of us would dare to seize them and slay them?

There is the Lord of Slaughter[2] always ready for this task, and to do it in his stead is like thrusting oneself into the master-carpenter's place and doing his chipping for him. Now "he who tries to do the master-carpenter's chipping for him is lucky if he does not cut his hand."[3]

151

第七十五章

大中华文库

【原文】

民之饥，以其上食税之多，是以饥。

民之难治，以其上之有为，是以难治。

民之轻死，以其上求生之厚，是以轻死。

夫唯无以生为者，是贤于贵生。

【今译】

人民之所以饥饿，就是由于统治者吃税太多，因此陷于饥饿。

人民之所以难治，就是由于统治者强作妄为，因此难以管治。

人民之所以轻死，就是由于统治者过分追求享受，因此轻于犯死。

只有不求一己私利的人，要胜过自我奉养奢厚的人。

Chapter 75

The people starve because those above them eat too much tax-grain. That is the only reason why they starve.

The people are difficult to keep in order because those above them interfere. That is the only reason why they are so difficult to keep in order.

The people attach no importance to death, because those above them are too grossly absorbed in the pursuit of life. That is why they attach no importance to death.

And indeed, in that their hearts are so little set on life they are superior to those who set store by life.

第七十六章

【原文】

人之生也柔弱，其死也坚强。

草木之生也柔脆，其死也枯槁。

故坚强者死之徒，柔弱者生之徒。

是以兵强则灭，木强则折。

强大处下，柔弱处上。

【今译】

人活着的时候身体是柔软的，死了的时候就变成僵硬了。

草木生长的时候形质是柔脆的，死的时候就变成干枯了。

所以坚强的东西属于死亡的一类；柔弱的东西属于生存的一类。

因此用兵逞强就会遭受灭亡，树木强大就会遭受砍伐。

凡是强大的，反而居于下位，凡是柔弱的，反而占在上面。

Chapter 76

When he is born, man is soft and weak; in death he becomes stiff and hard. The ten thousand creatures[1] and all plants and trees while they are alive are supple and soft, but when they are dead they become brittle and dry. Truly, what is stiff and hard is a "companion of death" ; what is soft and weak is a "companion of life." Therefore "the weapon that is too hard will be broken,[2] the tree that has the hardest wood will be cut down." Truly, the hard and mighty are cast down; the soft and weak set on high.

大中华文库

第七十七章

【原文】

　　天之道，其犹张弓与？

　　高者抑之，下者举之；

　　有余者损之，不足者补之。

　　天之道，损有余而补不足。

　　人之道，则不然，损不足以奉有余。

　　孰能有余以奉天下，唯有道者。

　　（是以圣人为而不恃，

　　功成而不处，其不欲见贤。）

【今译】

　　自然的规律，岂不就像拉开弓弦一样吗？弦位高了，就把它压低，弦位低了就把它升高；有余的加以减少，不足的加以补充。自然的规律，减少有余，用来补充不足。社会的法规，就不是这样，却要剥夺不足，而用来供奉有余的人。

　　谁能够把有余的拿来供给天下不足的？这只有有道的人才能做到。

　　（因此有道的人作成万物而不自恃己能；有所成就而不以功自居，他不想表现自己的聪明才智。）

156

Chapter 77

Heaven's way is like the bending of a bow. When a bow is bent the top comes down and the bottom-end comes up.[1]

So too does Heaven take away from those who have too much, and give to those that have not enough. But if it is Heaven's way to take from those who have too much and give to those who have not enough, this is far from being man's way. He takes away from those that have not enough in order to make offering to those who already have too much. One there is and one only, so rich that he can afford to make offerings to all under heaven. Who is this? It is the possessor of Tao. (If, then, the Sage "though he controls does not lean, and when he has achieved his aim does not linger," it is because he does not wish to reveal himself as better than others.)[2]

大中华文库

第七十八章

【原文】

天下莫柔弱于水，

而攻坚强者莫之能胜，

以其无以易之。

弱之胜强，柔之胜刚，

天下莫不知，莫能行。

是以圣人云：

"受国之垢，是谓社稷主；

受国不祥，是谓天下王。"

正言若反。

【今译】

世间没有比水更柔弱的，冲激坚强的东西没有能胜过它，因为没有什么能代替它。

弱胜过强，柔胜过刚，天下没有人不知道，但是没有人能够实行。

因此有道的人说："承担全国的屈辱，才配称国家的君主；承担全国的祸难，才配做天下的君王。"正面的话好像反话一样。

Chapter 78

Nothing under heaven is softer or more yielding than water; but when it attacks things hard and resistant there is not one of them that can prevail. For they can find no way of altering it.[1]

That the yielding conquers the resistant and the soft conquers the hard is a fact known by all men, yet utilized by none.

Yet it is in reference to this that the Sage said "Only he who has accepted the dirt of the country can be lord of its soil-shrines; only he who takes upon himself the evils of the country can become a king among those what dwell under heaven." Straight words seem crooked.[2]

159

第七十九章

【原文】

(报怨以德，)

和大怨，必有余怨；

安可以为善？

是以圣人执左契，

而不责于人。

有德司契，无德司彻。

天道无亲，常与善人。

【今译】

(用德来报答怨恨，)调解深重的怨恨，必然还有余留的怨恨；这怎能算是妥善的办法呢？

因此"圣人"保存借据的存根，但是并不向人索取偿还。有"德"的人只是管理借据(而不索债)；无"德"的人则实行税收(强行索取)。

自然的规律是没有偏爱的，经常帮助善良的人。

Chapter 79

(To requite injuries with good deeds.)[1]

To allay the main discontent, but only in a manner that will certainly produce further discontents can hardly be called successful.

Therefore the Sage behaves like the holder of the left-hand tally, who stays where he is and does not go round making claims on people.[2]

For he who has the "power" of Tao is the Grand Almoner; he who has not the "power" is the Grand Perquisitor. "It is Heaven's way, without distinction of persons, to keep the good perpetually supplied."

161

第八十章

【原文】

小国寡民。
使有什伯之器而不用；
使民重死而不远徙。
虽有舟舆，无所乘之；
虽有甲兵，无所陈之。
使民复结绳而用之。
甘其食，美其服，
安其居，乐其俗。
邻国相望，鸡犬之声相闻，
民至老死，不相往来。

【今译】

国土狭小人民稀少。即使有各种器具，却并不使用；使人民重视死亡而不向远方迁移。虽然有船只车辆，却没有必要去乘坐；虽然有铠甲武器，却没有机会去陈列。使人民回复到结绳记事的状况。

人民有甜美的饮食，美观的衣服，安适的居所，欢乐的习俗。邻国之间可以互相看得见，鸡鸣狗吠的声音可以相互听得着，人民从生到死，互相不往来。

Chapter 80

Given a small country with few inhabitants, he could bring it about that though there should be among the people contrivances requiring ten times, a hundred times less labour,[1] they would not use them. He could bring it about that the people would be ready to lay down their lives and lay them down again[2] in defence of their homes, rather than emigrate. There might still be boats and carriages, but no one would go in them; there might still be weapons of war but no one would drill with them. He could bring it about that "the people should have no use for any form of writing save knotted ropes, should be contented with their food, pleased with their clothing, satisfied with their homes, should take pleasure in their rustic tasks. The next place might be so near at hand that one could hear the cocks crowing in it, the dogs barking; but the people would grow old and die without ever having been there."[3]

第八十一章

【原文】

信言不美，美言不信。

善者不辩，辩者不善。

知者不博，博者不知。

圣人不积，既以为人己愈有，

既以与人己愈多。

天之道，利而不害；

人之道，为而不争。

【今译】

真实的言词不华美，华美的言词不真实。

行为善良的人不巧辩，巧辩的人不善良。

真正了解的人不广博，广博的人不能深入了解。

“圣人”不私自积藏，他尽量帮助别人，自己反而更充足；他尽量给与别人，自己反而更丰富。

自然的规律，利物而无害，人间的法则，施为而不争夺。

Chapter 81

True words are not fine-sounding;

Fine-sounding words are not true.

The good man does not prove by argument;

And he who proves by argument is not good.

True wisdom is different from much learning;

Much learning means little wisdom.

The Sage has no need to hoard;

When his own last scrap has been used up on behalf of others,

Lo, he has more than before!

When his own last scrap has been used up in giving to others,

Lo, his stock is even greater than before!

For heaven's way is to sharpen without cutting,[1]

And the Sage's way[2] is to act without striving.

165

附录　　Appendixes

马王堆汉墓帛书《德道经》甲本*

德　　经

　　【·上德不德，是以有德。下德不失德，是以无】德。上德无【为而】无以为也。上仁为之【而无】以为也。上义为之而有以为也。上礼【为之而莫之应也，则】攘臂而乃(扔)之。故失道。失道矣而后德，失德而后仁，失仁而后义，【失】义而【后礼。夫礼者，忠信之薄也】，而乱之首也。【前识者，】道之华也，而愚之首也。是以大丈夫居其厚而不居其泊(薄)，居其实不居其华。故去皮(彼)取此。昔之得一者，天得一以清，地得【一】以宁，神得一以需(灵)，浴【谷】得一以盈，侯【王得一】而以为正。其致之也，胃(谓)天毋已清将恐【裂】，胃(谓)地毋【已宁】将恐【发】，胃(谓)神毋已需(灵)将恐歇，胃(谓)浴(谷)毋已盈将恐渴(竭)，胃(谓)侯王毋已贵【以高将恐蹶】。故必贵而以贱为本，必高矣而以下为基。夫是以侯王自胃(谓)【曰】孤寡不䅽(穀)，此其贱【之本】与？非【也】？故致数与(誉)无与(誉)。是故不欲【禄禄】若玉，硌硌【若石】。【上士闻道，勤能行之。中士闻道，若存若亡。下士闻道，大笑之。弗笑，不足以为道。是以建言有之曰：明道如费，进道如退，夷道如类。上德如谷，大白如辱，广德如不足。建德如偷，质真如渝，大方无隅。大器晚成，大音希声，大象无形，道褒无名。夫唯】道，善【始且善成。反也者】，道之动也。弱也者，道之用也。天【下之物生于有，有生于无。道生一，一生二，二生三，三生万物。万物负阴而抱阳】，中气以为和。天下之所恶，唯孤寡不䅽(穀)，而王公以自名也。勿(物)或敗(损)之【而益，益】之而敗(损)。故人【之所】教，

---

　　*马王堆汉墓帛书《德道经》甲本、乙本系由湖南省博物馆提供，原载《马王堆汉墓帛书(壹)》，文物出版社1980年3月出版。"【】"中的文字系缺损部分，由甲、乙两本互补，若两本俱残或彼此字数有出入时，则选用传世诸本补入。"·"系帛书甲本的分段符号。

夕(亦)议而教人。故强良(梁)者不得死，我【将】以为学父。天下之至柔，【驰】骋于天下之致(至)坚。无有入于无间。五(吾)是以知无为【之有】益也。不【言之】教，无为之益，【天】下希能及之矣。名与身孰亲?身与货孰多?得与亡孰病?甚【爱必大费，多藏必厚】亡。故知足不辱，知止不殆，可以长久。大成若缺，其用不幣(敝)。大盈若盅(冲)，其用不窘(窘)。大直如诎(屈)，大巧如拙，大赢如炳。趮(躁)胜寒，靓(静)胜炅(热)。请(清)靓(静)，可以为天下正。·天下有道，【却】走马以粪。天下无道，戎马生于郊。·罪莫大于可欲，旤(祸)莫大于不知足，咎莫憯于欲得。【故知足之足】，恒足矣。不出于户，以知天下。不规(窥)于牖，以知天道。其出也弥远，其【知弥少。是以圣人不行而知，不见而名】，弗为而【成】。为【学者日益，闻道者日损。损】之又损，以至于无为，无为而无不为。【将欲】取天下也，恒【无事，及其有事也，又不足以取天下矣。圣人恒无心】，以百【姓】之心为【心】。善者善之，不善者亦善【之，得善也。信者信之，不信者亦信之，得】信也。【圣人】之在天下，惵惵焉，为天下浑心，百姓皆属耳目焉，圣人皆咳之。【出】生，【入死。生之徒十】有【三，死之】徒十有三，而民生生，动皆之死地之十有三。夫何故也?以其生生也。盖【闻善】执生者，陵行不【避】矢(兕)虎，入军不被甲兵。矢(兕)无所楇(揣)其角，虎无所昔(措)其蚤(爪)，兵无所容【其刃，夫】何故也?以其无死地焉。·道生之而德畜之，物刑(形)之而器成之。是以万物尊道而贵【德。道】之尊，德之贵也，夫莫之爵(爵)而恒自然也。·道生之，畜之，长之，遂之，亭之，□之，【养之，覆之。生而】弗有也，为而弗寺(恃)也，长而弗宰也，此之谓玄德。·天下有始，以为天下母。愍(既)得其母，以知其【子】，复守其母，没身不殆。·塞其闷(兑)，闭其门，终身不堇(勤)。启其闷，济其事，终身【不棘。见】小曰【明】，守柔曰强。用其光，复归其明。毋道〈遗〉身央(殃)，是胃(谓)袭常。·使我挈(挈)有知也，【行于】大道，唯【施是畏。大道】甚夷，民甚好解。朝甚除，田甚芜，仓甚虚;服文采，带利【剑。厌】食，货【财有余。是谓盗夸。盗夸，非道也】。善建【者不】拔，【善抱者不脱】，子孙以祭祀【不绝。修之身，其德乃真。修之家，其德有】余。修之【乡，其德乃长，修之邦，其德乃丰。修

167

之天下，其德乃溥】。以身【观】身，以家观家，以乡观乡，以邦观邦，以天【下】观【天下。吾何以知天下之然哉？以此。含德】之厚【者】，比于赤子。逢（蜂）虿（螫）蝎（虺）地（蛇）弗螫，攫鸟猛兽弗搏。骨弱筋柔而握固。未知牝牡【之会】而朘【怒】，精【之】至也。终日〈日〉号而不嗄，和之至也。和曰常，知和〈常〉曰明，益生曰祥，心使气曰强。【物壮】即老，胃（谓）之不道，不【道早已。知者】弗言，言者弗知。塞其闷，闭其【门，和】其光，同其坒（尘），坐（挫）其阅（锐），解其纷，是胃（谓）玄同。故不可得而亲，亦不可得而疏；不可得而利，亦不可得而害；不可【得】而贵，亦不可得而浅（贱）。故为天下贵。·以正之（治）邦，以畸（奇）用兵，以无事取天下。吾何【以知其然】也戈（哉）？夫天下【多忌】讳，而民弥贫。民多利器，而邦家兹（滋）昏。人多知（智），而何（奇）物兹（滋）【起。法物滋章，而】盗贼【多有。是以圣人之言曰】：我无为也，而民自化。我好静，而民自正。我无事，民【自富。我欲不欲，而民自朴。其政闵闵，其邦屯屯】。其正（政）察察，其邦夬（缺）夬（缺）。祸（祸）；福之所倚；福，祸（祸）之所伏；【孰知其极？其无正也？正复为奇，善复为妖。人之迷也，其日固久矣。是以方而不割，廉而不刺，直而不绁，光而不曜。治人事天，莫若啬。夫惟啬，是以早服。早服是谓重积德。重积德则无不克，无不克则莫知其极。莫知其极】，可以有国。有国之母，可以长久。是胃（谓）深槿（根）固氐（柢），长【生久视之】道也。【治大国若烹小鲜。以道莅】天下，其鬼不神。非其鬼不神也，其神不伤人也。非其申（神）不伤人也，圣人亦弗伤【也。夫两】不相【伤，故】德交归焉。大邦者，下流也，天下之牝。天下之郊（交）也，牝恒以靓（静）胜牡。为其靓（静）【也，故】宜为下。大邦【以】下小【邦】，则取小邦。小邦以下大邦，则取于大邦。故或下以取，或下而取。【故】大邦者不过欲兼畜人，小邦者不过欲入事人。夫皆得其欲，【故大邦者宜】为下。【道】者，万物之注也，善人之琛（宝）也，不善人之所琛（保）也。美言可以市，尊行可以贺（加）人。人之不善也，何弃【之】有？故立天子，置三卿，虽有共之璧以先驷马，不善〈若〉坐而进此。古之所以贵此者何也？不胃（谓）【求以】得，有罪以免舆（与）？故为天下贵。·为无为，事无事，味无未（味）。大小多少，报怨以德。图难乎【其易也，为大

乎其细也】。天下之难作于易，天下之大作于细。是以圣人冬（终）不
为大，故能【成其大。夫轻诺者必寡信。多易】必多难，是【以圣】
人献（犹）难之，故终于无难。·其安也，易持也。【其未兆也】，易
谋【也。其脆也，易判也。其微也，易散也。为之于其未有，治之于
其未乱也。合抱之木，生于】毫末。九成之台，作于赢（蔂）土。百仁
（仞）之高，台（始）于足【下。为之者败之，执之者失之。圣人无为】
也，【故】无败【也】；无执也，故无失也。民之从事也，恒于其成
事而败之。故慎终若始，则【无败事矣。是以圣人】欲不欲，而不贵
难得之肠（赇）；学不学，而复众人之所过；能辅万物之自【然，而】
弗敢为。故曰：为道者非以明民也，将以愚之也。民之难【治】也，
以其知（智）也。故以知（智）知邦，邦之贼也；以不知（智）知邦，【邦
之】德也；恒知此两者，亦稽式也。恒知稽式，此胃（谓）玄德。玄德
深矣，远矣，与物【反】矣，乃【至大顺。江】海之所以能为百浴
（谷）王者，以其善下之，是以能为百浴（谷）王。是以圣人之欲上民
也，必以其言下之；其欲先【民也】，必以其身后之。故居前而民弗
害也，居上而民弗重也。天下乐隼（推）而弗猒（厌）也，非以其无静
（争）与？故【天下莫能与】静（争）。·小邦寡（寡）民，使十百人之器
毋用。使民重死而远送〈徙〉。有车周（舟）无所乘之，有甲兵无所陈
【之。使民复结绳而】用之。甘其食，美其服，乐其俗，安其居。粼
（邻）邦相壁〈望〉，鸡狗之声相闻，民【至老死不相往来。信言不
美，美言】不【信。知】者不博，【博】者不知。善【者不多，多】
者不善。·圣人无积，【既】以为【人，己愈有；既以予人，己愈
多。故天之道，利而不害；人之道，为而弗争。天下皆谓我大，不
肖】。夫唯【大】，故不宵（肖）。若宵（肖），细久矣。我恒有三葆
（宝），之，一曰兹（慈），二曰检（俭），【三曰不敢为天下先。夫慈，
故能勇；【俭】，故能广；不敢为天下先，故能为成事长。今舍其兹
（慈），且勇；舍其后，且先；则必死矣。夫兹（慈），【以战】则胜，
以守则固。天将建之，女（如）以兹（慈）垣之。善为士者不武，善战者
不怒，善胜敌者弗【与】，善用人者为之下。【是】胃（谓）不静（争）
之德，是胃（谓）用人，是胃（谓）天，古之极也。·用兵有言曰：吾不
敢为主而为客，吾不进寸而芮（退）尺。是胃（谓）行无行，襄（攘）无
臂，执无兵，乃（扔）无敌矣。旤（祸）莫于〈大〉于无適（敌），无適

(敌)斤(近)亡吾葆(宝)矣。故称兵相若,则哀者胜矣。吾言甚易知也,甚易行也;而人莫之能知也,而莫之能行也。言有君,事有宗。夫唯无知也,是以不【我知。知者希,则】我贵矣。是以圣人被褐而裹(怀)玉。知不知,尚矣;不知不知,病矣。是以圣人之不病,以其【病病。是以不病。民之不】畏畏(威),则大【威将至】矣。·母(毋)闸(狎)其所居,毋猒(厌)其所生。夫唯弗猒(厌),是【以不厌。是以圣人自知而不自见也,自爱】而不自贵也。故去被(彼)取此。·勇于敢者【则杀,勇】于不敢者则栝(活)。【知此两者,或利或害。天之所恶,孰知其故?天之道,不战而善胜】,不言而善应,不召而自来,弹(坦)而善谋。【天网恢恢,疏而不失。若民恒且不畏死】,奈何以杀思(惧)之也?若民恒是〈畏〉死,则而为者吾将得而杀之,夫孰敢矣!若民【恒且】必畏死,则恒有司杀者。夫伐〈代〉司杀者杀,是伐〈代〉大匠斫也。夫伐〈代〉大匠斫者,则【希】不伤其手矣。·人之饥也,以其取食逡之多也,是以饥。百姓之不治也,以其上有以为【也】,是以不治。·民之巠(轻)死,以其求生之厚也,是以巠(轻)死。夫唯无以生为者,是贤贵生。·人之生也柔弱,其死也菫仞贤(坚)强。万物草木之生也柔脆,其死也棒(枯)薨(槁)。故曰:"坚强者,死之徒也;柔弱微细,生之徒也。"兵强则不胜,木强则恒。强大居下,柔弱微细居上。天下【之道,犹张弓】者也,高者印(抑)之,下者举之,有余者敃(损)之,不足者补之。故天之道,敃(损)有【余而补不足;人之道则】不然,敃(损)【不足以】奉有余。孰能有余而有以取奉于天者乎?【唯有道者乎?是以圣人为而弗有,成功而弗居也。若此其不欲】见贤也。天下莫柔【弱于水,而攻】坚强者莫之能【先】也,以其无【以】易【之也。故柔胜刚,弱】胜强,天【下莫不知,而莫能】行也。故圣人之言云,曰:受邦之訽(诟),是胃(谓)社稷之主;受邦之不祥,是胃(谓)天下之王。【正言】若反。和大怨,必有余怨,焉可以为善?是以圣右介(契)而不以责于人。故有德司介(契),【无】德司彻(彻)。夫天道无亲,恒与善人。

道　经

·道，可道也，非恒道也。名，可名也，非恒名也。无名，万物之始也。有名，万物之母也。【故】恒无欲也，以观其眇（妙）；恒有欲也，以观其所噭。两者同出，异名同胃（谓）。玄之有（又）玄，众眇（妙）之【门】。天下皆知美为美，恶已；皆知善，訾（斯）不善矣。有、无之相生也，难、易之相成也，长、短之相刑（形）也，高、下之相盈也，意〈音〉、声之相和也，先、后之相隋（随），恒也。是以声（圣）人居无为之事，行【不言之教。万物作而弗始】也，为而弗志（恃）也，成功而弗居也。夫唯居，是以弗去。不上贤，【使民不争。不贵难得之货，使】民不为【盗】。不【见可欲，使】民不乱。是以声（圣）人之【治也，虚其心，实其腹；弱其志】，强其骨。恒使民无知无欲也。使【夫知不敢弗为而已，则无不治矣。道冲，而用之又弗】盈也。潚（渊）呵始（似）万物之宗。锉（挫）其，解其纷，和其光，同【其尘。湛呵似】或存。吾不知【谁】子也，象帝之先。天地不仁，以万物为刍狗。声（圣）人不仁，以百省（姓）【为刍】狗。天地【之】间，【其】犹橐籥舆（与）？虚而不淈（屈），踵（动）而俞（愈）出。多闻数穷，不若守于中。浴（谷）神【不】死，是胃（谓）玄牝。玄牝之门，是胃（谓）【天】地之根。绵绵呵若存，用之不堇（勤）。天长，地久。天地之所以能【长】且久者，以其不自生也，故能长生。是以声（圣）人芮（退）其身而身先，外其身而身存。不以其无【私】舆（与）？故能成其私。上善治（似）水。水善利万物而有静（争），居众之所恶，故几于道矣。居善地，心善潚（渊），予善信，正（政）善治，事善能，踵（动）善时。夫唯不静（争），故无尤。揁（持）而盈之，不【若其已。揣而】□之□之，□可长葆之。金玉盈室，莫之守也。贵富而驕（骄），自遗咎也。功述（遂）身芮（退），天【之道也。戴营魄拘一，能毋离乎？榑气至柔】，能婴儿乎？脩（涤）除玄蓝（鉴），能毋疵乎？爱【民活国，能毋以知乎？天门启阖，能为雌乎？明白四达，能毋以为乎】？生之，畜之。生而弗【有，长而弗宰，是谓玄】德。卅【辐同一毂，当】其无【有，车】之用【也】。然（埏）埴为器，当其无有，埴器【之用也。凿户牖】，当其无有，【室】之用也。故有之以为利，无之以为用。五色使人目明〈盲〉，驰骋田腊（猎）使人【心发狂】，难得之赁（货）使人之行方（妨），五味使人之口唡（爽），五音使人之耳聋。是以声（圣）人之治也，为腹不【为目】。故去罢（彼）耳〈取〉此。龙（宠）辱若惊，贵大梡（患）若身。苛（何）胃（谓）龙（宠）辱若惊？龙（宠）之为下，得之若惊，失【之】若惊，是胃（谓）龙（宠）辱若惊。何胃（谓）贵大梡（患）若身？吾所以有大梡（患）者，为吾有身也。及吾无身，有何梡（患）？故贵为身于为天下，若可以迵（托）天下矣；爱以身为天下，女何〈可〉以寄天下。视之而弗见，名之曰微。听之而弗闻，名之曰希。揹之而弗得，名之曰夷。三者不可至（致）计（诘），故囷【而为一】。一者，其上不攸，其下不忽。寻寻呵不可名也，复归于无物。是胃（谓）无状之状，无物之【象。是谓忽恍。随而不见其后，迎】而不见其首。执今之道，以御今之有，以知古始，是胃（谓）【道纪。古之善为道者，微妙玄达】，深不可志（识）。夫唯不可志（识），故强为之容，曰：与呵其若冬【涉水，犹呵其若】畏四【邻，严】呵其若客，涣呵其若淩（凌）泽（释），□呵其若楃（朴），湷【呵其若浊，湉呵其】若浴（谷）。浊而情（静）之，余（徐）清。女〈安〉以重（动）之，余（徐）生。葆此道不欲盈。夫唯不欲【盈，是】以能【敝而不】成。至虚极也，守情（静）表也。万物旁（并）作，吾以观其复也。天物云云，各复归于其【根，曰静。】情（静），是胃（谓）复命。复命，常也。知常，明也。不知常，茫（妄），茫（妄）作凶。知常容，容乃公，公乃王，王乃天，天乃道，【道乃久】，沕（没）身不怠。大上下知有之，其次亲誉之，其次畏之，其下母（侮）之。信不足，案有不信。【犹呵】其贵言也。成功遂事，而百省（姓）胃（谓）我自然。故大道广，案有仁义。知（智）快（慧）出，案有大伪。六亲不和，案有畜（孝）兹（慈）。邦家閭（昏）乱，案有贞臣。绝声（圣）弃知（智），民利百负（倍）。绝仁弃义，民复畜（孝）兹（慈）。绝巧弃利，盗贼无有。此三言也，以为文未足，故令之有所属。见素抱【朴，少私寡欲。绝学无忧】。唯与诃，其相去几何？美与恶，其相去何若？人之【所畏】，亦不【可以不畏。恍呵其未央哉】·众人配（熙）配（熙），若乡（飨）于大牢，而春登台。我泊焉未佻（兆），若【婴儿未咳】。累呵如【无所归。众人】皆有余，我独遗。我禺（愚）人之心也，蠢蠢呵。鬻（俗）【人昭昭，我独若】闻（昏）呵。鬻（俗）人蔡（察）蔡（察），我独闷（闷）闷（闷）呵。忽呵其若【海】，望（恍）呵其若无所止。【众人皆有以，我独顽】以悝（俚）。吾欲独异于人，而贵食母。孔德之容，唯道是从。道之物，唯望（恍）唯忽。【忽呵恍】呵，中有象呵。望（恍）呵忽呵，中有物呵。潀（幽）呵鸣（冥）呵，中有请（精）吔〈呵〉。其请（精）甚真，其中【有信】。自今及古，其名不去，以顺众仪（父）。吾何以知众仪（父）之然？以此。炊者不立，自视（示）不章，【自】见者不明，自伐者无功，自矜者不长。其在道，曰："粽（余）食、赘行。"物或恶之，故有欲者【弗】居。曲则金（全），枉则定（正），洼则盈，敝则新。少则得，多则惑。是以声（圣）人执一，以为天下牧。不【自】视（示）故明，不自见故章，不自伐故有功，弗矜故能长。夫唯不争，故莫能与之争。古【之所谓曲全者几】语才（哉），诚金（全）归之。希言自然。飘风不冬（终）朝，暴雨不冬（终）日。孰为此？天地，【而弗能久，又况】于【人乎】？故从事而道者同于道，德（得）者同于德（得），者〈失〉者同于失。同德（得）【者】，道亦德（得）之。同于失者，道亦失之。有物昆成，先天地生。绣（寂）呵缪（寥）呵，独立【而不改】，可以为天地母。吾未知其名，字之曰道。吾强为之名曰大。【大】曰筮（逝），筮（逝）曰【远，远曰反。道大】，天大，地大，王亦大。国中有四大，而王居一焉。人法地，【地】法【天】，天法【道，道】法【自然。重】为巠（轻）根，清（静）为趮（躁）君。是以君子众（终）日行，不离其甾（辎）重，唯（虽）有环官，燕处【则昭】若。若何万乘之王而以身巠（轻）于天下？巠（轻）则失本，趮（躁）则失君。善行者无犙（辙）迹，【善】言者无瑕適（谪），善数者不以梼（筹）筭（策）。善闭者无闲（关）籥（闩）而不可启也，善结者【无纆】约而不可解也。是以声（圣）人恒善怵（救）人，而无弃人，物无弃财，是胃（谓）愧明。故善【人，善人】之师；不善人，善人之齎（资）也。不贵其师，不爱其齎（资），唯（虽）知（智）乎大眯（迷）。是胃（谓）眇（妙）要。知其雄，守其雌，为天下溪。为天下溪，恒德不鸡〈离〉。恒〈德〉不鸡〈离〉，复归婴儿。知其白，守其辱，为天下。为天下浴（谷），恒德乃【足】。德乃【足，复归于朴】。知其，守其黑，为天下式。为天下式，恒德不贰（忒）。德不贰

(忒），复归于无极。楃（朴）散【则为器，圣】人用则为官长。夫大制无割。将欲取天下而为之，吾见其弗【得已。夫天下，神】器也，非可为者也。为者败之，执者失之。物或行或随，或炅（热）或【吹，或强或挫】，或坏（培）或撱（堕）。是以声（圣）人去甚，去大，去楮（奢）。以道佐人主，不以兵强【于】天下。【其事好还，师之】所居，楚朸（棘）生之。善者果而已矣，毋以取强焉。果而毋驕（骄），果而勿矜，果而【勿伐】，果而毋得已居，是胃（谓）【果】而不强。物壮而老，是胃（谓）之不道，不道蚤（早）已。夫兵者，不祥之器【也】。物或恶之，故有欲者弗居。君子居则贵左，用兵则贵右。故兵者非君子之器也。【兵者】不祥之器也，不得已而用之，铦袭为上，勿美也。若美之，是乐杀人也。夫乐杀人，不可以得志于天下矣。是以吉事上左，丧事上右；是以便（偏）将军居左，上将军居右，言以丧礼居之也。杀人众，以悲依（哀）立（莅）之；战胜，以丧礼处之。道恒无名，楃（朴）唯（虽）【小而天下弗敢臣。侯】王若能守之，万物将自宾。天地相谷〈合〉，以俞甘洛（露）。民莫之【令，而自】均焉。始制有【名。名亦既】有，夫【亦将知止，知止】所以不【殆】。俾（譬）道之在天【下也，犹小】浴（谷）之与江海也。知人者，知（智）也。自知【者，明也。胜人】者，有力也。自胜者，【强也。】知足者，富也。强行者，有志也。不失其所者，久也。死不忘者，寿也。道泛【呵其可左右也，成功】遂事而弗名有也。万物归焉而弗为主，则恒无欲也，可名于小。万物归焉【而弗】为主，可名于大。是【以】声（圣）人之能成大也，以其不为大也，故能成大。执大象，【天下】往。往而不害，安平大。乐与饵，过格（客）止。故道之出言也，曰："谈（淡）呵其无味也。【视之】，不足见也。听之，不足闻也。用之，不可既也。"将欲拾（翕）之，必古（固）张之。将欲弱之，【必固】强之。将欲去之，必古（固）与之。将欲夺之，必古（固）予之。是胃（谓）微明。友弱胜强，鱼不脱于潚（渊），邦利器不可以视（示）人。道恒无名，侯王若守之，万物将自愿（化）。愿（化）而欲【作，吾将镇之以无】名之楃（朴）。【镇之以】无名之楃（朴），夫将不辱。不辱以情（静），天地将自正。

马王堆汉墓帛书《德道经》乙本

德　　经

　　上德不德，是以有德。下德不失德，是以无德。上德无为而无以为也。上仁为之而无以为也。上德〈义〉为之而有以为也。上礼为之而莫之应也，则攘臂而乃（扔）之。故失道而后德，失德而句（后）仁，失仁而句（后）义，失义而句（后）礼。夫礼者，忠信之泊（薄）也，而乱之首也。前识者，道之华也，而愚之首也。是以大丈夫居【其厚不】居其泊（薄），居其实而不居其华。故去罢（彼）而取此。昔得一者，天得一以清，地得一以宁，神得一以需（灵），浴（谷）得一盈，侯王得一以为天下正。其至也，胃（谓）天毋已清将恐莲（裂），地毋已宁将恐发，神毋【已灵将】恐歇，谷毋已【盈】将渴（竭），侯王毋已贵以高将恐欮（蹶）。故必贵以贱为本，必高矣而以下为基。夫是以侯王自胃（谓）孤寡不橐（穀），此其贱之本与？非也？故至数舆无舆。是故不欲禄禄若玉，硌硌若石。上【士闻】道，堇（勤）能行之。中士闻道，若存若亡。下士闻道，大笑之。弗笑【不足】以为道。是以建言有之曰：明道如费，进道如退，夷道如类。上德如浴（谷），大白如辱，广德如不足。建德如【偷】，质【真如渝】，大方无禺（隅），大器免（晚）成，大音希声，天〈大〉象无刑（形），道褒无名。夫唯道，善始且善成。反也者，道之动也。【弱也】者，道之用也。天下之物生于有，有【生】于无。道生一，一生二，二生三，三生【万物。万物负阴而抱阳，中气】以为和。人之所亚（恶），唯孤寡不橐（穀），而王公以自【称也。物或益之而】云（损），云（损）之而益。【人之所教，亦议而教人。强梁者不得其死】，吾将以【为学】父。天下之至【柔】，驰骋乎天下【之至坚。出于无有，入于】无间。吾是以【知无为之有益】也。不【言之教，无为之益，天下希能及之】矣。名与【身孰亲？身与货孰多？得与亡孰病？甚爱必大费，多藏必厚亡。故知足不辱，知止不殆，可以长久。大成如缺，其用不敝。大】盈如冲，其

【用不穷。大直如诎，大辩如讷，大】巧如拙，【大赢如】绌。趮
（躁）朕（胜）寒，【静胜热。知清静，可以为天下正。天下有】道，却
走马【以】粪。无道，戎马生于郊。罪莫大可欲，祸【莫大于不知
足，咎莫憯于欲得。故知足之足，恒】足矣。不出于户，以知天下。
不窥（窥）于【牖，以】知天道。其出笉（弥）远者，其知笉（弥）【鲜。
是以圣人不行而知，不见】而名，弗为而成。为学者日益，闻道者日
云（损），云（损）之有（又）云（损），以至于无【为，无为而无不为矣。
将欲】取天下，恒无事，及其有事也，【又不】足以取天【下矣。
圣】人恒无心，以百省（姓）之心为心。善【者善之，不善者亦善之，
得】善也。信者信之，不信者亦信之，德（得）信也。耵（圣）人之在天
下也欱（歙）欱（歙）焉，【为天下浑心，百】生（姓）皆注其【耳目焉，
圣人皆咳之。出】生，入死。生之【徒十有三，死】之徒十又（有）
三，而民生生，僮（动）皆之死地之十有三。【夫】何故也？以其生
生。盖闻善执生者，陵行不辟（避）兕虎，入军不被兵革。兕无【所椯
其角，虎无所措】其蚤（爪），兵【无所容其刃，夫何故】也？以其无
【死地焉】。道生之，德畜之，物刑（形）之而器成之。是以万物尊道
而贵德。道之尊也，德之贵也，夫莫之爵也，而恒自然也。道生之，
畜【之，长之，育】之，亭之，毒之，养之，复（覆）【之。生而弗
有，为而弗恃，长而】弗宰，是胃（谓）玄德。天下有始，以为天下
母。既得其母，以知其子，既○知其子，复守其母，没身不佁（殆）。
塞其闷，闭其门，冬（终）身不堇（勤）。启其闷，齐其【事，终身】不
棘。见小曰明，守【柔曰】强。用【其光，复归其明。无】遗身央
（殃），是胃（谓）【袭】常。使我介有知，行于大道，唯他（施）是畏。
大道甚夷，民甚好懈。朝甚除，田甚芜，仓甚虚；服文采，带利剑，
猒（厌）食而齎（资）财【有余，是谓】盗□。【盗】□，非【道】也。
善建者【不拔，善抱者不脱】，子孙以祭祀不绝。脩之身，其德乃
真。脩之家，其德有余。脩之乡，其德乃长。脩之国，其德乃夆
（丰）。脩之天下，其德乃博（溥）。以身观身，以家观【家，以国观】
国，以天下观天下。吾何【以】知天下之然兹（哉）？以【此】。含德
之厚者，比于赤子。蜂（蜂）疠（虿）虫（虺）蛇弗赫（螫），据鸟孟（猛）兽
弗捕（搏），骨筋弱柔而握固。未知牝牡之会而朘怒，精之至也。冬
（终）日号而不嚘，和【之至也。知和曰】常，知常曰明，益生【曰】

祥，心使气曰强。物【壮】则老，胃(谓)之不道，不道蚤(早)已。知者弗言，言者弗知。塞其堄，闭其门，和其光，同其尘，锉(挫)其兑(锐)而解其纷，是胃(谓)玄同。故不可得而亲也，亦【不可】得而【疏；不可】得而〇利，【亦不可】得而害；不可得而贵，亦不可得而贱。故为天下贵。以正之(治)国，以畸(奇)用兵，以无事取天下。吾何以知其然也才(哉)?夫天下多忌讳，而民弥贫。民多利器，【而国家滋】昏。【人多智慧，而奇物滋起。法】物兹(滋)章，而盗贼【多有】。是以【圣】人之言曰：我无为而民自化，我好静而民自正，我无事而民自富，我欲不欲而民自朴。其正(政)閜(闵)閜(闵)，其民屯屯。其正(政)察察，其【民缺缺】。福，【祸】之所伏，孰知其极?【其】无正也?正【复为奇】，善复为【妖。人】之悉(迷)也，其日固久矣。是以方而不割，兼(廉)而不刺，直而不绁，光而不眺(耀)。治人事天，莫若啬。夫唯啬，是以蚤(早)服。蚤(早)服是胃(谓)重积【德】。重【积德则无不克，无不克则】莫知其【极】。莫知其【极，可以】有国。有国之母，可【以长】久。是胃(谓)【深】根固氐(柢)，长生久视之道也。治大国若亨(烹)小鲜。以道立(莅)天下，其鬼不神。非其鬼不神也，其神不伤人也。非其神不伤人也，【圣人亦】弗伤也。夫两【不】相伤，故德交归焉。大国【者，下流也，天下之】牝也。天下之交也，牝恒以静朕(胜)牡。为其静也，故宜为下也㉖。故大国以下【小】国，则取小国。小国以下大国，则取于大国。故或下【以取，或】下而取。故大国者不【过】欲并畜人，小国不【过】欲人事人。夫【皆得】其欲，则大者宜为下。道者，万物之注也，善人之琛(宝)也，不善人之所保也。美言可以市，尊行可以贺(加)人。人之不善，何【弃之有?故】立天子，置三乡〈卿〉，虽有【共之】璧以先四马，不若坐而进此。古【之所以贵此道者何也】?不胃(谓)求以得，有罪以免与?故为天下贵。为无为，【事无事，味无味。大小多少，报怨以德。图难乎其易也，为大】乎其细也。天下之【难作于】易，天下之大【作于细。是以圣人终不为大，故能成其大】。夫轻若(诺)【必寡】信，多易必多难，是以耵(圣)人【犹难】之，故【终于无难。其安也易持，其未兆也易谋，其脆也易判，其微也易散。为之于其未有也，治之于其未乱也。合抱之】木，作于毫末。九成之台，作于虆(蔂)土。百千之高，始于足下。为之者败之，执者失之。是以耵（圣）人无为【也，故无败也；无执也，故无失也】。民之从事也，恒于其成而败之。故曰："慎冬（终）若始，则无败事矣。"是以耵（圣）人欲不欲，而不贵难得之货；学不学，复众人之所过；能辅万物之自然，而弗敢为。古之为道者，非以明【民也，将以愚】之也。夫民之难治也，以其知（智）也。故以知（智）知国，国之贼也；以不知（智）知国，国之德也；恒知此两者，亦稽式也。恒知稽式，是胃（谓）玄德。玄德深矣、远矣，【与】物反也，乃至大顺。江海所以能为百浴（谷）【王者，以】其【善】下之也，是以能为百浴（谷）王。是以耵（圣）人之欲上民也，必以其言下之；其欲先民也，必以其身后之。故居上而民弗重也，居前而民弗害。天下皆乐谁（推）而弗猒（厌）也，不【以】其无争与？故天下莫能与争。小国寡民，使有十百人器而勿用，使民重死而远徙。又（有）周（舟）车无所乘之，有甲兵无所陈之。使民复结绳而用之。甘其食，美其服，乐其俗，安其居。㷼（邻）国相望，鸡犬之【声相】闻，民至老死不相往来。信言不美，美言不信。知者不博，博者不知。善者不多，多者不善。耵（圣）人无积，既以为人，己俞（愈）有；既以予人矣，己俞（愈）多。故天之道，利而不害；人之道，为而弗争。天下【皆】胃（谓）我大，大而不宵（肖）。夫唯不宵（肖），故能大。若宵（肖），久矣其细也夫。我恒有三琛（宝），市（持）而琛（宝）之，一曰兹（慈），二曰检（俭），三曰不敢为天下先。夫兹（慈），故能勇；检（俭），敢〈故〉能广；不敢为天下先，故能为成器长。今舍其兹（慈），且勇；舍其检（俭），且广；舍其后，且先；则死矣。夫兹（慈），以单（战）则朕（胜），以守则固。天将建之，如以兹（慈）垣之。故善为士者不武，善单（战）者不怒，善朕（胜）敌者弗与，善用人者为之下。是胃（谓）不争【之】德。是胃（谓）用人，是胃（谓）肥（配）天，古之极也。用兵又（有）言曰：吾不敢为主而为客，不敢进寸而退尺。是胃（谓）行无行，攘无臂，执无兵，乃（扔）无敌。祸莫大于无敌。无敌近〇亡吾琛（宝）矣。故抗兵相若，而依（哀）者朕（胜）【矣】。吾言易知也，易行也；而天下莫之能知也，莫之能行也。夫言又（有）宗，事又（有）君。夫唯无知也，是以不我知。知者希，则我贵矣。是以耵（圣）人被褐而裹（怀）玉。知不知，尚矣；不知知，病矣。是以耵（圣）人之不【病】也，以其病病也，是以不病，民之不畏畏（威），则大畏（威）将至矣。

毋伊（狎）其所居，毋猒（厌）其所生。夫唯弗猒（厌），是以不猒（厌）。是以耵（圣）人自知而不自见也，自爱而不自贵也。故去罢（彼）而取此。勇于敢则杀，勇于不敢则栝（活），【此】两者或利或害。天之所亚（恶），熟知其故？天之道，不单（战）而善朕（胜），不言而善应，弗召而自来，单（坦）而善谋。天罔（网）恲恲，疏而不失。若民恒且〇不畏死，若何以杀瞿（惧）之也？使民恒且畏死，而为畸（奇）者【吾】得而杀之，夫孰敢矣！若民恒且必畏死，则恒又（有）司杀者。夫代司杀者杀，是代大匠斫。夫代大匠斫，则希不伤其手。人之饥也，以其取食跣之多，是以饥。百生（姓）之不治也，以其上之有以为也，【是】以不治。民之轻死也，以其求生之厚也，是以轻死。夫唯无以生为者，是贤贵生。人之生也柔弱，其死也䐤信坚强。万【物草】木之生也柔桴（脆），其死也榑（枯）槁。故曰："坚强，死之徒也；柔弱，生之徒也"。【是】以兵强则不朕（胜），木强则兢。故强大居下，柔弱居上。天之道，酉（犹）张弓也，高者印（抑）之，下者举之，有余（馀）者云（损）之，不足者【补之。故天下之道】，云（损）有余（馀）而益不足；人之道，云（损）不足而奉又（有）余（馀）。夫孰能又（有）余（馀）而【有以】奉于天者，唯又（有）道者乎？是以耵（圣）人为而弗又（有），成功而弗居也。若此其不欲见贤也。天下莫柔弱于水，【而攻坚强者莫之能先】，以其无以易之也。水之朕（胜）刚也，弱之朕（胜）强也，天下莫弗知也，而【莫之能行】也。是故耵（圣）人之言云，曰：受国之詢（诟），是胃（谓）社稷之主。受国之不祥，是胃（谓）天下之王。正言若反。禾（和）大【怨，必有余怨，安可以】为善？是以耵（圣）人执左芥（契）而不以责于人。故又（有）德司芥（契），无德司镢（彻）。【天道无亲，常与善人】。《德》三千册一。

道　　经

道，可道也，【非恒道也。名，可名也，非】恒名也。无名，万物之始也。有名，万物之母也。故恒无欲也，【以观其妙】；恒又（有）欲也，以观其所噭。两者同出，异名同胃（谓）。玄之又玄，众眇

（妙）之门。天下皆知美之为美，亚（恶）已。皆知善，斯不善矣。【有、无之相】生也，难、易之相成也，长、短之相刑（形）也，高、下之相盈也，音、声之相和也，先、后之相隋（随），恒也。是以耴（圣）人居无为之事，行不言之教。万物昔（作）而弗始①，为而弗侍（恃）也，成功而弗居也。夫唯弗居，是以弗去。不上贤，使民不争。不贵难得之货，使民不为盗。不见可欲，使民不乱。是以耴（圣）人之治也，虚其心，实其腹；弱其志，强其骨。恒使民无知无欲也。使夫知不敢弗为而已，则无不治矣。道冲，而用之有（又）弗盈也。渊呵佁（似）万物之宗。铧（挫）其兑（锐），解其芬（纷）；和其光，同其尘。湛呵佁（似）或存。吾不知其谁之子也，象帝之先。天地不仁，以万物为刍狗。耴（圣）人不仁，【以】百姓为刍狗。天地之间，其猷（犹）橐籥舆（与）？虚而不淈（屈），动而俞（愈）出。多闻数穷，不若守于中。浴（谷）神不死，是胃（谓）玄牝。玄牝之门，是胃（谓）天地之根。绵绵呵其若存，用之不堇（勤）。天长，地久。天地之所以能长且久者，以其不自生也，故能长生。是以耴（圣）人退其身而身先，外其身而身先，外其身而身存。不以其无私舆（与）？故能成其私。上善如水。水善利万物而有争，居众人之所亚（恶），故几于道矣。居善地，心善渊，予善天，言善信，正（政）善治，事善能，动善时。夫唯不争，故无尤。植（持）而盈之，不若其已。掘（揣）而允之，不可长葆也。金玉盈室，莫之能守也。贵富而骄，自遗咎也。功遂身退，天之道也。戴营袙（魄）抱一，能毋离乎？槫（抟）气至柔，能婴儿乎？脩（涤）除玄监（鉴），能毋有疵乎？爱民栝（活）国，能毋以知乎？天门启阖，能为雌乎？明白四达，能毋以知乎？生之，畜之，生而弗有，长而弗宰也，是胃（谓）玄德。卅楅（辐）同一毂，当其无有，车之用也。燃（埏）埴而为器，当其无有，埴器之用也。鑿户牖，当其无有，室之用也。故有之以为利，无之以为用。五色使人目盲，驰骋田腊（猎）使人心发狂，难得之货○使人之行仿（妨）。五味使人之口爽，五音使人之耳（聋）。是以耴（圣）人之治也，为腹而不为目。故去彼而取此。弄（宠）辱若惊，贵大患若身。何胃（谓）弄（宠）辱若惊？弄（宠）之为下也，得之若惊，失之若惊，是胃（谓）弄（宠）辱若惊。何胃（谓）贵大患若身？吾所以有大患者，为吾有身也。及吾无身，有何患？故贵为身于为天下，若可以橐（托）天下【矣】；爱以身为天下，女可以寄天下矣。视之而弗见，

【名】之曰微。听之而弗闻，命（名）之曰希。〇搐之而弗得，命（名）之曰夷。三者不可至（致）计（诘），故绲而为一。一者，其上不谬，其下不忽。寻寻呵不可命（名）也，复归于无物。是胃（谓）无状之状，无物之象。是胃（谓）沕（忽）望（恍）。隋（随）而不见其后，迎而不见其首。执今之道，以御今之有。以知古始，是胃（谓）道纪。古之□为道者，微眇（妙）玄达，深不可志（识）。夫唯不可志（识），故强为之容，曰：与呵其若冬涉水，猷（犹）呵其若畏四英（邻），严呵其若客，涣呵其若凌（凌）泽（释），沌呵其若朴，湷呵其若浊，湷呵其若浴（谷）。浊而静之，徐清。女〈安〉以重（动）之，徐生。葆此道【者不】欲盈。是以能襒（敝）而不成。至虚极也，守静督也。万物旁（并）作，吾以观其复也。天物祘（魂）祘（魂），各复归于其根。曰静。静，是胃（谓）复命。复命，常也。知常，明也。不知常，芒（妄），芒（妄）作凶。知常容，容乃公，公乃王，【王乃】天，天乃道，道乃。没身不殆。大上下知又（有）【之】，其【次】亲誉之，其次畏之，其下母（侮）之。信不足，安有不信。猷（犹）呵其贵言也。成功遂事，而百姓胃（谓）我自然。故大道废，安有仁义。知（智）慧出，安有【大伪】。六亲不和，安又（有）孝兹（慈）。国家閔（昏）乱，安有贞臣。绝耵（圣）弃知（智），而民利百倍。绝仁弃义，而民复孝兹（慈）。绝巧弃利，盗贼无有。此三言也，以为文未足，故令之有所属。见素抱朴，少私而寡欲。绝学无忧。唯与呵，其相去几何？美与亚（恶），其相去何若？人之所畏，亦不可以不畏人。望（恍）呵其未央才（哉）！众人䁔（熙）䁔（熙），若乡（飨）于大牢，而春登台。我博（泊）焉未挑（兆），若婴儿未咳。累呵佁（似）无所归。众人皆又（有）余（馀）。我愚人之心也，湷湷呵。鬻（俗）人昭昭，我独若閔（昏）呵。鬻（俗）人察察，我独闽（闵）闽（闵）呵。沕（忽）呵其若海，望（恍）呵若无所止。众人皆有以，我独门元（顽）以鄙。吾欲独异于人，而贵食母。孔德之容，唯道是从。道之物，唯望（恍）唯沕（忽）。沕（忽）呵望（恍）呵，中又（有）象呵。望（恍）呵沕（忽）呵，中有物呵。幼（窈）呵冥呵，其中有请（精）呵。其请（精）甚真，其中有信。自今及古，其名不去，以顺众父。吾何以知众父之然也？以此。炊者不立。自视（示）者不章，自见者不明，自伐者无功，自矜者不长。其在道也，曰："粽（馀）食、赘行"。物或亚（恶）之，故有欲者弗居。曲则全，汪（枉）则正，洼则盈，襒（敝）则新。少则得，多则惑。是以耶（圣）人执一，以为天下牧。不自视（示）故章，不自见也故明，不自伐故有功，弗矜故能长。夫唯不争，故莫能与之争。古之所胃（谓）曲全者几语才（哉），诚全归之。希言自然。飘（飘）风不冬（终）朝，暴雨不冬（终）日。孰为此？天地，而弗能久，有（又）兄（况）于人乎？故从事而道者同于道，德（得）者同于德（得），失者同于失。同于德（得）者，道亦德（得）之；同于失者，道亦失之。有物昆成，先天地生。萧（寂）呵漻（寥）呵，独立而不玹（改），可以为天地母。吾未知其名也，字之曰道。吾强为之名曰大。大曰筮（逝），筮（逝）曰远，远曰反。道大，天大，地大，王亦大。国中有四大，而王居一焉。人法地，地法天，天法道，道法自然。重为轻根，静为趮（躁）君。是以君子冬（终）日行，不远其甾（辎）重，虽有环官（馆），燕处则昭若。若何万乘之王而以身轻于天下？轻则失本，趮（躁）则失君。善行者无达迹，善言者无瑕适（谪），善数者不用梼（筹）诧（策）。善○闭者无关籥（钥）而不可启也，善结者无纆约而不可解也。是以耶（圣）人恒善怵（救）人，而无弃人，物无弃财，是胃（谓）曳（袭）明。故善人，善人之师；不善人，善人之资也。不贵其师，不爱其资，虽知（智）乎大迷。是胃（谓）眇（妙）要。知其雄，守其雌，为天下鸡（溪）。为天下鸡（溪），恒德不离。恒德不离，复【归于婴儿。知】其白，守其辱，为天下○浴（谷）。为天下浴（谷），恒德乃足。恒德乃足，复归于朴。知其白，守其黑，为天下式。为天下式，恒德不贷（忒）。恒德不贷（忒），复归于无极。朴散则为器，耶（圣）人用则为官长。夫大制无割。将欲取【天下而为之，吾见其弗】得已。夫天下，神器也，非可为者也。为之者败之，执之者失之。○物或行或隋（随），或热，或硅，或陪（培）或堕。是以耶（圣）人去甚，去大，去诸（奢）。以道佐人主，不以兵强于天下。其【事好还，师之所处，荆】棘生之。善者果而已矣，毋以取强焉。果而毋骄，果而勿矜，果【而毋】伐，果而毋得已居，是胃（谓）果而强。物壮而老，胃（谓）之不道，不道蚤（早）已。夫兵者，不祥之器也。物或亚（恶）【之，故有欲者弗居。君】子居则贵左，用兵则贵右。故兵者非君子之器。兵者不祥【之】器也，不得已而用之，铦袭为上，勿美也。若美之，是乐杀人也。夫乐杀人，不可以得志于天下矣。是以吉事【上左，丧事上右】；是以偏将军居左，而上将军居右，言以丧礼居之也。杀【人众，以悲哀】立

（茈）【之；战】朕（胜）而以丧礼处之。道恒无名，朴唯（虽）小而天下弗敢臣。侯王若能守之，万物将自宾。天地相合，以俞甘洛（露）。【民莫之】令，而自均焉。始制有名，名亦既有，夫亦将知止，知止所以不殆。卑（譬）【道之】在天下也，猷（犹）小浴（谷）之与江海也。知人者，知（智）也。自知，明也。朕（胜）人者，有力也。自朕（胜）者，强也。知足者，富也。强行者，有志也。不失其所者，久也。死而不忘者，寿也。道，沨（泛）呵其可左右也，成功遂【事而】弗名有也。万物归焉而弗为主，则恒无欲也，可名于小。万物归焉而弗为主，可命（名）于大。是以耵（圣）人之能成大也，以其不为大也，故能成大。执大象，天下往。往而不害，安平大。乐与【饵】，过格（客）止。故道之出言也，曰："淡呵其无味也。视之，不足见也。听之，不足闻也。用之不可既也"。将欲擒（翕）之，必古（固）张之。将欲弱之，必古（固）○强之。将欲去之，必古（固）与之。将欲夺之，必古（固）予【之】。是胃（谓）微明。柔弱朕（胜）强。鱼不可说（脱）于渊，国利器不可以示人。道恒无名，侯王若能守之，万物将自化。化而欲作，吾将阒（镇）之以无名之朴。阒（镇）之以无名之朴，夫将不辱。不辱以静，天地将自正。《道》二千四百廿六

索 引　　Index

　　本索引的原则是：凡书中所出现的重要概念一概收入，每个概念下详列实例。按汉语拼音字母顺序排列。每例后均在括号里注明章号和页码。如：道可道非常道 the Way that can be told of is not an Unvarying Way (1.2)。圆点前的数字为章号，之后的数字为页码。

A

爱

爱民治国 love the people and rule the land (10.20)

爱以身为天下 in dealing with the empire loves his subjects as one should love one's body (13.26)

不爱其资 not take care of his stock-in-trade (27.54)

甚爱必大费 he who grudges expense pays dearest in the end (44.90)

自爱不自贵 knows his value, does not put himself on high (72.146)

B

兵

不以兵强天下 oppose all conquest by force of arms (30.60)

夫兵者不祥之器 fine weapons are none the less ill-omened things (31.62)

用兵则贵右 in war the right-hand side is the place of honour (31.62)

兵者不祥之器 weapons are ill-omened things (31.62)

入军不被甲兵 in battle he is not touched by weapons of war (50.102)

兵无所容其刃 a weapon would find no place for its point to enter in (50.102)

以奇用兵 battles can only be won if rules are broken (57.116)

用兵有言 the strategists have the sayings (69.140)

执无兵 a host that can confront, yet presents no battle-front (69.140)

故抗兵相若 when armies are raised and issues joined (69.140)

兵强则灭 the hard and mighty are cast down (76.154)

虽有甲兵无所陈之 there might still be weapons of war but no one would drill with them (80.162)

C

长

长短相形 long and short test one another (2.4)

天长地久 Heaven is Eternal, the Earth everlasting (7.14)

天地所以能长且久者 how come they to be so (7.14)

以其不自生故能长生 they do not foster their own lives; that is why they live so long (7.14)

不可长保 you will find it soon grows dull (9.18)

不自矜故长 he is not proud of his work, and therefore it endures (22.44)

自矜者不长 he who is proud of his work, achieves nothing that endures (24.48)

知止不殆可以长久 stops in time nothing can harm he is forever safe and secure (44.90)

修之于乡其德乃长 apply it to the village, and the village will be made secure (54.110)

有国之母可以长久 he who having the kingdom goes to the Mother can keep it long (59.120)

长生久视之道 making life long by fixed staring (59.120)

常

道可道非常道 the Way that can be told of is not an Unvarying Way

(1.2)

名可名非常名 the names that can be named are not unvarying names (1.2)

故常无欲以观其妙 only he that rids himself forever of desire can see the Secret Essences (1.2)

常有欲以观其徼 he that has never rid himself of desire can see only the Outcomes (1.2)

常使民无知无欲 ever striving to make the people knowledgeless and desireless (3.6)

复命曰常 what has submitted to Fate has become part of the always-so (16.32)

知常曰明 to know the always-so is to be illumined (16.32)

不知常妄作凶 not to know the always-so means to go blindly to disaster (16.32)

知常容 he who knows the always-so (16.32)

是以圣人常善救人 the Sage is all the time in the most perfect way helping men (27.54)

常善救物 he is all the time in the most perfect way helping creatures (27.54)

道常无名 Tao is eternal, but has no fame (32.64)

常无欲 asks for nothing from them (34.68)

道常无为而无不为 Tao never does; yet through it all things are done (37.74)

故知足之足常足矣 he who has once known the contentment that comes simply through being content, will never again be otherwise than contented (46.94)

取天下常以无事 those who of old won the adherence of all who live under heaven, all did so by not interfering (48.98)

圣人无常心 the Sage has no heart of his own (49.100)

常自然 it was always and of itself so (51.104)

是谓袭常 this is called resorting to the always-so (52.106)

知和曰常 to understand such harmony is to understand the always-so
(55.112)

知常曰明 to understand the always-so is to bo illumined (55.112)

牝常以静胜牡 the female by quiescence conquers the male (61.124)

常于几成而败之 constantly spoil things when within an ace of completing them (64.130)

常知稽式 to be always able to apply this test and standard (65.132)

若使民常畏死 even supposing people were generally frightened of death
(74.150)

常有司杀者杀 there is the Lord of Slaughter always ready for this task
(74.150)

天道无亲常与善人 it is Heaven's way, without distinction of persons,
to keep the good perpetually supplied (79.160)

常德

常德不离 he knows all the time a power that he never calls upon in vain (28.56)

常德不忒 he has all the time a power that never errs (28.56)

常德乃足 he has all the time a power that suffices (28.56)

成

难易相成 difficult and easy complete one another (2.4)

功成而弗居 achieves his aim, but does not call attention to what he
does (2.4)

故能成其私 that all his personal ends are fulfilled (7.14)

故能敝而新成 they are like a garment that endures all wear and need never to be renewed (they are able to be rejuvenating) (15.30)

功成事遂 when his task is accomplished, his work done (17.34)

有物混成 there are something formless yet complete (25.50)

功成而不有 having produced them, it does not take possession of them (34.68)

故能成其大 in fact achieves greatness (34.68)

大器晚成 the greatest vessel takes the longest to finish (41.84)

夫唯道善贷且成 Tao alone supports all things and brings them to fulfilment (41.84)

大成若缺 what is most perfect seems to have something missing (45.92)

不为而成 does nothing, yet achieves everything (47.96)

势成之 perfected them, giving to each its strength (their environment completes them) (51.104)

故能成其大 and so achieves greatness (63.128)

常于几成而败之 constantly spoil things when within an ace of completing them (64.130)

故能成器长 is truly able to become chief of all Ministers (67.136)

功成而不处 when he has achieved his aim does not linger (77.156)

D

大

贵大患若身 high rank hurts keenly as our bodies hurt (13.26)

何谓贵大患若身 what does it mean to say that high rank hurts keenly as our bodies hurt (13.26)

吾所以有大患者 the only reason that we suffer hurt (13.26)

大道废 it was when the Great Way declined (18.36)

有大伪 the Great Artifice began (18.36)

强为之名曰大 were I forced to say to what class of things it belongs I should called it Great (25.50)

大曰逝 now ta also means passing on (25.50)

故道大 as Tao has this greatness (25.50)

天大 as heaven has it (25.50)

地大 as earth has it (25.50)

人亦大 so may the ruler also have it (so may man have it) (25.50)

域中有四大 within the realm there are four portions of greatness (25.50)

虽智大迷 much learning though he may possess, is far astray (27.54)

故大制不割 the greatest carver does the least cutting (28.56)

大军之后 the raising of a great host (30.60)

大道泛兮 Great Tao is like a boat that drifts (34.68)

可名为大 it is called the Great (34.68)

以其终不自为大故能成其大 the Sage just because he never at any time makes a show of greatness in fact achieves greatness (34.68)

执大象 he who holding the Great Form (35.70)

是以大丈夫处其厚 therefore the full-grown man takes his stand upon the solid substance (38.76)

189

下士闻道大笑之 when the man of low capacity hears Tao he laughs loudly at it (41.84)

大白若辱 what is sheerest white looks blurred (41.84)

大方无隅 the largest square has no corners (41.84)

大器晚成 the greatest vessel takes the longest to finish (41.84)

大音希声 great music has the faintest notes (41.84)

大象无形 the Great Form is without shape (41.84)

甚爱必大费 he who grudges expense pays dearest in the end (44.90)

大成若缺 what is most perfect seems to have something missing (45.92)

大盈若冲 what is most full seems empty (45.92)

大直若屈 what is most straight seems crooked (45.92)

祸莫大于轻敌 the greatest of all calamities is to attack and find no enemy (69.140)

民不畏威则大威至 never mind if the people are not intimidated by your authority, a Mightier Authority will deal with them in the end (when the people no longer show fear for the intimitation of the authority, then calamities are on the way)(72.146)

代大匠斫 thrusting oneself into the master-carpenter's place and doing his chipping for him (74.150)

夫代大匠斫者 he who tries to do the master-carpenter's chipping for him (74.150)

强大处下 the hard and mighty are cast down (76.154)

和大怨必有余怨 to ally the main discontent but only in a manner that will certainly produce further discontents (79.160)

道

道可道非常道 the Way that can be told of is not an Unvarying Way (1.2)

道冲 the Way is like an empty vessel (4.8)

故几于道 that makes water so near to the Way (8.16)

天之道也 such is Heaven's Way (9.18)

执古之道 by seizing on the Way that was (14.28)

是谓道纪 this is called the essence of the Way (14.28)

保此道者 those who possess this Tao (15.30)

天乃道 to be of heaven is to be in Tao (16.32)

道乃久 Tao is forever (16.32)

大道废 it was when the Great Way declined (18.36)

惟道是从 it alone can act through the Way (21.42)

道之为物惟恍惟惚 the Way is a thing impalpable, incommensurable

(21.42)

故从事于道者同于道 if one uses the Way as one's instrument, the results will be like the Way (23.46)

同于道者道亦乐得之 to those who have conformed themselves to the Way, the Way readily lends it power (23.46)

其在道也 from the standpoint of the Way (24.48)

故有道者不处 that is why he that possesses Tao does not linger (24.48)

强字之曰道 "Way" is the by-name that we give it (25.50)

故道大 Tao has "this greatness" (25.50)

天法道 the ways of heaven (are conditioned) by those of Tao (25.50)

道法自然 the ways of Tao (are conditioned) by the Self-so (25.50)

以道佐人主者 he who by Tao purposes to help a ruler of men (30.60)

物壮则老是谓不道 what has a time of vigour also has a time of decay, this is against Tao (30.60)

不道早已 what is against Tao will soon perish (30.60)

故有道者不处 those in possession of the Tao do not depend on them(31.62)

道常无名 Tao is eternal, but has no fame (name) (32.64)

譬道之在天下 to Tao all under heaven will come (32.64)

大道泛兮 great Tao is like a boat that drifts (34.68)

道之出口淡乎其无味 how different the words that Tao gives forth! so thin, so flavourless (35.70)

道常无为 Tao never does (37.74)

故失道而后德 after Tao was lost, then came the "power" (38.76)

前识者道之华 foreknowledge may be the "flower of doctrine" (38.76)

反者"道"之动 in Tao the only motion is returning (40.82)

弱者"道"之用 the only useful quality, weakness (40.82)

上士闻道 when the man of highest capacities hears Tao (41.84)

193

house (62.126)

不如坐进此道 better were it, as can be done without moving from one's seat, to send this Tao (62.126)

古之所以贵此道者何 what did the ancients say of this Tao, how did they prize it (62.126)

古之善为道者 in the days of old those who practised Tao with success (65.132)

道大似不肖 our Way is greatly like folly (67.136)

天之道不争而善胜 it is the way of Heaven not to strive but none the less to conquer (73.148)

天之道其犹张弓与 Heaven's way is like the bending of a bow (77.156)

天之道 it is Heaven's way (77.156)

人之道则不然 far from being man's way. (77.156)

唯有道者 one there is and one only... it is the possessor of Tao (77.156)

天之道 heaven's way (81.164)

人之道 the Sage's way (81.164)

德

是谓玄德 this is called the Mysterious Power (10.20)

孔德之容 such the scope of the All-pervading Power (21.42)

德者同于德 if one uses the "power" as one's instrument, the results will be like the "power" (23.46)

同于德者德亦乐得之 to those who have conformed themselves to the power, the power readily, lends more power (23.46)

常德不离 a power that he never calls upon in vain (28.56)

常德不忒 he has all the time a power that never errs (28.56)

常德乃足 he has all the time a power that suffices (28.56)

上德不德是以有德 the man of highest "power" does not reveal him-

195

早服谓之重积德 "quickly absorbing" means doubling one's garnered "power" (59.120)

重积德 double your garnered power(59.120)

故德交归焉 their "power" could converge towards a common end(60.122)

报怨以德 requites injuries with good deeds (63.128)

是谓玄德 is called the mysterious "power" (65.132)

玄德深矣 the mysterious "power," so deep-penetrating (65.132)

是谓不争之德 this is called the power that comes of not contending (68.138)

报怨以德 to requite injuries with good deeds (79.160)

有德司契 he who has the "power" of Tao is the Grand Almoner (79.160)

无德司彻 he who has not the "power" is the Grand Perquisitor (79.160)

地

天地不仁 Heaven and Earth are ruthless (5.10)

天地之间 Heaven and Earth and all that lies between(5.10)

是为天地根 is the base from which Heaven and Earth sprang (6.12)

天长地久 Heaven is eternal, the Earth everlasting(7.14)

天地所以能长且久者 how come they to be so(7.14)

居善地 if men think the ground the best place for building a house upon (8.16)

天地 it is Heaven-and-Earth (23.46)

天地尚不能久 even Heaven-and-Earth cannot blow or pour for long (23.46)

地大 earth has it (this greatness) (25.50)

人法地 the ways of men are conditioned by those of earth (25.50)

地法天 the ways of earth (are conditioned) by those of heaven (25.50)

地得一以宁 earth (through such understanding) remains steady (39.80)

动之于死地 the (death-spots) in man's life and activity (50.102)

以其无死地 because such men have no "death-spots" in them (50.102)

E

二

一生二 the One gave birth successively to two things (42.86)

二生三 two (gave birth to) three things (42.86)

二曰俭 the second, frugality (67.136)

恶

斯恶矣 that the idea of ugliness exists (2.4)

美之与恶相去何若 can it be compared to the difference between good and bad (20.40)

物或恶之 people despise them (31.62)

197

F

法

人法地 the ways of men are conditioned by those of earth (25.50)

地法天 the ways of earth (are conditioned) by those of heaven (25.50)

天法道 the ways of heaven (are conditioned) by those of Tao (25.50)

道法自然 the ways of Tao (are conditioned) by the Self-so (25.50)

法令滋彰 the more laws are promulgated (57.116)

福

祸兮福之所倚 it is upon bad fortune that good fortune leans (58.118)

福兮祸之所伏 upon good fortune that bad fortune rests (58.118)

国之福 bring a stock of good fortune to the land (65.132)

复

吾以观复 I have beheld them, whither they go back (16.32)

民复孝慈 the people will be dutiful and compassionate (19.38)

复守其母 will hold all the tighter to the mother (52.106)

正复为奇 every straight is doubled by a crooked (58.118)

善复为妖 every good by an ill (58.118)

复众人之所过 turning all men back to the things they have left behind (64.130)

复结绳而用之 have no use for any form of writing save knotted ropes (80.162)

复命

静曰复命 quietness is called submission to Fate (16.32)

复命曰常 what has submitted to Fate has become part of the always-so (16.32)

复归

复归于无物 on the way back to where there is nothing (14.28)

复归其根 return to the root from which they grew (16.32)

复归于婴儿 this is returning to the state of infancy (28.56)

复归于无极 he returns to the Limitless (28.56)

复归于朴 he returns to the state of the Uncarved Block (28.56)

复归其明 return to the inner-light (52.106)

G

根

天地根 the base from which Heaven and Earth sprang (6.12)

复归其根 return to the root from which they grew (16.32)

归根曰静 this return to the root is called Quietness (16.32)

重为轻根 as the heavy must be the foundation of the light (26.52)

轻则失根 if he is light, the foundation is lost (26.52)

深根固柢 making the roots strike deep (59.120)

功

功成而弗居 achieves his aim, but does not call attention to what he does (2.4)

功遂身退 when your work is done, then withdraw (9.18)

功成事遂 when his task is accomplished, his work done (17.34)

不自伐故有功 he does not boast of what he will do, therefore he succeeds (22.44)

自伐者无功 he who boasts of what he will do succeeds in nothing (24.48)

功成而不有 having produced them, it does not take possession of them (34.68)

功成而不处 when he has achieved his aim (the Sage) does not linger (77.156)

谷

谷神不死 the Valley Spirit never dies (6.12)

旷兮其若谷 receptive as a hollow in the hills (15.30)

为天下谷 becomes like a valley (28.56)

为天下谷 being such a valley (28.56)

犹川谷之于江海 as streams and torrents flow into a great river or sea (32.64)

谷得一以盈 the abyss (through such understanding) is replenished (39.80)

谷无以盈将恐竭 were it not for this replenishment, the abyss would soon go dry (39.80)

上德若谷 the "power" that is really loftiest looks like an abyss (41.84)

江海之所以能为百谷王者 how did the great rivers and seas get their kingship over the hundred lesser streams (66.134)

故能为百谷王 that was how they got their kingship (66.134)

寡

少私寡欲 give them selflessness and fewness of desires (19.38)

孤寡不穀 "the Orphan," "the Needy," "the Ill-provided" (39.80)

孤寡不穀 to be orphaned, needy, ill-provided (42.86)

夫轻诺必寡信 light assent inspires little confidence (63.128)

小国寡民 a small country with few inhabitants (80.162)

观

以观其妙 can see the Secret Essences (1.2)

以观其徼 can see only the Outcomes (1.2)

吾以观复 I have beheld them, whither they go back (16.32)

虽有荣观 however magnificent the view (26.52)

以身观身 through oneself one may contemplate Oneself (54.110)

以家观家 through the household one may contemplate the Household (54.110)

以乡观乡 through the village one may contemplate the Village (54.110)

以国观国 through the kingdom one may contemplate the Kingdom (54.110)

以天下观天下 through the empire one may contemplate the Empire (54.110)

归

归根曰静 this return to the root is called Quietness (16.32)

无所归 as though I belonged nowhere (20.40)

诚全而归之 true wholeness can only be achieved by return (22.44)

万物归焉 the ten thousand creatures obey it (34.68)

德交归焉 their "powers" could converge towards a common end (60.122)

鬼

其鬼不神 not let an evil spirit with them display its powers (60.122)

非其鬼不神 not only that the evil spirit did not display its powers (60.122)

国

爱民治国 love the people and rule the land (10.20)

国家昏乱 till fatherland was dark with strife (18.36)

国之利器 the State's sharpest weapons (36.72)

以正治国 kingdoms can only be governed if rules are kept (57.116)

国家滋昏 the more benighted will the whole land grow (57.116)

可以有国 huge enough to keep a whole kingdom in its grasp (59.120)

有国之母 he who having the kingdom goes to the Mother (59.120)

治大国 ruling a large kingdom (60.122)

以智治国国之贼 those who seek to rule by giving knowledge are like bandits preying on the land (65.132)

不以智治国国之福 those who rule without giving knowledge bring a stock of good fortune to the land (65.132)

受国之垢 he who has accepted the dirt of the country (78.158)

受国不祥 he who takes upon himself the evils of the country (78.158)

小国寡民 a small country with few inhabitants (80.162)

邻国相望 the next place might be so near at hand (80.162)

和

音声相和 pitch and mode give harmony to one another (2.4)

和其光 all glare tempered (4.8)

六亲不和 when the six near ones were no longer at peace (18.36)

冲气以为和 on this blending of the breaths that their harmony depends (42.86)

和之至也 the harmony is at its perfection (55.112)

知和曰常 to understand such harmony is to understand the always-so (55.112)

和其光 all glare tempered (56.114)

和大怨 to allay the main discontent (79.160)

厚

大丈夫处其厚 the full-grown man takes his stand upon the solid substance (38.76)

多藏必厚亡 he who has hoarded most will suffer the heaviest loss (44.90)

以其生生之厚 it is because men feed life too grossly (50.102)

含德之厚 the impunity of things fraught with the "power" (55.112)

以其上求生之厚 because those above them are too grossly absorbed in the pursuit of life (75.152)

化

万物将自化 the ten thousand creatures would at once be transformed (37.74)

化而欲作 having been transformed they should desire to act (37.74)

民自化 the people will of themselves be transformed (57.116)

患

贵大患若身 high rank hurts keenly as our bodies hurt (13.26)

何谓贵大患若身 what does it mean to say that high rank hurts keenly as our bodies hurt (13.26)

吾所以有大患者 the only reason that we suffer hurt (13.26)

及吾无身吾有何患 if we had no bodies, how could we suffer (13.26)

J

极

致虚极 push far enough towards the Void (16.32)

复归于无极 he returns to the Limitless (28.56)

孰知其极 though few know it (58.118)

莫知其极 it knows no bounds (59.120)

莫知其极 only what knows no bounds (59.120)

是谓配天古之极 the secret of being mated to heaven, to what was of old (68.138)

203

教

行不言之教 carries on wordless teaching (2.4)

人之所教我亦教之 others use in their teaching I too will use in mine (42.86)

吾将以为教父 I will take him for my teacher (42.86)

不言之教 there can be teaching without words (43.88)

静

孰能浊以静之徐清 which of you can assume such murkiness, to become in the end still and clear (15.30)

守静笃 hold fast enough to Quietness (16.32)

归根曰静 this return to the root is called Quietness (16.32)

静曰复命 quietness is called submission to Fate (16.32)

静为躁君 quietness is lord and master of activity (26.52)

不欲以静 to be dispassionate is to be still (37.74)

静胜躁 staying still overcomes heat (movement) (45.92)

我好静 so long as I love quietude (57.116)

牝常以静胜牡 the female by quiescence conquers the male (61.124)

以静为下 by quiescence gets underneath (61.124)

净

清净为天下正 he by his limpid calm puts right everything under heaven (45.92)

L

礼

言以丧礼处之 which is arranged on the rites of mourning (31.62)

战胜以丧礼处之 he that has conquered in battle is received with rites of mourning (31.62)

上礼为之 he who is best versed in ritual (38.76)

失义而后礼 after morality was lost, then came ritual (38.76)

夫礼者忠信之薄 now ritual is the mere husk of loyalty and promise keeping (38.76)

利

水善利万物 the goodness of water is that it benefits the ten thousand creatures. (8.16)

有之以为利 just as we take advantage of what is (11.22)

民利百倍 the people will be benefited a hundredfold (19.38)

M

205

民

使民不争 there will be no more jealousies among the people (3.6)

使民不为盗 there will be no more thieves (3.6)

使民心不乱 their hearts will remain placid and undisturbed (3.6)

常使民无知无欲 ever striving to make the people knowledgeless and desireless (3.6)

爱民治国 love the people and rule the land (10.20)

民利百倍 the people will be benefited a hundredfold (19.38)

民复孝慈 the people will be dutiful and compassionate (19.38)

民莫之令而自均 without law or compulsion, men would dwell in harmony (32.64)

民弥贫 the poorer the people will be (57.116)

民自化 the people will of themselves be transformed (57.116)

民自正 the people will of themselves go straight (57.116)

民自富 the people will of themselves become prosperous (57.116)

民自朴 the people will of themselves return to the "state of the Uncarved Block" (57.116)

其民淳淳 the people will be happy and satisfied (58.118)

其民缺缺 the people will be carping and discontented (58.118)

民之从事 the people of the world, at their tasks (64.130)

非以明民 not enlighten the people (65.132)

民之难治 the harder they are to rule (65.132)

是以圣人欲上民 the Sage in order to be above the people (66.134)

欲先民 in order to guide them (66.134)

民不重 the people not be crushed by his weight (66.134)

民不害 the people not be led into harm (66.134)

民不畏威 if the people are not intimidated by your authority (72.146)

民不畏死 the people are not frightened of death (74.150)

若民常畏死 even supposing people were generally frightened of death (74.150)

民之饥 the people starve (75.152)

民之难治 the people are difficult to keep in order (75.152)

民之轻死 the people attach no importance to death (75.152)

小国寡民 a small country with few inhabitants (80.162)

使民重死 the people would be ready to lay down their lives (80.162)

使民复结绳而用之 the people should have no use for any form of writing save knotted ropes (80.162)

民至老死 the people would grow old and die (80.162)

名

名可名非常名 the names that can be named are not unvarying names (1.2)

无名天地之始 it was from the Nameless that Heaven and Earth sprang (1.2)

有名万物之母 the named is but the mother that rears the ten thousand creatures, each after its kind (1.2)

同出而异名 issued from the same mould, but nevertheless are different in name (1.2)

名曰夷 it is called elusive (14.28)

名曰希 it is called the rarefied (14.28)

名曰微 it is called the infinitesimal (14.28)

绳绳兮不可名 endless the series of things without name (14.28)

其名不去 its charge has not departed (21.42)

吾不知其名 its true name we do not know (25.50)

强为之名 were I forced to say to what class of things it belongs (25.50)

道常无名 Tao is eternal, but has no fame (name) (32.64)

207

始制有名 once the block is carved, there will be names (32.64)

名亦既有 so soon as there are names (32.64)

可名为小 it may be called the Lowly (34.68)

可名为大 it is called the Great (34.68)

无名之朴 the blankness of the Unnamed (37.74)

道隐无名 Tao is hidden and nameless (41.84)

名与身 fame or one's own self (44.90)

不见而名 sees all without looking (47.96)

母

万物之母 the mother that rears the ten thousand creatures (1.2)

贵食母 prize no sustenance that comes not from the Mother's breast (20.40)

为天地母 the mother of all things under heaven (25.50)

为天下母 the "mother" of all things (52.106)

既得其母 apprehends the mother (52.106)

复守其母 hold all the tighter to the mother (52.106)

有国之母 he who having the kingdom goes to the Mother (59.120)

P

朴

敦兮其若朴 blank, as a piece of uncarved wood (15.30)

见素抱朴 give them Simplicity to look at, the Uncarved Block to hold (19.38)

复归于朴 returns to the state of the Uncarved Block (28.56)

朴散则为器 when a block is sawed up it is made into implements (28.56)

朴小 the Uncarved Block, though seemingly of small account (32.64)

无名之朴 the blankness of the Unnamed (37.74)

大中华文库

民自朴 the people will of themselves return to the "state of the Uncarved Block" (57.116)

Q

气

专气至柔能如婴儿乎 concentrating your breath, make it soft like that of a little child (10.20)

冲气 this blending of the breaths (42.56)

心使气 the heart makes calls upon the life-breath (55.112)

器

埏埴以为器 turn clay to make a vessel (11.22)

当其无有器之用 it is on the space where there is nothing that the usefulness of the vessel depends (11.22)

朴散则为器 when a block is sawed up it is made into implements (28.56)

天下神器 that which is under heaven is like a holy vessel (29.58)

夫兵者不祥之器 fine weapons are none the less ill-omened things (31.62)

兵者不祥之器 weapons are ill-omened things (31.62)

非君子之器 the superior man should not depend on (31.62)

国之利器 the State's sharpest weapons (36.72)

大器晚成 the Greatest vessel takes the longest to finish (41.84)

人多利器 the "more sharp weapons" there are (57.116)

故能成器长 truly able to become chief of all Ministers (67.136)

什伯之器 contrivances requiring ten times, a hundred times less labour (80.162)

强

强其骨 toughening their sinews (3.6)

故强为之容 I can but tell of them as they appeared to the world (15.30)

强为之名 were I forced to say to what class of things it belongs (25.50)

或强或羸 some are feeling vigorous just when others are worn out (29.58)

不以兵强天下 oppose all conquest by force of arms (30.60)

不敢以取强 he does not take further advantage of his victory (30.60)

果而勿强 fulfils his purpose, but without violence (30.60)

自胜者强 to conquer oneself is harder still (33.66)

强行者有志 he that works through violence may get his way (33.66)

必固强之 must begin by being made strong (36.72)

柔弱胜刚强 it is thus the soft overcomes the hard, and the weak, the strong (36.72)

强梁者不得其死 a man of violence that came to a good end (42.86)

守柔曰强 strength means holding on to what is weak (52.106)

心使气曰强 if the heart makes calls upon the life-breath, rigidity follows (55.112)

其死也坚强 in death he becomes stiff and hard (76.154)

故坚强者死之徒 what is stiff and hard is a "companion of death" (76.154)

兵强则灭 the weapon that is too hard will be broken (76.154)

木强则折 the tree that has the hardest wood will be cut down (76.154)

强大处下 the hard and mighty are cast down (76.154)

而攻坚强者 when it attacks things hard and resistant (78.158)

弱之胜强 the yielding conquers the resistant (78.158)

轻

重为轻根 the heavy must be the foundation of the light (26.52)

以身轻于天下 allow himself to be lighter than these he rules (26.52)

轻则失根 if he is light, the foundation is lost (26.52)

夫轻诺必寡信 light assent inspires little confidence (63.128)

祸莫大于轻敌 the greatest of all calamities is to attack and find no enemy (69.140)

轻敌几丧吾宝 I can have no enemy at the price of losing my treasure (69.140)

民之轻死 the people attach no importance to death (75.152)

是以轻死 that is why they attach no importance to death (75.152)

穷

多言数穷 the force of words is soon spent (5.10)

其用不穷 its use will never fail (45.92)

取

故去彼取此 he rejects that but takes this (12.24)

将欲取天下 those that would gain what is under heaven (29.58)

不敢以取强 he does not take further advantage of his victory (30.60)

故去彼取此 truly, he rejects that and takes this (38.78)

取天下 those who of old won the adherence of all who live under heaven (48.98)

不足以取天下 they would never have won this adherence (48.98)

以无事取天下 the adherence of all under heaven can only be won by letting-alone (57.116)

则取小邦 win the adherence of the small kingdom (61.124)

则取大邦 win the adherence of large kingdoms (61.124)

故或下以取或下而取 the one must get underneath in order to do it; the other is underneath and therefore does it (61.124)

取彼去此 he rejects that but takes this (72.146)

211

R

人

处众人之所恶 is content with the places that all men disdain (8.16)

令人目盲 confuse the eye (12.24)

令人耳聋 dull the ear (12.24)

令人口爽 spoil the palate (12.24)

令人心发狂 makes minds go mad (12.24)

令人行妨 impede their owner's movements (12.24)

人之所畏 what others avoid (20.40)

众人熙熙 all men are wreathed in smiles (20.40)

众人皆有余 all men have enough and to spare (20.40)

我愚人之心也哉 Mine is indeed the mind of a very idiot, so dull am I (20.40)

俗人昭昭 the world is full of people that shine (20.40)

俗人察察 they look lively and self-assured (20.40)

众人皆有以 all men can be put to some use (20.40)

我独异于人 I most am different from men (20.40)

而况于人乎 how much less in his utterance should man (23.46)

人亦大 so may the ruler (men) also have it (25.50)

人法地 the ways of men are conditioned by those of earth (25.50)

常善救人故无弃人 is all the time in the most perfect way helping men, he certainly does not turn his back on men (27.54)

故善人者不善人之师 the perfect man is the teacher of the imperfect (27.54)

不善人者善人之资 the imperfect is the stock-in-trade of the perfect man (27.54)

人之不善何弃之有 even the bad let slip no opportunity to acquire them (62.126)

复众人之所过 turning all men back to the things they have left behind (64.130)

善用人者 the best user of men (68.138)

用人之力 the capacity to use men (68.138)

人之生也柔弱 when he is born, man is soft and weak (76.154)

人之道则不然 far from being man's way (77.156)

而不责于人 not go round making claims on people (79.160)

常与善人 to keep the good perpetually supplied (79.160)

既以为人 his own last scrap has been used up on behalf of others (81.164)

既以与人 his own last scrap has been used up in giving to others (81.164)

人之道 the Sage's way (81.164)

仁

天地不仁 Heaven and Earth are ruthless (5.10)

圣人不仁 the Sage is ruthless (5.10)

与善仁 in friendship they value gentleness (8.16)

大道废有仁义 when the Great Way declined that human kindness and morality arose (18.36)

绝仁弃义 banish human kindness, discard morality (19.38)

上仁 the man of highest humanity (38.76)

失德而后仁 after the "power" was lost, then came human kindness (38.76)

失仁而后义 after human kindness was lost, then came morality (38.76)

柔

专气致柔 can you, when concentrating your breath, make it soft (10.20)

柔弱胜刚强 the soft overcomes the hard, and the weak, the strong (36.72)

天下之至柔 what is of all things most yielding (43.88)

守柔曰强 strength means holding on to what is weak (52.106)

骨弱筋柔 its bones are soft, its sinews weak (55.112)

人之生也柔弱 when he is born, man is soft and weak (76.154)

草木之生也柔弱 all plants and trees while they are alive are supple and soft (76.154)

柔弱者生之徒 what is soft and weak is a "companion of life" (76.154)

柔弱处上 the soft and weak set on high (76.154)

天下莫柔弱于水 nothing under heaven is softer or more yielding than water (78.158)

柔之胜刚 the soft conquers the hard (78.158)

辱

宠辱若惊 favour and disgrace goad as it were to madness (13.26)

何谓宠辱若惊 what does it mean to say that favour and disgrace goad as it were to madness (13.26)

是谓宠辱若惊 that is what is meant by saying favour and disgrace goad as it were to madness (13.26)

知其荣守其辱 he who knows glory, yet cleaves to ignominy (28.56)

大白若辱 what is sheerest white looks blurred (41.84)

知足不辱 be content with what you have and are, and no one despoil you (44.90)

弱

弱其志 weakening their intelligence (3.6)

大中华文库

将欲弱之 whatever is to be weakened (36.72)

柔弱胜刚强 the soft overcomes the hard, and the weak, the strong (36.72)

弱者道之用 the only useful quality, weakness (40.82)

骨弱筋柔 its bones are soft, its sinews weak (55.112)

人之生也柔弱 when he is born, man is soft and weak (76.154)

柔弱者生之徒 what is soft and weak is a "companion of life" (76.154)

柔弱处上 the soft and weak set on high (76.154)

天下莫柔弱于水 nothing under heaven is softer or more yielding than water (78.158)

弱之胜强 the yielding conquers the resistant (78.158)

S

三

此三者不可致诘 these three cannot be further scrutinized (14.28)

此三者 when these three things are done (19.38)

二生三 two things (gave birth to) three things (42.86)

三生万物 three things (gave birth to) ten thousand (42.86)

生之徒十有三 the "companions of life" are thirteen (three-tenths) (50.102)

死之徒十有三 the "companions of death" are thirteen (three-tenths) (50.102)

人之生动之于死地亦十有三 the "death-spots" in man's life and activity are also thirteen (three-tenths) (50.102)

置三公 the installation of the three officers of State (62.126)

我有三宝 here are my three treasures (67.136)

三曰不敢为天下先 the third, refusal to be "foremost of all things under heaven" (67.136)

善

皆知善之为善斯不善矣 if evey one recognized virtue as virtue, this would merely create fresh conceptions of wickedness (2.4)

上善若水 the highest good is like that of water (8.16)

水善利万物 the goodness of water is that it benefits the ten thousand creatures (8.16)

居善地 the ground the best place for building a house upon (8.16)

心善渊 thoughts they value those that are profound (8.16)

与善仁 in friendship they value gentleness (8.16)

言善信 in words (they value) truth (8.16)

政善治 in government (they value) good order (8.16)

事善能 in deeds (they value) effectiveness (8.16)

动善时 in actions (they value) timeliness (8.16)

古之善为道者 of old those that were the best officers of Court (15.30)

善行 perfect activity (27.54)

善言 perfect speech (27.54)

善数 perfect reckoner (27.54)

善闭 perfect door (27.54)

善结 perfect knot (27.54)

常善救人 in the most perfect way helping men (27.54)

常善救物 in the most perfect way helping creatures (27.54)

故善人者不善人之师 the perfect man is the teacher of the imperfect (27.54)

不善人者善人之资 the imperfect is the stock-in-trade of the perfect man (27.54)

善者果而已 a good general effects his purpose and then stops (30.60)

夫唯道善贷且成 Tao alone supports all things and brings them to fulfilment (41.84)

217

善者吾善之 of the good man I approve (49.100)

不善者吾亦善之德善 of the bad I also approve, and thus he gets goodness (49.100)

盖闻善摄生者 it is said that he who has a true hold on life (50.102)

善建者不拔 what Tao plants cannot be plucked (54.110)

善抱者不脱 what Tao clasps, cannot slip (54.110)

善复为妖 every good (is doubled) by an ill (58.118)

善人之宝 it is the treasure of the good man (62.126)

不善人之所保 the support of the bad (62.126)

人之不善何弃之有 even the bad let slip no opportunity to acquire them (62.126)

古之善为道者 in the days of old those who practised Tao with success (65.132)

以其善下之 through merit of being lower than they (66.134)

善为士者不武 the best charioteers do not rush ahead (68.138)

善战者不怒 the best fighters do not make displays of wrath (68.138)

善胜敌者不与 the greatest conqueror wins without joining issue (68.138)

善用人者为之下 the best user of men acts as though he were their inferior (68.138)

天之道不争而善胜 it is the way of Heaven not to strive but none the less to conquer (73.148)

不言而善应 not to speak, but none the less to get an answer (73.148)

繟然而善谋 one who says little, yet none the less has laid his plans (73.148)

安可以为善 can hardly be called successful (79.160)

常与善人 to keep the good perpetually supplied (79.160)

善者不辩 the good man does not prove by argument (81.164)

辩者不善 he who proves by argument is not good (81.164)

上

上善若水 the highest good is like that of water (8.16)

其上不皎 its rising brings no light (14.28)

太上不知有之 Of the highest the people merely know that such a one exists (17.34)

恬淡为上 the best attitude is to remain tranquil and peaceful (31.62)

上将军居右 the supreme general stands on the right (31.62)

上德不德 the man of highest "power" does not reveal himself as a possessor of "power" (38.76)

上德无为 the man of highest "power" neither acts (38.76)

上仁为之 the man of highest humanity, though he acts (38.76)

上义为之 a man of even the highest morality acts (38.76)

上礼为之 he who is best versed in ritual not merely acts (38.76)

上士闻道 when the man of highest capacities hears Tao (41.84)

上德若谷 the "power" that is really loftiest looks like an abyss (41.84)

欲上民 in order to be above the people (66.134)

处上而民不重 only thus can the Sage be on top and the people not be crushed by his weight (66.134)

以其上食税之多 because those above them eat too much tax-grain (75.152)

以其上之有为 because those above them interfere (75.152)

以其上求生之厚 because those above them are too grossly absorbed in the pursuit of life (75.152)

柔弱处上 the soft and weak set on high (76.154)

身

后其身而身先 puts himself in the background; but is always to the fore (7.14)

外其身而身存 remains outside; but is always there (7.14)

功遂身退天之道 when your work is done, then withdraw (9.18)

贵大患若身 high rank hurts keenly as our bodies hurt (13.26)

何谓贵大患若身 what does it mean to say that high rank hurts keenly as our bodies hurt (13.26)

为吾有身 that we have bodies (13.26)

及吾无身吾有何患 if we had no bodies, how could we suffer (13.26)

贵以身为天下 he who in dealing with the empire regards his high rank as though it were his body (13.26)

爱以身为天下 he who in dealing with the empire loves his subjects as one should love one's body (13.26)

没身不殆 though his body ceases, is not destroyed (16.32)

以身轻于天下 allow himself to be lighter than these he rules (26.52)

名与身孰亲 fame or one's own self, which matters to one most (44.90)

身与货孰多 one's own self or things bought, which should count most (44.90)

没身不殆 to the end of his days suffer no harm. (52.106)

终身不勤 till the end your strength shall not fail (52.106)

终身不救 till your last day no help shall come to you (52.106)

无遗身殃 is thereby preserved from all harm (52.106)

修之于身 apply it to yourself (54.110)

以身观身 through oneself one may contemplate Oneself (54.110)

必以身后之 he must put himself behind them (66.134)

神

谷神不死 the Valley Spirit never dies (6.12)

天下神器 that which is under heaven is like a holy vessel (29.58)

神得一以灵 the spirits (through such understanding) keep their holiness(39.80)

神无以灵 were it not for their (the spirits') holiness (39.80)

其鬼不神 not let an evil spirit within them display its powers (60.122)

非其鬼不神 not only the evil spirit did not display its powers (60.122)

其神不伤人 neither was the Sage's good spirit used to the hurt of other men (60.122)

非其神不伤人 nor was it only that his good spirit was not used to harm other men (60.122)

生

有无相生 Being and Not-being grow out of one another (2.4)

生而弗有 he rears them, but does not lay claim to them (2.4)

以其不自生 because they do not foster their own lives (7.14)

故能长生 that is why they live so long (7.14)

生之畜之 rear them, then, feed them (10.20)

生而不有 rear them, but do not lay claim to them (10.20)

孰能安以动之徐生 which of you can make yourself inert, to become in the end full of life and stir (15.30)

先天地生 that existed before heaven and earth (25.50)

荆棘生焉 thorn and brambles grow (30.60)

万物恃之以生 the ten thousand creatures owe their existence to it (34.68)

万物得一以生 the ten thousand creatures (through such understanding) bear their kind (39.80)

万物无以生 were it not that the ten thousand creatures can bear their kind (39.80)

天下万物生于有 all creatures under heaven are the products of Being (40.82)

有生于无 Being itself is the product of Not-being (40.82)

道生一 Tao gave birth to the One (42.86)

一生二 the One gave birth successively to two things (42.86)

二生三 two things (gave birth to) three things (42.86)

三生万物 three things (gave birth) up to ten thousand (42.86)

戎马生于郊 war horses will be reared even on the sacred mounds below the city walls (46.94)

出生入死 he who aims at life achieves death (50.102)

生之徒 the "companions of life" (50.102)

人之生动之于死地 the "death-spots" in man's life and activity (50.102)

以其生生之厚 it is because men feed life too grossly (50.102)

善摄生者 he who has a true hold on life (50.102)

道生之 Tao gave them birth (51.104)

故道生之 therefore as Tao bore them (51.104)

生而不有 rear them, but not lay claim to them (51.104)

益生曰祥 to fill life to the brim is to invite omens (55.112)

长生久视 making life long by fixed staring (59.120)

生于毫末 began as a tiny sprout (64.130)

无厌其所生 do not harrass their lives (72.146)

以其上求生之厚 because those above them are too grossly absorbed in the pursuit of life (75.152)

夫唯无以生为者是贤于贵生 in that their hearts are so little set on life they are superior to those who set store by life (75.152)

人之生 when he (man) is born (76.154)

草木之生 while they (all plants and trees) are alive (76.154)

生之徒 a "companion of life" (76.154)

圣人

圣人处无为之事 the Sage relies on actionless activity (2.4)

圣人之治 the Sage rules (3.6)

圣人不仁 the Sage too is ruthless (5.10)

圣人后其身 the Sage puts himself in the background (7.14)

圣人为腹 the Sage considers the belly (12.24)

圣人抱一 the Sage clasps the Primal Unity (22.44)

圣人常善救人 the Sage is all the time in the most perfect way helping men (27.54)

圣人用之 when the Sage uses it (28.56)

圣人去甚 the Sage discards the absolute (29.58)

圣人不行而知 the Sage arrives without going (47.96)

圣人常无心 the Sage has no heart of his own (49.100)

圣人之在天下 the Sage in his dealing with the world (49.100)

圣人皆孩之 the Sage all the time sees and hears no more than an infant sees and hears (49.100)

故圣人云 therefore a sage has said (57.116)

圣人方而不割 the Sage squares without cutting (58.118)

圣人亦不伤人 the Sage himself was thus saved from harm (60.122)

圣人终不为大 the Sage never has to deal with the great (63.128)

圣人犹难之 the Sage knows too how to make the easy difficult (63.128)

圣人无为 the Sage does not act (64.130)

圣人欲不欲 the Sage wants only things that are unwanted (64.130)

圣人欲上民 the Sage in order to be above the people (66.134)

圣人处上 can the Sage be on top (66.134)

圣人被褐 the Sage wears hair-cloth on top (70.142)

圣人不病 he who recognizes this disease as a disease (71.144)

圣人自知 the Sage knows himself (72.146)

圣人犹难之 the Sage too disallows it (73.148)

圣人为而不恃 the Sage though he controls does not lean (77.156)

圣人云 the Sage said (78.158)

223

inefficacy readily lends its ineffectiveness (23.46)

轻则失根 if he is light, the foundation is lost (26.52)

躁则失君 if he is active, the lord and master is lost (26.52)

执者失之 those that grab at it, lose it (29.58)

不失其所者久 only what stays in its place can endure (33.66)

下德不失德 the man of inferior "power" cannot rid it of the appearance of "power" (38.76)

故失道而后失德 after Tao was lost, then came the "power" (38.76)

失德而后仁 after the "power" was lost, then came human kindness (38.76)

失仁而后义 after human kindness was lost, then came morality (38.76)

失义而后礼 after morality was lost, then came ritual (38.76)

执者失之 he who grabs, lets slip (64.130)

无执故无失 does not grab, and so does not let slip (64.130)

疏而不失 coarse are the meshes, yet nothing slips through (73.148)

225

始

无名万物之始 it was from the Nameless that Heaven and Earth sprang (1.2)

能知古始 to know what once there was, in the Beginning (14.28)

始制有名 once the block is carved, there will be names (32.64)

愚之始 it is the beginning of folly (38.76)

天下有始 that which was the beginning of all things under heaven (52.106)

千里之行始于足下 the journey of a thousand leagues began with what was under the feet (64.130)

慎终如始 heed the end no less than the beginning (64.130)

事

圣人处无为之事 the Sage relies on actionless activity (2.4)

事善能 in deeds (they value) effectiveness (8.16)

功成事遂 when his task is accomplished, his work done (17.34)

从事于道者 if one uses the Way as one's instrument (23.46)

其事好还 such things are wont to rebound (30.60)

吉事尚左 in happy events, the left-hand is the place of honour (31.62)

凶事尚右 in grief and mourning, the right-hand is the place of honour (31.62)

常以无事 all did so by not interfering (48.98)

及其有事 had they interfered (48.98)

开其兑济其事 open up the passages, increase your doings (52.106)

以无事取天下 the adherence of all under heaven can only be won by letting-alone (57.116)

我无事 so long as I act only by inactivity (57.116)

治人事天 rule men and serve heaven (59.120)

小国不过欲入事人 what small countries need is some place where their surplus inhabitants can go and get employment (the small nation wants nothing more than to be accepted by and to serve the large nation) (61.124)

事无事 does without doing (63.128)

难事必作于易 everything difficult must be dealt with while it is still easy (63.128)

大事必作于细 everything great must be dealt with while it is still small (63.128)

民之从事 the people of the world, at their tasks (64.130)

则无败事 and your work will not be spoiled (64.130)

事有君 my deeds have a lord (70.142)

视

视之不见 the eye gazes but can catch no glimpse of it (14.28)

视之不足见 if one looks for Tao, there is nothing solid to see (35.70)

长生久视 making life long by fixed staring (59.120)

水

上善若水 the highest good is like that of water (8.16)

水善利 the goodness of water is that it benefits (8.16)

天之莫柔弱于水 nothing under heaven is softer or more yielding than water (78.158)

损

故物或损之而益 things are often increased by seeking to diminish them (42.86)

或益之而损 diminished by seeking to increase them (42.86)

为道日损 the practice of Tao consists in substracting day by day (48.98)

损之又损 substracting and yet again substracting (48.98)

有余者损之 take away from those who have too much (77.156)

天之道损有余 it is heaven's way to take from those who have too much (77.156)

损不足 takes away from those that have not enough (77.156)

T

太

太上不知有之 of the highest the people merely know that such a one exists (17.34)

如享太牢 as though feasting after the Great Sacrifice (20.40)

安平太 all is peace, quietness and security (35.70)

天

天长地久 Heaven is eternal, the Earth everlasting (7.14)

天门开阖 can you in opening and shutting the heavenly gates (10.20)

全乃天 to be kingly is to be of heaven (16.32)

天乃道 to be of heaven is to be in Tao (16.32)

天大 heaven has it (this greatness) (25.50)

地法天 the ways of earth (are conditioned) by those of heaven (25.50)

天法道 the ways of heaven (are conditioned) by those of Tao (25.50)

天得一以清 the sky through such understanding remains limpid (39.80)

天无以清 were it (the sky) not so limpid (39.80)

治人事天 rule men and serve heaven (59.120)

天将救之以慈卫之 Heaven arms with pity those whom it would not see destroyed (67.136)

是谓配天 the secret of being mated to heaven (68.138)

天之所恶 Heaven hates what it hates (73.148)

天网恢恢 Heaven's net is wide (73.148)

228

天道

天之道 such is Heaven's Way (9.18)

见天道 he knows all the ways of heaven (47.96)

天之道 it is the way of Heaven (73.148)

天之道其犹张弓与 Heaven's way is like the bending of a bow (77.156)

天之道 it is Heaven's way (77.156)

天道无亲 it is Heaven's way, without distinction of persons (79.160)

天之道 heaven's way (81.164)

天地

天地之始 that Heaven and Earth sprang (1.2)

天地不仁 Heaven and Earth are ruthless (5.10)

天地之间其犹橐籥乎 Heaven and Earth and all that lies between is like a bellows (5.10)

是谓天地根 is the base from which Heaven and Earth sprang (6.12)

天地所以能长且久者 how come they to be so (7.14)

天地 it is Heaven-and-Earth (23.46)

天地尚不能久 even Heaven-and-Earth cannot blow or pour for long (23.46)

先天地生 that existed before heaven and earth (25.50)

天地相合 Heaven-and-Earth would conspire (32.64)

天下

天下皆知美之为美 every one under Heaven recognizes beauty as beauty (2.4)

贵以身为天下 in dealing with the empire regards his high rank as though it were his body (13.26)

若可托天下 the best person to be entrusted with rule (13.26)

爱以身为天下 in dealing with the empire loves his subjects as one should love one's body (13.26)

若可寄天下 the best person to whom one can commit the empire (13.26)

为天下式 testing by it everything under heaven (22.44)

故天下莫能与之争 for that very reason no one under heaven can contend with him (22.44)

可以为天下母 one may think of it as the mother of all things under heaven (25.50)

以身轻天下 allow himself to be lighter than these he rules (26.52)

为天下溪 like a ravine, receiving all things under heaven (28.56)

为天下溪 being such a ravine (28.56)

为天下式 becomes the standard by which all things are tested (28.56)

为天下式 and being such a standard (28.56)

为天下谷 becomes like a valley that receives into it all things under heaven (28.56)

为天下谷 and being such a valley (28.56)

将欲取天下 those that would gain what is under heaven (29.58)

天下神器 that which is under heaven is like a holy vessel (29.58)

不以兵强天下 oppose all conquest by force of arms (30.60)

不可得志于天下矣 never get what he looks for out of those that dwell under heaven (31.62)

天下莫能臣 is greater than anything that is under heaven (32.64)

譬道之在天下 to Tao all under heaven will come (32.64)

天下往 goes about his work in the empire (35.70)

天下将自正 the whole empire will be at rest (37.74)

侯王得一以为天下正 barons and princes (through such understanding) direct their people (39.80)

天下之物生于有 all creatures under heaven are the products of Being (40.82)

天下之至柔 what is of all things most yielding (43.88)

驰骋天下之至坚 overwhelm that which is of all things most hard (43.88)

天下希及之 few indeed can understand (43.88)

清净为天下正 he by his limpid calm puts right everything under heaven (45.92)

天下有道 when there is Tao in the empire(46.94)

天下无道 when there is not Tao in the empire(46.94)

不出户知天下 without leaving his door, he knows everything under heaven(47.96)

取天下常以无事 won the adherence of all who live under heaven, all

231

不敢为天下先 refusal to be "foremost of all things under heaven" (67.136)

不敢为天下先 he that refuses to be foremost of all things (67.136)

天下莫能知 no one under heaven understands them (70.142)

孰能有余以奉天下 one there is and one only, so rich that he can afford to make offerings to all under heaven (77.156)

天下莫柔弱于水 nothing under heaven is softer or more yielding than water (78.158)

天下莫不知 a fact known by all men (78.158)

是谓天下王 a king among those what dwell under heaven (78.158)

同

同出而异名 These two things issued from the same mould, but nevertheless are different in name (1.2)

同谓之玄 this "same mould" we can but call the Mystery (1.2)

同其尘 all dust soothed (4.8)

同于道 the results will be like the Way (23.46)

同于德 the results will be like the "power" (23.46)

同于失 the results will be the reverse of the"power" (23.46)

同于道者 those who have conformed themselves to the Way (23.46)

同于德者 those who have conformed themselves to the power (23.46)

同于失者 those who conform themselves to inefficacy (23.46)

同其尘 all dust smoothed (56.114)

是谓玄同 This is called the mysterious levelling (56.114)

W

万物

万物之母 the mother that rears the ten thousand creatures (1.2)

万物作焉 the myriad creatures are worked upon by him (2.4)

万物之宗 the very progenitor of all things in the world (4.8)

以万物为刍狗 the Ten Thousand Things are but as straw dogs (5.10)

水善利万物 the goodness of water is that it benefits the ten thousand creatures (8.16)

万物并作 of the ten thousand things none but can be worked on by you (16.32)

万物将自宾 the ten thousand creatures would flock to do them homage (32.64)

万物恃之以生 the ten thousand creatures owe their existence to it (34.68)

衣养万物 it covers the ten thousand things like a garment (34.68)

万物归焉 the ten thousand creatures obey it (34.68)

万物将自化 the ten thousand creatures would at once be transformed (37.74)

万物得一以生 the ten thousand creatures (through such understanding) bear their kind (39.80)

万物无以生 were it not that the ten thousand creatures can bear their kind (39.80)

三生万物 three things (gave birth) up to ten thousand (42.86)

万物负阴 these ten thousand creatures cannot turn their back to the shade (42.86)

万物莫不尊道 of the ten thousand things there is not one that does not worship Tao (51.104)

道者万物之奥 Tao in the Universe is like the south-west corner in the house (62.126)

以辅万物之自然 the ten thousand creatures may be restored to their Self-so (64.130)

王

而王公以为称 princes and dukes style themselves so (42.86)

江海之所以能为百谷王者 How did the great rivers and seas get their kingship over the hundred lesser streams? (66.134)

故能为百谷王 that was how they got their kingship (66.134)

为天下王 become a king among those what dwell under heaven (78.158)

无

无名天地之始 it was from the Nameless that Heaven and Earth sprang (1.2)

常无欲以观其妙 only he that rids himself forever of desire can see the Secret Essences (from eternal non-existence, therefore, we serenely observe the mysterious beginning of the Universe) (1.2)

有无相生 Being and Non-being grow out of one another (2.4)

为无为则无不治 through his actionless activity all things are duly regulated (3.6)

非以其无私邪 it is not just because he does not strive for any personal end (7.14)

夫唯不争故无尤 because they prefer what does not lead to strife, and therefore does not go amiss (8.16)

能无离乎 can you... from straying (10.20)

能无疵乎 can you... till all is without blur (10.20)

当其无 it is on the space where there is nothing (11.22)

无之以为用 we should recognize the usefulness of what is not (11.22)

及吾无身 if we had no bodies (13.26)

是谓无状之状 they are called shapeless shapes (14.28)

盗贼无有 thieves and robbers will disappear (19.38)

绝学无忧 banish learning, and there will be no more grieving (19.38)

兕无所投其角 a buffalo that attacked him would find nothing for its horns to butt (50.102)

虎无所措其爪 a tiger would find nothing for its claws to tear (50.102)

兵无所容其刃 a weapon would find no place for its point to enter in (50.102)

以其无死地 because such men have no "death-spots" in them (50.102)

无遗身殃 is thereby preserved from all harm (50.102)

其无正也 there is a bourn where there is neither right nor wrong (58.118)

则无不克 it acquires a strength that nothing can overcome (59.120)

无不克 if there is nothing it cannot overcome (59.120)

故终无难矣 by doing so avoid all difficulties (63.128)

圣人无为故无败 the Sage does not act and so does not harm (64.130)

无执故无失 does not grab, and so does not let slip (64.130)

则无败事 your work will not be spoiled (64.130)

是谓行无行 this latter is what we call to march without moving (69.140)

攘无臂 to roll the sleeve, but present no bare arm (69.140)

扔无敌 a host that can confront, yet presents no battle-front (69.140)

执无兵 the hand that seems to hold, yet had no weapon in it (69.140)

无狎其所居 do not narrow their dwellings (72.146)

无厌其所生 (do not) harass their lives (72.146)

夫唯无以生 their hearts are so little set on life (75.152)

以其无以易之 they can find no way of altering it (78.158)

无德司彻 he who has not the "power" is the Grand Perquisitor (79.160)

天道无亲 it is Heaven's way, without distinction of persons (79.160)

无所乘之 no one would go in them (80.162)

无所陈之 no one would drill with them (80.162)

无极

复归于无极 he returns to the Limitless (28.56)

无名

道常无名 Tao is eternal, but has no fame (name) (32.64)

无名之朴 the blankness of the Unnamed (37.74)

道隐无名 Tao is hidden and nameless (41.84)

无事

取天下常以无事 won the adherence of all who live under heaven... by not interfering (48.98)

以无事取天下 the adherence of all under heaven can only be won by letting-alone (57.116)

我无事而民自富 so long as I act only by inactivity the people will of themselves become prosperous (57.116)

事无事 does without doing (63.128)

无为

圣人处无为之事 the Sage relies no actionless activity (2.4)

为无为则无不治 through his actionless activity all things are duly regulated (3.6)

道常无为而无不为 Tao never does; yet through it all things are done(37.74)

上德无为而无以为 the man of highest "power" neither acts nor is there any who so regards him (38.76)

下德无为而有以为 the man of inferior "power" both acts and is so regarded (38.76)

吾是以知无为之有益 That is how I know the value of action that is

大中华文库

actionless (43.88)

无为之益　value in action that is actionless (43.88)

以至于无为　till one has reached inactivity (48.98)

无为而无不为　by this very inactivity, everything can be activated (48.98)

我无为而民自化　so long as I "do nothing" the people will of themselves be transformed (57.116)

为无为　it acts without action (63.128)

圣人无为　the Sage does not act (64.130)

无不为

道常无为而无不为　Tao never does; yet through it all things are done (37.74)

无为而无不为　by this very inactivity, everything can be activated (48.98)

无以为

上德无为而无以为　the man of highest "power" neither acts nor is there any who so regards him (38.76)

上仁为之而无以为　the man of highest humanity, though he acts, is not so regarded (38.76)

无味

淡乎其无味　so thin, so flavourless (35.70)

味无味　finds flavour in what is flavourless (63.128)

无物

复归于无物　on the way back to where there is nothing (14.28)

无物之象　forms without form (14.28)

无形

大象无形 the Great Form is without shape (41.84)

无欲

使民无知无欲 striving to make the people knowledgeless and desireless (3.6)

常无欲 asks for nothing from them (34.68)

我无欲而民自朴 so long as I have no wants the people will of themselves return to the "state of the Uncarved Block" (57.116)

无知

常使民无知无欲 ever striving to make the people knowledgeless and desireless (3.6)

夫惟无知 because men do not understand this (70.142)

勿

果而勿矜 fulfils his purpose and does not glory in what he has done (30.60)

果而勿伐 fulfils his purpose and does not boast of what he has done (30.60)

果而勿骄 fulfils his purpose, but takes no pride in what he has done (30.60)

果而勿强 fulfils his purpose, but without violence (30.60)

物

复归于无物 on the way back to where there is nothing (14.28)

无物之象 forms without form (14.28)

夫物云云 all things howsoever they flourish (16.32)

道之为物 the Way is a thing (21.42)

其中有物 within it are entities (21.42)

物或恶之 no creature but will reject them in disgust (24.48)

有物混成 there was something formless yet complete (25.50)

常善救物 all the time in the most perfect way helping creatures (27.54)

故无弃物 certainly does not turn his back on creatures (27.54)

夫物或行或随 among the creatures of the world some go in front, some follow (29.58)

物壮则老 what has a time of vigour also has a time of decay (30.60)

物或恶之 people despise them (31.62)

物或损之而益 things are often increased by seeking to diminish them (42.84)

物形之 shaped them according to their kinds (51.104)

物壮则老 whatever has a time of vigour also has a time of decay (55.112)

奇物滋起 the more pernicious contrivances will be invented (57.116)

与物反矣 that can follow things back (65.132)

X

下

高下相倾 high and low determine one another (2.4)

宠为下 a ruler's subjects (favour is an inferior matter) (13.26)

其下不昧 its sinking (brings) no darkness (14.28)

下德 the man of inferior "power" (38.76)

高以下为基 the low is the foundation upon which the high is laid (39.80)

下士闻道 when the man of low capacity hears Tao (41.84)

大邦者下流 a large kingdom must be like the low ground towards which all streams flow down (61.124)

以静为下 by quiescence gets underneath (61.124)

大邦以下小邦 if a large kingdom can in the same way succeed in getting underneath a small kingdom (61.124)

小邦以下大邦 because small kingdoms are by nature in this way underneath large kingdoms (61.124)

故或下以取 the one must get underneath in order to do it (61.124)

或下而取 the other is underneath and therefore does it (61.124)

大者宜为下 the large kingdom must "get underneath" (61.124)

千里之行始于足下 the journey of a thousand leagues began with what was under the feet. (64.130)

以其善下之 through the merit of being lower than they (66.134)

必以言下之 must speak as though he were lower than the people (66.134)

善用人者为之下 the best user of men acts as though he were their inferior. (68.138)

强大处下 the hard and mighty are cast down (76.154)

下者举之 the bottom-end comes up (77.156)

先

象帝之先 as a substanceless image it existed before the Ancestor (4.8)

后其身而身先 puts himself in the background; but is always to the fore (7.14)

先天地生 that existed before heaven and earth (25.50)

虽有拱璧以先驷马 rather than send a team of four horses, preceded by a disc of jade (62.126)

欲先民 in order to guide them (the people) (66.134)

不敢为天下先 refusal to be "foremost of all things under heaven" (67.136)

不敢为天下先 refuses to be foremost of all things (67.136)

舍后且先死矣 your vanguard (is not based) on your rear and this is death (67.136)

贤

不尚贤 stop looking for "persons of superior morality" (3.6)

是贤于贵生 they are superior to those who set store by life (75.152)

其不欲见贤 he does not wish to reveal his aim as better than others (77.156)

小

虽小天下莫能臣 though seemingly of small account, is greater than anything that is under heaven (32.64)

可名为小 therefore it may be called the Lowly (34.68)

见小曰明 good sight means seeing what is very small (52.106)

治大国若烹小鲜 ruling a large kingdom is indeed like cooking small fish (60.122)

故大邦以下小邦 if a large kingdom can in the same way succeed in getting underneath a small kingdom (61.124)

则取小国 it will win the adherence of the small kingdom (61.124)

小邦以下大邦 small kingdoms are by nature in this way underneath large kingdoms (61.124)

小邦不过欲入事人 what small countries need is some place where their surplus inhabitants can go and get employment (the small nation wants nothing more than to be accepted and serve the large nation) (61.124)

大小多少 make the small great and the few many (63.128)

小国寡民 a small country with few inhabitants (80.162)

心

使民心不乱 their hearts will remain placid and undisturbed (3.6)

大中华文库

修

修之于身 apply it (Tao) to yourself (54.110)

修之于家 apply it (Tao) to your household (54.110)

修之于乡 apply it (Tao) to the village (54.110)

修之于邦 apply it (Tao) to the kingdom (54.110)

修之于天下 apply it (Tao) to an empire (54.110)

虚

虚其心 emptying their hearts (3.6)

虚而不屈 it is empty, but gives a supply that never fails (5.10)

致虚极 push far enough towards the Void (16.32)

岂虚言哉 was no idle word (22.44)

仓甚虚 their granaries stand empty (53.108)

玄

同谓之玄 we can but call the Mystery (1.2)

玄之又玄 rather the "Darker than any Mystery" (1.2)

是谓玄牝 it is named the Mysterious Female (6.12)

玄牝之门 the Doorway of the Mysterious Female (6.12)

涤除玄鉴 wipe and cleanse your vision of the Mystery (10.20)

是谓玄德 this is called the Mysterious Power (10.20)

微妙玄通 subtle, abstruse, mysterious, penetrating (15.30)

是谓玄德 this is called the mysterious power (51.104)

是谓玄同 this is called the mysterious levelling (56.114)

是谓玄德 is called the mysterious "power" (65.132)

玄德深矣 the mysterious "power," so deep-penetrating (65.132)

245

Y

一

载营魄抱一 keep the unquiet physical-soul from straying, holding fast to the Unity (10.20)

三十辐共一毂 put thirty spokes together and call it a wheel (11.22)

故混而为一 blend into one (14.28)

圣人抱一 the Sage clasps the Primal Unity (22.44)

而人居其一焉 and one belongs to the king (25.50)

昔之得一者 the things that from of old have understood the Whole (39.80)

天得一以清 the sky through such understanding remains limpid (39.80)

地得一以宁 earth remains steady (39.80)

神得一以灵 the spirits keep their holiness (39.80)

谷得一以盈 the abyss is replenished (39.80)

万物得一以生 the ten thousand creatures bear their kind (39.80)

侯王得一以为天下正 barons and princes direct their people (39.80)

道生一 Tao gave birth to the One (42.86)

一生二 the One gave birth successively to two things (42.86)

一曰慈 the first is pity (67.136)

义

大道废有仁义 when the Great Way declined that human kindness and morality arose (18.36)

绝仁弃义 banish human kindness, discard morality (19.38)

上义 a man of the highest morality (38.76)

失仁而后义 after human kindness was lost, then came morality (38.76)

先义而后礼 after morality was lost, then came ritual (38.76)

益

物或损之而益 things are often increased by seeking to diminish them (42.86)

或益之而损 and diminished by seeking to increase them (42.86)

无为之有益 the value of action that is actionless (43.88)

无为之益 value in action that is actionless (43.88)

为学日益 learning consists in adding to one's stock day by day (48.98)

益生曰祥 to fill life to the brim is to invite omens (55.112)

盈

用之或不盈 be drawn from without ever needing to be filled (4.8)

持而盈之 stretch a bow to the very full (9.18)

不欲盈 not try to fill themselves to the brim (15.30)

夫唯不盈 because they do not try to fill themselves to the brim (15.30)

洼则盈 to become full, be hollow (22.44)

谷得一以盈 the abyss (through such understanding) is replenished (39.80)

谷无以盈 were it (the abyss) not for this replenishment (39.80)

大盈若冲 what is most full seems empty (45.92)

247

有

有名万物之母 the named is but the mother that rears the ten thousand creatures (1.2)

常有欲以观其徼 he that has never rid himself of desire can see only the Outcomes (1.2)

有无相生 Being and Non-being grow out of one another (2.4)

生而弗有 he rears them, but does not lay claim to them (2.4)

生而不有 rear them, but do not lay claim to them (10.20)

当其无有车之用 it is on the space where there is nothing that the usefulness of the wheel depends (11.22)

当其无有器之用 it is on the space where there is nothing that the usefulness of the vessel depends (11.22)

当其无有室之用 it is on these spaces where there is nothing that the usefulness of the house depends (11.22)

故有之以为利 therefore just as we take advantage of what is (11.22)

吾所以有大患者为吾有身 the only reason that we suffer hurt is that we have bodies (13.26)

及吾无身吾有何患 if we had no bodies, how could we suffer (13.26)

执古之道以御今之有 by seizing on the Way that was you can ride the things that are now (14.28)

太上不知有之 of the highest the people merely know that such a one exists (17.34)

信不足焉有不信 it is by not believing people that you turn them into liars (17.34)

大道废有仁义 it was when the Great Way declined that human kindness and morality arose (18.36)

智慧出有大伪 it was when intelligence and knowledge appeared that the Great Artifice began (18.36)

六亲不和有孝慈 it was when the six near ones were no longer at peace that there was talk of "dutiful sons" (18.36)

国家昏乱有忠臣 nor till fatherland was dark with strife did we hear of "loyal slaves" (18.36)

绝巧弃利盗贼无有 banish skill, discard profit, and thieves and robbers will disappear (19.38)

故令有所属 then let them have accessories (19.38)

众人皆有余 all men have enough and to spare (20.40)

众人皆有以 all men can be put to some use (20.40)

其中有象 latent in it are forms (21.42)

其中有物 within it are entities (21.42)

其中有精 within it there is a force (21.42)

其精甚真其中有信 a force that though rarefied is none the less efficacious (21.42)

不自伐故有功 he does not boast of what he will do, therefore he succeeds (22.44)

信不足焉有不信 it is by not believing in people that you turn them into
liars (23.46)

故有道者不处 he that possesses Tao does not linger (24.48)

有物混成 there was something formless yet complete (25.50)

域中有四大 within the realm there are four portions of greatness (25.50)

虽有荣观燕处超然 however magnificent the view, he sits quiet and
dispassionate (26.52)

大军之后必有凶年 the raising of a great host is followed by a year of
dearth (30.60)

故有道者不处 those in possession of the Tao do not depend on them
(31.62)

始制有名 once the block is carved, there will be names (32.64)

名亦既有 so soon as there are names (32.64)

胜人者有力 to conquer others needs strength (33.66)

强行者有志 he that works through violence may get his way (33.66)

功成而不有 having produced them, it does not take possession of them
(34.68)

上德不德是以有德 the man of highest "power" does not reveal himself as a possessor of "power" ; therefore he keeps his "power" (38.76)

下德无为而有以为 the man of inferior "power" both acts and is so

regarded (38.76)

上义为之而有以为 a man of even the highest morality both acts and is so regarded (38.76)

天下万物生于有 all creatures under heaven are the products of Being (40.82)

有生于无 Being itself is the product of Not-being (40.82)

故建言有之 therefore the proverb has it (41.84)

无有入无间 being substanceless it can enter even where there is no space (43.88)

吾是以知无为之有益 that is how I know the value of action that is actionless (43.88)

天下有道 when there is Tao in the empire (46.94)

及其有事不足以取天下 had they interfered, they would never have won this adherence (48.98)

生之徒十有三 if the "companions of life" are thirteen (three-tenths) (50.102)

死之徒十有三 so likewise are the "companions of death"thirteen (three-tenths) (50.102)

人之生动之于死地亦十有三 the "death-spots" in man's life and activity are also thirteen (those who could have lived long but walk into death of their own accord also number about three-tenths) (50.102)

生而不有 rear them, but not lay claim to them (51.104)

天下有始 that which was the beginning of all things under heaven (52.106)

使我介然有知 he who has the least scrap of sense (53.108)

财货有余 have more possessions than they can use (53.108)

法令滋彰盗贼多有 the more laws are promulgated, the more thieves and bandits there will be (57.116)

tents (79.160)

有德司契 he who has the "power" of Tao is the Grand Almoner (79.160)

使有什伯之器 there should be among the people contrivances requiring ten times, a hundred times less labour (80.162)

虽有舟舆 there might still be boats and carriages (80.162)

虽有甲兵 there might still be weapons of war (80.162)

既以为人己愈有 when his own last scrap has been used up on behalf of others, lo, he has more than before (81.164)

欲

常无欲以观其妙 he that rids himself forever of desire can see the Secret Essences (1.2)

常有欲以观其徼 he that has never rid himself of desire can see only the Outcomes (1.2)

不见可欲 if the people never see such things as excite desire (3.6)

保此道者不欲盈 those who possess this Tao do not try to fill themselves to the brim (15.30)

少私寡欲 give them selflessness and fewness of desires (19.38)

将欲取天下而为之 those that would gain what is under heaven by tampering with it (29.58)

将欲歙之必固张之 what is in the end to be shrunk must first be stretched (36.72)

将欲弱之必固强之 whatever is to be weakened must begin by being made strong (36.72)

将欲废之必固兴之 what is to be overthrown must begin by being set up (36.72)

将欲取之必固与之 he who would be a taker must begin as a giver (36.72)

化而欲作 if having been transformed they should desire to act (37.74)

无名之朴夫将不欲 the blankness of the Unnamed brings dispassion (37.74)

不欲以静天下将自正 to be dispassionate is to be still, and so, of itself, the whole empire will be at rest (37.74)

不欲琭琭如玉 they did not want themselves to tinkle like jade-bells (39.80)

罪莫大于可欲 no lure is greater than to possess what others want (46.94)

咎莫大于欲得 no presage of evil greater than that men should be wanting to get more (46.94)

大邦不过欲兼畜人 what large countries really need is more inhabitants (61.124)

小邦不过欲入事人 what small countries need is some place where their surplus inhabitants can go and get employment (61.124)

夫两者各得所欲 each gets what it needs (61.124)

圣人欲不欲 the Sage wants only things that are unwanted (64.130)

圣人欲上民 the Sage in order to be above the people (66.134)

欲先民必以身后之 in order to guide them he must put himself behind them (66.134)

其不欲见贤 because he does not wish to reveal himself as better than others (77.156)

渊

渊兮似万物之宗 it is bottomless; the very progenitor of all things in the world (4.8)

心善渊 among thoughts they value those that are profound (8.16)

鱼不可脱于渊 it is best to leave the fish down in his pool (36.72)

253

Z

长

长而不宰 be chief among them, but do not manage them (10.20)

圣人用之则为官长 when the Sage uses it, it becomes Chief of all Ministers (28.56)

长之育之 made them grow, fostered them (51.104)

长而不宰 be chief among them, but not manage them (51.104)

故能成器长 (he) is truly able to become chief of all Ministers (67.136)

真

其精甚真 (within it) a force that though rarefied (21.42)

质真若渝 what is in its natural, pure state looks faded (41.84)

其德乃真 by its power you will be freed from dross (54.110)

正

清净为天下正 he by his limpid calm puts right everything under heaven (45.92)

以正治国 kingdoms can only be governed if rules are kept (57.116)

我好静而民自正 so long as I love quietude, the people will of themselves go straight (57.116)

其无正也 there is a bourn where there is neither right nor wrong (58.118)

正复为奇 in a realm where every straight is doubled by a crooked (58.118)

正言若反 straight words seem crooked (78.158)

知

天下皆知美之为美 because every one under Heaven recognizes beauty as beauty (2.4)

皆知善之为善 equally if every one recognized virtue as virtue (2.4)

常使民无知无欲 ever striving to make the people knowledgeless and desireless (3.6)

吾不知谁之子 was it too the child of something else? we cannot tell (4.8)

爱民治国能无为乎 can you love the people and rule the land, yet remain unknown (10.20)

能知古始是谓道纪 to know what once there was, in the Beginning, this is called the essence of the Way (14.28)

知常曰明 to know the always-so is to be illumined (16.32)

不知常妄作凶 not to know it, means to go blindly to disaster (16.32)

知常容 he who knows the always-so has room in him for everything (16.32)

太上不知有之 of the highest the people merely know that such a one exists (17.34)

吾何以知众甫之状哉 how do I know that the many warriors are so (21.42)

吾不知其名 its true name we do not know (25.50)

知其雄守其雌 he who knows the male, yet cleaves to what is female (28.56)

知其白守其黑 he who knows the white, yet cleaves to the black (28.56)

知其荣守其辱 he who knows glory, yet cleaves to ignominy (28.56)

夫亦将知止 know that it is time to stop (32.64)

知止可以不殆 only by knowing when it is time to stop can danger be avoided (32.64)

知人者智 to understand others is to have knowledge (33.66)

自知者明 to understand oneself is to be illumined (33.66)

知足者富 to be content with what one has is to be rich (33.66)

治

是以圣人之治 therefore the Sage rules (3.6)

为无为则无不治 through his actionless activity all things are duly regulated (3.6)

正善治 in government (they value) good order (8.16)

爱民治国能无为乎 can you love the people and rule the land, yet remain unknown (10.20)

以正治国 kingdoms can only be governed if rules are kept (57.116)

治人事天莫若啬 you cannot rule men nor serve heaven unless you have laid up a store (59.120)

治大国若烹小鲜 ruling a large kingdom is indeed like cooking small fish (60.122)

治之于未乱 put them in order before they have got into confusion (64.130)

民之难治以其智多 the more knowledge people have, the harder they are to rule (65.132)

故以智治国 those who seek to rule by giving knowledge (65.132)

不以智治国 those who rule without giving knowledge (65.132)

民之难治以其上之有为 the people are difficult to keep in order because those above them interfere (75.152)

是以难治 that is the only reason why they are so difficult to keep in order (75.152)

智

使夫智者不敢为也 indeed he sees to it that if there be any who have knowledge they dare not interfere (3.6)

智慧出有大伪 when intelligence and knowledge appeared that the Great Artifice began (18.36)

绝圣弃智 banish wisdom, discard knowledge (19.38)

虽智大迷 much learning though he may possess, is far astray (27.54)

知人者智 to understand others is to have knowledge (33.66)

民之难治以其智多 the more knowledge people have, the harder they are to rule (65.132)

故以智治国 those who seek to rule by giving knowledge (65.132)

不以智治国 those who rule without giving knowledge (65.132)

中

不如守中 far better is it to keep what is in the heart (5.10)

其中有象 yet latent in it are forms (21.42)

其中有物 yet within it are entities (21.42)

其中有精 yet within it there is a force (21.42)

其中有信 is none the less efficacious (21.42)

中士闻道 when the man of middling capacity hears Tao (41.84)

259

重

重为轻根 as the heavy must be the foundation of the light (26.52)

行不离辎重 travels all day, will not let himself be separated from his baggage-wagon (26.52)

早服谓之重积德 "quickly absorbing" means doubling one's garnered "power" (59.120)

重积德 double your garnered power (59.120)

民不重 the people not be crushed by his weight (66.134)

使民重死 the people would be ready to lay down their lives (80.162)

主

万乘之主 the lord of ten thousand chariots (26.52)

以道佐人主者 he who by Tao purposes to help a ruler of men (30.60)

不为主 makes no claim to be master over them (34.68)

万物归焉而不为主 the ten thousand creatures obey it, though they know not that they have a master (34.68)

吾不敢为主 when you doubt your ability to meet the enemy's attack (69.140)

是谓社稷主 can become a king among those what dwell under heaven (78.158)

自

以其不自生 it is because they do not foster their own lives (7.14)

自遗其咎 that brings ruin in its train (9.18)

自今及古 from the time of old till now (21.42)

不自见故明 he does not show himself; therefore he is seen everywhere (22.44)

不自是故彰 he does not define himself, therefore he is distinct (22.44)

不自伐故有功 he does not boast of what he will do, therefore he succeeds (22.44)

不自矜故长 he is not proud of his work, and therefore it endures (22.44)

自见者不明 he who does his own looking sees little (24.48)

自是者不彰 he who defines himself is not therefore distinct (24.48)

自伐者无功 he who boasts of what he will do succeeds in nothing (24.48)

自矜者不长 he who is proud of his work, achieves nothing that endures (24.48)

万物将自宾 the ten thousand creatures would flock to do them homage (32.64)

民莫之令而自均 without law or compulsion, men would dwell in harmony (32.64)

自知者明 to understand oneself is to be illumined (33.66)

自胜者强 to conquer oneself is harder still (33.66)

以其终不自为大故能成其大 the Sage just because he never at any time makes a show of greatness in fact achieves greatness (34.68)

天下将自正 of itself, the whole empire will be at rest (37.74)

侯王自称 that is why barons and princes refer to themselves as (39.80)

民自正 the people will of themselves go straight (57.116)

民自富 the people will of themselves become prosperous (57.116)

民自朴 the people will of themselves return to the "state of the Uncarved Block" (57.116)

自知不自见 knows himself but does not show himself (72.146)

自爱不自贵 knows his own value, but does not put himself on high (72.146)

不召而自来 not to beckon; yet things come to it of themselves (73.148)

自化

万物将自化 the ten thousand creatures would at once be transformed (37.74)

我无为而民自化 so long as I "do nothing" the people will of themselves be transformed (57.116)

自然

我自然 it happened of its own accord (17.34)

希言自然 to be always talking is against nature (23.46)

道法自然 the ways of Tao (are conditioned) by the Self-so (25.50)

常自然 it was always and of itself so (51.104)

以辅万物之自然 the ten thousand creatures may be restored to their Self-so (64.130)

注释　Notes

Chapter 1

1　For these two sentences, there are usually two different interpretations. In Wang Bi text, they are read as"无名，天地之始；有名，万物之母",thus Waley's translation follows it, which is different from Wang Anshi text as "有，名天地之始；有，名万物之母",the translation should be"'Non-being'names this beginning of Heaven and Earth;'Being'names the mother of the myriad things" by Rhett Young and Roger Ames.

2　The usual understanding of these two sentences should be "From eternal non-existence, therefore, we serenely observe the mysterious beginning of the Universe; From eternal existence we clearly see the apparent distinctions" by Chu Dagao.

3　For" 玄之又玄 ",there are different translations, for instance, "More mystical than the most mystical" by Paul Lin;"even more profound than the profound" by Robert Henricks.

4　As to" 众妙之门 ",we can take for reference that"the gate of all mysteries"by Young and Ames; and"gate whence comes the beginning of all parts of the Universe"by Chu Dagao.

Chapter 2

1　Some people interpret these two sentences as" 天下都知道美之为美，就成了丑；天下都知道善之为善，就成了恶 "which is translated as"The whole world recognizes the beautiful as beautiful, yet this is only the ugly; the whole world recognizes the good as the good, yet this is only the bad" by D.C.Lau.

2 The accepted translation for"善"is goodness, and "德",virtue; while in Waley's translation they are virtue and power respectively.

3 Gao Heng suspects this"therefore" was added by some later scholar for the lines above are not consistent in style and meaning with the following. The first part is on relativity, and the second on government.

4 Chen Guying holds that the proper word for" 无为 " should be non-action translated by W. T. Chan. Chan explains: "Non-action (wuwei) is not meant literally 'inactivity'but rather 'taking no action that is contrary to Nature'in other words, letting Nature take its own course." (*A Source Book in Chinese Philosophy* P.136)

5 For " 万物作而弗始 ", we can take for reference that "He lets all things rise without dominating them" by Paul Lin and "The Sage permits the myriad things to arise of themselves, but does not attempt to be their master." by Rhett Young and Roger Ames.

Chapter 3

263

1 The accepted translation for "贤" is "the worthy," "men of worth" or "superiormen."

2 For " 虚其心 ", W.T.Chan explains, "Literally, 'empty'(hsu) means absolute peace and purity of mind, freedoom from worry and selfish desires."

Chapter 4

1 " 似万物之宗 ", this sentence can be translated in different ways such as "as if it were the first ancestor of the myriad things" by Young and

Ames,"it is like the ancestor of the myriad creatures" by D.C.Lau.

2 The lines in parentheses belong to Chapter 56.

3 This sentence " 湛兮，似或存 " is regarded consistent in syntactic structure with " 渊兮！似万物之宗 ", thus English translation can be "In its profundity it seems to be the origin of all things. In its depth it seems ever to remain" by Chu Dagao.

4 Waley thinks that "The Ancestor (帝)in question is almost certainly the Yellow Ancestor who seperated Earth from Heaven and destroyed the Primal Unity," but Wang Bi says, "it is God in heaven." So the different versions are provided here for reference, "it images the forefather of God" by D.C.Lau, "But it looks like the predecessor of Nature" by Chu Dagao, and "It seems to be the predecessor of the gods" by Young and Ames.

Chapter 5

1 Wang Bi says, "Heaven and Earth follow a natural course and accord with non-action and non-creation, the myriad things grow and die of their own accord, thus Heaven and Earth are ruthless." Chen Guying explains, " 天地不仁 means that Heaven and Earth are without favourites. That is, Heaven and Earth are only a physical and natural existence, and do not possess any human emotions. The myriad things between Heaven and Earth simply comply with the natural law. However, theists think Heaven and Earth show particular favour (rejection) towards some things. In fact, this is only the projection of human sentiments onto the cosmic order."

2 " 刍狗 " is a dog-like figure made of straw, used usually for sacrificial ceremony. Lin Xiyi says, "The straw dogs are made for the occasion of sacrifice, when it is finished, they are abandoned. The analogy shows they receive no particular favour and are easily forgotten.··· Some scholars ex-

plain this sentence as treating people as straws, certainly they are mistaken."

3 Paul Lin remarks, "The Sage, joining in the virtue of Heaven and Earth, compares the people to straw dogs."

4 According to Yan Lingfeng, " 守中 "should be " 守冲 ", so this sentence may be translated as "Is it not better to keep tranquility".

Chapter 6

1 Yan Fu explains, "Because it is empty, it is called 'valley'; because it is changeable and inexhaustible, it is called 'spirit'; because it changes unceasingly, it 'never dies'." (*Comments and A Textual Study of Dao De Jing*)

2 " 玄牝 " here refers to the creative nature of Tao. It (the valley spirit) gives birth to Heaven, Earth and myriad things but there is nowhere to find the primordial womb.

3 For the last two sentences, we can take for reference that "Perpetual and without end is its invisible existence; Its functions are inexhautible"; and "Dimly visible, it seems as if it were there, Yet use will never drain it" by D.C.Lau.

Chapter 7

1 Robert Henricks translated these two sentences as "The reason why Heaven and Earth can endure and last a long time—Is that they do not live for themselves."

2 In some Chinese editions, the two words are " 长久 ", there can be subtle difference for the rendition as "they are able to remain perpetually existent" by Young and Ames.

3 A better version can be like that "Put self-concern out of his mind, yet finds that his self-concern is preserved" by Robert Henricks.

4 An alternative translation can be that "Is it not because of his selflessness that he completes his own" by Paul Lin.

Chapter 8

1 Heshang Gong says, "Men of supreme goodness resemble the nature of water."

2 D.C.Lau put these seven sentences as:

In a home it is the site that matters;

In quality of mind it is depth that matters;

In an ally it is benevolence that matters;

In speech it is good faith that matters;

In government it is order that matters;

In affairs it is ability that matters;

In action it is timeliness that matters.

Chapter 9

1 Waley's note: The expression used can also apply to filling a vessel to the brim, but "stretching a bow" makes a better parallel to "sharpening a sword."

2 It should be "gold."

3 Wang Zhen comments, "'身退'does not mean one should retire from his office and leave, but does not claim the deed for himself."

4 Paul Lin explains,"The four seasons evolve in turn, each completing its role and then moving on."

Chapter 10

1 Fan Yingyuan explains,"' 营魄 'are spititual and sentient souls." *The Book of Internal Perception* says,"What controls the body in movement is the spiritual soul, whereas what keeps the body in tranquility is the sentient soul."

2 Chen Guying changed this word "玄览" to "玄鉴" based on the Silk Text B and Gao Heng's explanation. A possible translation for it can be "Profound mirror".

3 This is a good translation, but other versions can provide us with some reference as "Can you love the people and govern the state by non-action" by Chu Dagao; and "One should love his people and order the country properly, But can he accord with 'non-action'" by Young and Ames.

4 The sentences in parentheses are repeated in Chapter 51, they are irrelevant in meaning to the text above.

Chapter 11

1 This sentence can be translated as "Thirty spokes unite in one hub" by Henricks.

2 We can take the following for reference:"Therefore, on the one hand we have the benefit of existence, and on the other, we make use of non-existence" by Chu Dagao, and "Therefore, being constitutes utility, While non-being constitutes function" by Young and Ames.

Chapter 12

1 Excessive riding and hunting cause one to lose his sense of restraint.

2 "That" refers to a life "on behalf of what the eyes desire", while "this", a life "on behalf of what the stomach needs."

Chapter 13

1 This sentence is better understood as "Concern keenly for one's body as one does for a greater disaster."

2 This sentence should read as "Favour is an inferior matter, if one gets..."

3 Young and Ames translated the sentence as "when one can govern the empire with the same attitude as he esteems his own person."

Chapter 14

1 Alternative translations can be "Its surface is not dazzling bright, Nor is its underside dark," by Young and Ames, and "Its upper part is not dazzling, Its lower part is not obscure" by D.C.Lau.

Waley's notes:

2 i.e. dominate.

3 Macrocosmically, in the Universe. Microcosmically, in oneself.

4 Literally, main-thread.

5 Different translations can be read as "By adhering to the Tao of the past You will master the existence of the present And be able to know the origin of the past. This is called the clue of Tao" by Chu Dagao; "Grasp the Tao of antiquity to superintend present existence: Being able to understand

the beginning of the universe Is called the major principle of the Tao" by Young and Ames.

Chapter 15

1 In Wang Bi text, it is "士", but in Silk Manuscript Text B and Fu Yi text, it is "道". Therefore, in Chen Guyin text it is "善为道者", the perfect man of Tao.

2 "澹兮其若海，飂兮若无止" is moved from the twentieth chapter to follow this sentence according to the explanation given by Yan Lingfeng.

3 Young and Ames' translation for the last four sentences may provide for the reference:"Who is able to slowly become perspicacious through tranquility while dwelling in a situation of turbidity? Who is able to slowly advance through motion while dwelling in a situation of stability? Those who maintain these principles do not seek self-satisfaction. Only because they are not self-satisfied are they able to be rejuvenating."

269

Chapter 16

1 In Wang Bi text it is "kingly" (王), but his comment is "Nothing is not encompassed." So according to Lao Jian, we should adopt "complete" (全)here.

2 "天" here should be "nature," so the sentence can be translated as "To be complete is to be in accord with nature."

3 A proper translation will be that "to the end of his days, he will suffer no harm."

Chapter 17

1 In Wang Bi text, it is "the people merely know"(下知有之), but in many other texts, such as Wu Cheng's, Zhu Yuanzhang's, Jiao Hong's, etc. it is "people do not know"(不知有之) which is consistent with the overall text and Laozi's philosophy.

2 A different rendition is that "When trust is insufficient, there will be no trust in return" by Robert Henricks.

Chapter 18

1 "仁义" is often translated as benevolence and righteousness.

2 Waley's note: father, son, elder brother, younger brother, husband and wife.

3 "孝慈" is usually translated as "filial piety and parental affection."

4 Waley's note: As Ministers called themselves.

Chapter 19

1 The first sentence of the twentieth chapter should be moved here. Gao Heng explains: This sentence belongs to Chapter 19, it can be verified at three points. Firstly, the similar syntactical structure between "banish learning and have no anxiety,""manifest simplicity and embrace genuinness"and "lessen self-interest and abate desires," it is quite different from other sentences in structure in Chapter 20; secondly, the same rhyme for " 忧 " with" 足、属、朴、欲 ", but there is not any other word with the same rhyme in Chapter 20; thirdly,"manifest simplicity and embrace genuinness" is consistent in the meaning with "banish learning and have no

anxiety," but if this sentence is put at the beginning of the twentieth chapter, the meaning seems irrelevant to the following sentences.

Chapter 20

1 According to Chen Guying, wei(唯) is the response made when a junior replies to an elder, while o (阿) is the response made when an elder replies to a junior. Some commentators consider that the word 阿 is a loanword for "to shout," "to scold" (诃), and thus explain it as a word of reproach.

2 This sentence should be understood as "Vast (is my spirit), as though interminate."

3 It should be "to be insufficient."

4 See Chapter 15.

5 Waley's note: i.e.the Way's. The image may equally well be that of a child in the womb,"feeding on the mother."

271

Chapter 21

1 " 精 " is usually translated as "essence", the most subtle and most fundamental substance.

2 According to Chen Guying's comment, these last four lines should be understood as "Its name has not been abandoned in discerning the origin of all things. How do I know the disposition of this origin of the myriad things? From it (the Way)."

Chapter 22

1 Waley's note: To the Way.

Chapter 23

1 Waley's note: Nature, as we should say.

2 Here it should be "the Way and its virtue."

3 See Chapter 17. Young and Ames translated this sentence as "When the integrity (of the ruler) is inadequate, There will be those who do not trust him."

Chapter 24

1 This sentence is often understood as "He who puts himself on display does not shine."

2 Waley's note: Over the scene of his successes, thus calling attention to them.

Chapter 25

1 Waley's note: Returning to "what was there at the Beginning."

2 Waley's note: Henceforward I shall use the Chinese word Tao instead of the Way, to do so avoids many inconvenience.

3 In Fan Yingyuan and Fu Yi texts, this word is "man." If we take the whole text into consideration, we would think "man" is a better choice.

4 Waley's note: The "unconditioned"; the "what-is-so-itself."

Chapter 26

1 In Chen Guying text, it is explained as "luxurious life."

2 Waley's note: i.e.more easily moved.

3 Waley's note: i.e. Quietness, the magical passivity that is also called non-action.

4 For the last two sentences, Young and Ames' translation reads as "If he is flippant he will lose the root; If he is agitated he will lose the way of being a ruler."

Chapter 27

1 According to Chen Guying, this sentence should be "A good traveller leaves no track" by Henricks.

2 i.e. counting sticks or tallies.

3 This is called "according with natural perspicacity" by Young and Ames.

4 D.C.Lau puts these two sentences as "Hence the good man is the teacher the bad learns from; And the bad man is the material the good works on."

5 Waley's note: The power to influence mankind through Tao. The commonest charge brought against Taoists was that of being merely interested in self-perfection without regard for the welfare of the community as a whole. The present chapter is devoted to rebutting that charge.

Chapter 28

1 The comments by Yi Shunding, Ma Xunlun and Gao Heng state that the sentences within the parentheses are probably the addition by later scholars.

2 Waley's note: Play on the double sense of this word which also means "a subordinate," "an instrument of government."

3 Waley's note: Play on " 制 ", "to carve" and "to rule." The secondary meaning is that the greatest ruler does the least chopping about.

Chapter 29

1 " 天下 " here means people under heaven.

2 Yi Shunding says, "After 'dangerous to temper with' there should be another sentence 'impossible to grab at,' I can list three examples to verify this. In the note to the *Introduction to History of Jin Dynasty* by Gan Bao, Li Shan quotes from *Wenzi*, 'Laozi says, "The world is great vessel, it cannot be grabbed at, and dangerous to temper with. He who tempers with it. damages it; he who grabs at it, lost it."' This is the first. Wang Bi in his notes says,'Therefore, they can be accorded with but not tempered with; they can be understood but not grabbed at.' Since Wang Bi quotes this sentence in his comment, we can be sure there is such a sentence in the original text. This is the second. In Chapter 64, we read, 'He who acts, harms; he who grabs, lets slip. Therefore, the Sage does not act, and so does not harm; Does not grab, and so does not let slip.' 'Does not act'means'cannot be tempered with';'does not grab'means'impossible to grab at.' Thus in Chapter 29, there is such a sentence. This is the third proof."

3 The sentences in parentheses are suspected to be misplaced bamboo slips in Chapter 64, according to Xi Dong, they are moved here.

4 Chen Guying explains "物" as man.

5 This sentence should be "discards the extreme, the extravagant, the excessive."

Chapter 30

1 Waley's note: Lit."To be reversed." He who overcomes by violence will himself be overcome by violence.

Chapter 31

1 Chen Guying revised "fine weapons" to "weapons" based on Silk Texts A and B.

2, 3, 4 For this chapter, Waley held that a considerable amount of commentary had been inextricably confused with the text. So he reconstructed the text which was fairly close to that of Ma Xulun (1924). The sentences in the parentheses are my additions based on Chen Guying text with the reference of different translations.

275

Chapter 32

1 For the beginning sentences, we can take for reference that "The way is for ever nameless. Though the uncarved block is small, No one in the world dare claim its allegiance" by D.C.Lau; and "The Tao is an eternally nameless genuinness. Although its manifestations are subtle, There is no one in the empire capable of making it his minister" by Young and Ames.

2 According to Chen Guying, this sentence should be translated as "There is no need for the people to command it, for it is equally distributed of its own accord."

3 Waley's note: i.e.to the possessor of Tao. The last two lines resume the thought of lines 4 and 5.

Chapter 33

1 "Violence" should be replaced with "tenacity" or "perseverence."

Chapter 34

1 Chu Takao's translation for this two sentences is "The great Tao pervades everywhere, both on the left and on the right."

2 "衣被" (to cover... like a garment) now in Chen Guying text is "衣养", which means "to clothe and nourish."

3 The parentheses are added to show that this sentence possibly was inserted by later scholars.

Chapter 35

1 Waley's comment: The Great Form that is formless, i.e. Tao.

2 According to Chen Guying, these first four lines should be translated as "Hold fast to the Great Form, and all the world will throng to you; They will throng to you, and yet will inflict no injury on each other; All will find contentment in concord and equanimity" by Young and Ames.

Chapter 36

1 It should be "subtle but clear" in the light of Fan Yingyuan's comment.

2 Different explanations for " 利器 ": Heshang Gong thinks it is the principle of authority; Han Fei believes it means rewards and punishments; Fan Yingyuan explicates it as sagacity, wisdom, benevolence, righteousness, artfulness and profits.

3 Young and Ames translated this sentence as "The sharp weapons of the state cannot be indiscriminately flaunted before the people."

Chapter 37

1 It should be "would be transformed of their own accord," "at once" is redundant here.

2 Waley's note: Literally,"the uncarven-wood-quality."

3 According to Gao Heng," 镇之以 " should be added to the beginning of this sentence, so the English translation should be added with "Refrain them by."

4 Consequently, this sentence should be "they will free from avarice."

5 Waley's note: If the sage is "still."

Chapter 38

1 Waley's note: Does not act separately and particularly, but only applies the "power" in a general way.

2 Waley's note: Regards him as possessor of power.

3 It should be "chaos."

4 A great man. Waley's note: Full grown in Tao.

Chapter 39

1 "寡" means "friendly," "不榖" means "unworthy" here.

2 In Chen Guying text, this sentence is "至誉无誉", That is, "highest praise is to be without praise." In Wang Bi text, it is "至舆无舆".

3 Waley's note: The sage of old.

4 This sentence may be understood like this: They would rather be like firm and jagged stones than like the glittering and dazzling precious jade.

Chapter 40

1 Chen Guying explains, "The meaning of non-being in this sentence is the same as that 'Non-being names this beginning of Heaven and Earth' in Chapter 1, but different from that 'Being and non-being grow out of one another' in Chapter 2 and that 'it is on the space where there is nothing that the usefulness of the wheel depends' in Chapter 11. The '无' in Chapters 2 and 11 refers to non-concrete and intangible aspect of phenomenal world, whereas '无' in this chapter refers to the metaphysical Tao. '有' and '无' in Chapters 2 and 11, if translated into English, '有' is equivalent to 'existence,' '无' is equivalent to 'non-existence.' However, '有' and '无' in this chapter and Chapter 1 are untranslatable, but if we are forced to translate them, usually, they are 'being' and 'non-being' respectively. (But, we must not confuse them with Parmenides' concepts of being and non-being, for Parmenides, there is only one unchanging, unmoving and indivisible real existence, he calls it 'being,' but there is no non-being for him.) Laozi pays attention both to being and non-being and holds their relation as comple-

mentary and continuous."

Chapter 41

1 Waley's note: Tao.

2 This sentence should be put after the sentence "What is in its natural, pure state looks faded" according to Zhang Songru.

Chapter 42

1 Waley's note: i.e. everything.

2 Waley's note: Which symbolizes the fact that they are themselves a mixture of light and dark, hard and soft, water and fire, etc.

3 See Chapter 39.

4 This chapter is divided into two paragraphs, but the meaning in the second paragraph seems irrelevant to the first. Gao Heng, Chen Zhu and Yan Lingfeng suspect the second paragraph belongs to Chapter 39.

279

Chapter 44

1 Waley's note: i.e. which is better, to get fame and wealth but injure oneself, or to lack fame and wealth and save oneself.

2 Young and Ames' translation will provide for our reference that "one who cherishes reputation to excess must certainly pay a heavy penalty."

Chapter 45

1 According to Jiang Xichang's commentary, these two lines should be

"still overcomes movement, and cold overcomes heat."

2 In accordance with Chen Guying's explanation, Young and Ames translated this sentence as "Clarity and tranquility become the upright models of the empire."

Chapter 46

1 There is no such sentence in Wang Bi and Chen Guying texts, but in the texts of Heshang Gong, Fu Yi, Fan Yingyuan, Jinglong Tablet, the Mawangdui Silk Manuscript Text A and B. Waley also translated this sentence. Therefore I add this sentence to Chen Guying text.

Chapter 47

1 Waley's note: Away from Tao; away from the Unity into the Multiplicity.

Chapter 48

1 We can take D.C.Lau's translation as reference: "In the pursuit of learning one knows more every day; In the pursuit of the way one does less every day. One does less and less until one does nothing at all, and when one does nothing at all there is nothing that is undone."

Chapter 49

1 Waley's note: Makes no judgements of his own.

2 It should be "common people."

3 The sentence can be revised as "the Sage regards them all as infants."

Chapter 50

1 This sentence can be revised as "Human life begins in birth, and ends in death."

2 Waley's note: "The four limbs and nine apertures that constitute the human apparatus." This is based on the explanation of Han Feizi. Actually, "十有三" should be "three-tenths."

3 The meaning for this sentence could be that "Those who could have lived long but walk into death of their own accord also number about three-tenths."

4 It is "rhinoceros."

Chapter 51

1 For the third and forth lines, we may take for reference the translation "The physical world gives form to them, and their environment completes them" by Young and Ames.

2 It should be "stablized and pacified."

3 For this sentence, different translations can be taken as reference: "It does things to assist them" by Young and Ames; "It benefits them" by D.C.Lau; and "It acts on their behalf " by Henricks.

4 See Chapter 10.

Chapter 52

Waley's note:

1 Tao, the One, the Whole.

2 the Many, the universe.

3 i.e. Tao.

Chapter 53

1 Waley's note: All this is of course metaphorical.

2 A different understanding for " 除 " is "to be rank with corruption."

Chapter 54

Waley's note:

1 Literally "what is well planted," i.e.planted by Tao.

2 The "power" of the ancestor's Tao carries the family on.

3 By delving back through the successive stages of one's own conscious one gets back to the Unity of the Whole which is one's Tao.

4 Waley's note: i.e.the Tao of the household. When one has had vision of the Tao (underlying essence) of a thing, one can control it. This catena (self—household—village, etc.) is found in every branch of Chinese philosophy, applied in a variety of ways.

Chapter 55

1 The usual understanding for this sentence should be that "He who is endowed with ample virtue may be compared to an infant" by Chu Dagao, and that "One who possesses virtue in abundance is comparable to a new born babe" by D.C.Lau.

2 For these two sentences, Chu Dagao translates them as "To know this

harmony is to approach eternity; To know eternity is to attain enlightenment."

Chapter 56

1 See Chapter 52.

2 Waley's note: In which there is a general perception not effected through particular senses.

Chapter 57

1 It is "unexpected manoeuvres."

2 Principle of Tao.

Chapter 58

283

1 Young and Ames' translation for the first two lines: "When the government is dull and sluggish, The people will be simple and sincere."

2 Waley's note: Through Tao he reaches his ends without use of means. To translate "shines without dazzling" is to misunderstand the whole sequence.

Chapter 59

1 Although "事天" literally can be translated as "serve heaven," in fact, it means "nurture one's own person," Wang Chunfu says, "serving heaven" means to fulfill that which has been endowed by Heaven, which in turn means "nurturing one's own person."

2 According to Chen Guying, this means frugality or thriftness.

3 Waley's note: i.e. going to Tao the Mother.

4 In Chen Guying text, "久视" means "to increase one's span of existence."

Chapter 60

1 Simply, gods or spirits.

2 Waley's understanding is different from that of Chen Guying's. According to Chen, this sentence can be translated as "also the sage will not injure others."

Chapter 61

1 In Silk Manuscript Text A, the third sentence is before the second sentence.

2 It should be "the protection."

3 For the sentences in the parentheses, the correct translation should be that "The large nation wants nothing more than to ally and nurture the people, While the small nation wants nothing more than to be accepted by and to serve the large nation" by Young and Ames.

Chapter 62

1 Waley's note: Where family worship was carried on; the pivotal point round which the household centered. This sentence is translated as "the sanctuary of the thousand things" by Young and Ames.

2 It is "three high ministers," i.e. the Grand Tutor, Deputy Grand Tutor,

and Senior Guardian of the Heir-Apparent.

Chapter 63

1 Some scholars suspect there are missing words here, for it is difficult to explain the sentence. Duyvendak put in English as: "to consider what is small as great, and a few as many."

2 This sentence is not fit for the context, according to Ma Xulun and Yan Lingfeng, it is moved to Chapter 79.

Chapter 64

1 See Chapter 29.

2 Chen Guying holds the sentences in the parentheses do not belong to this chapter, bacause their meaning are not consistent with those above.

285

Chapter 65

1 For "稽式", D.C.Lau translates it as "models," and Young and Ames put it as "principles."

Chapter 66

1 For "推", D.C.Lau translates it as "support," and Young and Ames as "promote."

Chapter 67

1 The sentences in the parentheses are not relevant in meaning to the following, so Yan Lingfeng thinks they can be moved to the end of Chapter 34.

2 Waley's note: The three rules that formed the practical, political side of the author's teaching— (1) abstention from aggressive was and capital punishment, (2) absolute simplicity of living, (3) refusal to assert active authority.

3 A different rendition will be "the leader of all things."

4 Waley's note: It means "Heaven deigned to help them; in its pity it protected them."

Chapter 68

1 Waley's note: Wang Bi says quite rightly that " 士 " is a "leader" of foot-soldiers. The leaders rode in war-chariots. However, Young and Ames' translation can be an alternative: "Those adept at being officers Do not display warlike emotions."

Chapter 69

1, 2 It is not "doubt," but "dare not."

3 These two lines can be translated as "This is what we call: To deploy troops as if without deploying, To strike out as if without an arm."

4 Waley's note: The Wang Bi commentary shows the order in which these clauses should come.

5 Waley's note: i.e. pity.

Chapter 70

1 Waley's note: To have "neither ancestors nor lord" was to be a wild man, a savage. This is a metaphorical way of saying that all the sage did and said was related to a definite system of thought.

2 "则" here means "emulate." This sentence should be understood as "Even fewer emulate me."

3 It is "coarse-colth."

Chapter 71

1 For "病病", Chen Guying translates them as "who recognizes sick-minded as sick-minded."

2 In Chen Guying text, these two sentences are moved to the end of the chapter based on the explanation by Jiang Xichang.

Chapter 72

1 Waley's note: Heaven.

2 Wang Bi comments on these two sentences: "When those in authority can not control the people, when the people can not put up with authority, then there will be a great disintegration in the relationship between the ruling and the ruled." So we might understand them as: "When the people no longer show fear for the intimitation of the authority, then calamities are on the way."

3 Waley's note: Literally "that whereby they live," their livelihoods.

Chapter 73

1 Henricks translated these three sentences as "If you're brave in being daring, you'll be killed, If you're brave in not being daring, you'll live. With these two things, in one case there's profit, in the other there's harm."

2 This line belongs to Chapter 63, according to Ma Xunlun and Gao Heng.

Chapter 74

1 Wang Bi says, "奇" means "to put in a turmoil with intrigues," so it can be translated as "those who commit felonies."

2 Waley's note: Heaven, or its agents (pestilence, famine, lightning, earthquake, etc.).

3 Waley's note: Adaptation of a proverb meaning "let every man stick to his task."

Chapter 76

1 Chen Guying explains that "万物" is redundant, for in many texts, there are no such two characters.

2 It is often understood as "the mighty and formidable army will be defeated."

Chapter 77

1 Here we take for reference the translation by Young and Ames: "Is not

the Tao of Heaven like the drawing of a bow? If the aim is high then we lower our sights; If the aim is low then we raise them."

2 The sentences in parentheses are considered irrelevant to the text above in meaning.

Chapter 78

1 D.C.Lau translates this sentence as "This is because there is nothing that can take its place."

2 Waley's note: Seem, as we should say, to be paradoxes.

Chapter 79

1 According to Ma Xulun, "To requite injuries with good deeds" should be put before the sentence "安可以为善" in this chapter. I have to put the sentence at the beginning for Waley translated the three sentences into one in English.

2 D.C.Lau understands this sentence as "Therefore the sage takes the left-hand tally (The left-hand tally is the half held by the creditor), but extracts no payment from the people."

Chapter 80

1 The explanations given by Yan Lingfeng and Zhang Songru are "tens of and hundreds of contrivances."

2 "重" should be "important" instead of "again" or "twice." It means that "to make people regard that to die (in their native place) is important."

3 Waley explains: "The passage in inverted commas occurs (with tri-

fling differences) in *Zhuangzi* (Ch.10) as a description of life under the rule of the legendary agricultural Sage Shennong. The whole chapter can be understood in the past, present or future tense, as the reader desires."

Chapter 81

1 This should be "to benefit without injuring." Waley's note: To achieve the end without using the material means.

2 Chen Guying deletes the word " 圣 " based on the Silk Text B.

参考书目

Bibliography

1. 陈鼓应《老子注译及评介》，中华书局，1984年。

2. 陈鼓应《老庄新论》，上海古籍出版社，1992年。

3. 张松如《老子校读》，吉林人民出版社，1981年。

4. 卢育三《老子释义》，天津古籍出版社，1987年。

5. 张玉春、金国泰《老子注译》，巴蜀书社，1991年。

6. 黄钊主编《道家思想史纳》，湖南师范大学出版社，1991年。

7. 任继愈主编《中国道教史》，上海人民出版社，1990年。

8. 张舜徽《周秦道论发微》。中华书局，1982年。

9. 张立文主编《道》，中国人民大学出版社1989年。

10. 詹剑峰《老子其人其书及其道论》，湖北人民出版社，1982年。

11. 亚瑟·韦利译著《道和德〈道德经〉及其在中国思想中的地位研究》，乔治·艾伦和安温有限公司，1934年。

12. 刘殿爵译《老子道德经》，企鹅丛书，1963年。

13. 杨有维、罗杰·艾米斯译《老子注译及其评介》，台湾中国资料中心，1981年。

14. 林振述译《老子道德经和王弼注英译》，密执安中国研究文献，1977年。

15. 初大告译《道德经》，海泽尔·沃森和维尼有限公司，1959年。

16. 赫里蒙·毛利尔译《道之道》，剑桥大学出版社，1982年。

17. 韩禄伯译《老子德道经马王堆帛书新译》，麦克米兰公司，1989年。

18. 刘殿爵《道德经马王堆帛书英译》，大卫·坎贝尔出版有限公司，1994年。

291

1. Chen Guying, *Annotations on Laozi with Contemporary Chinese Translation*, China Book Company, 1984.

2. Chen Guying, *A New Commentary on Laozi and Zhuang Zi*, Shanghai Classics Press, 1992.

3. Zhang Songru, *A Collation of Laozi with Textual Study*, Jilin People's Press, 1981.

4. Lu Yusan, *Exposition on Laozi*, Tianjin Classics Press, 1987.

5. Zhang Yuchun and Jin Guotai, *Annotation and Modern Chinese Translation of Laozi*, Bashu Press, 1991.

6. Huang Zhao, ed. *An Outline of Taoist Thought*, Hunan Normal University Press, 1991.

7. Ren Jiyu, ed. *A History of Chinese Taoist Religion*, Shanghai People's Press, 1990.

8. Zhang Shunhui, *Exposition on the Subtle Meanings of Taoism in the Zhou and Qin Dynasties*, China Book Company, 1982.

9. Zhang Liwen, ed. *Dao*, Chinese People's University Press, 1989.

10. Zhan Jianfeng, *Laozi, His Book and His Taoism*, Hubei People's Press, 1982.

11. Arthur Waley, *The Way and Its Power, A Study of the Tao Te Ching and Its Place in Chinese Thought*, George Allen and Unwin Lit., London, 1934.

12. D.C.Lau, *Lao Tzu Tao Te Ching*, Penguin Books, 1963.

13. Rhett Y.W.Young and Roger T.Ames, *Laozi, Text, Notes and Comments*, Chinese Material Center, Taiwan, 1981.

14. Paul J.Lin, *A Translation of Lao Tzu's Tao Te Ching and Wang Bi's Commentary*, Michigan Papers in Chinese Studies, 1977.

15. Chu Takao, *Tao Te Ching*, Hazel Watson and Viney Ltd., 1959.

16. Herrymon Maurer, *TAO: The Way of the Ways*, Cambridge Univer-

sity Press, 1982.

17. Robert Henricks, *Lao Tzu Te-Tao Ching, A New Translation Based on the Recently Discovered Ma-wang-tui Texts*, Macmillan Publishing Company, 1989.

18. D.C.Lau, *Tao Te Ching Translation of the Ma Wang Tui Manuscripts*, David Campbell Publishers Ltd., 1994.

LIBRARY OF CHINESE CLASSICS

图书在版编目(ＣＩＰ)数据

老子：汉英对照／陈鼓应 今译；傅惠生 校注；[英]韦利 英译

长沙：湖南人民出版社 1999.9

（大中华文库）

ISBN 7－5438－2089－7

Ⅰ.老… Ⅱ.①陈… ②傅… ③韦… Ⅲ.孟子－汉、英

Ⅳ.B223.1

中国版本图书馆 CIP 数据核字(1999)第 42249 号

责任编辑: 聂双武 戴 茵

审 校: 罗志野

大中华文库

老 子

[英]韦利 英译

陈鼓应 今译

傅惠生 校注

ⓒ1999 湖南人民出版社

出版发行者:

湖南人民出版社

（湖南省长沙市展览馆路 66 号）

邮政编码 410005

外文出版社

（中国北京百万庄大街 24 号）

邮政编码 100037

http://www.flp.com.cn

制版、排版者:

湖南省新华印刷三厂（湖南新华精品印务有限公司）

印制者:

深圳佳信达印务有限公司印刷

开本:960×640 1/16(精装) 印张:23.25 印数:3001－7300

2003 年第 1 版第 2 次印刷

（汉英） ISBN 7－5438－2089－7/B·50

定价:43.00 元